Harvard Historical Studies

Published under the direction
of the Department of History
from the income of the
Henry Warren Torrey Fund

VOLUME LXXXIX

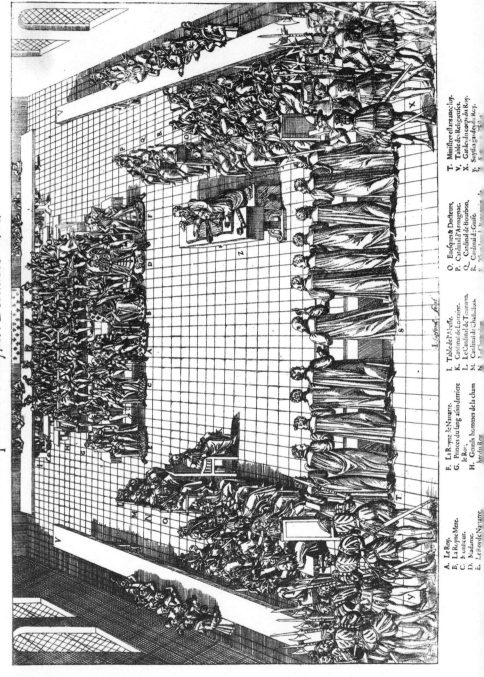

Le Colloque tenu a Poissy, le 9. Decembre · 1561.

A. Le Roy.
B. La Royne Mere.
C. Monsieur.
D. Madame.
E. Le Roy de Navarre.

F. La Royne le Navarre.
G. Prince du sang assis derriere le Roy.
H. Gentils hommes de la chambre du Roy.

I. Table de Messe.
K. Cardinal de Lorraine.
L. Le Cardinal de Tournon.
M. Gentils hommes de la chambre du Roy.
N. Le Chancelier.

O. Euesques & Docteurs.
P. Cardinal d'Armagnac.
Q. Cardinal de Bourbon.
R. Cardinal de Chastillon.

T. Ministre estans auec clug.
V. Table des Religieuses.
X. Gardes du corps du Roy.
Y. Suytte garde du Roy.

The Colloquy of Poissy
(Engraving by Tortorel
and Périssin)

DONALD NUGENT

Ecumenism in the Age of the Reformation:

The Colloquy of Poissy

Harvard University Press   Cambridge, Massachusetts   1974

BR
355
P64
N8
1974

In Memory of My Father

Acknowledgments

This study began as a doctoral dissertation at the University of Iowa in 1961, fourth centenary of the colloquy. Professor Robert Kingdon, now at the University of Wisconsin, first suggested the subject and wisely and generously steered it through to completion as a dissertation. I would like to express special gratitude for his kind advice and counsel and for that of Alain Dufour of the Librairie Droz, Geneva; Peter Fraenkel of the University of Geneva; Michel François of the École des Chartres, Institut Catholique, and the Sorbonne; Kilian McDonnell, O.S.B., of St. John's College; and Henri Meylan of the University of Lausanne. I appreciate the help of the following libraries and archives and of their staffs: the University of Iowa, the University of Kentucky, the Newberry Library, the Huntington Library, the Archives Nationales, Bibliothèque Nationale, and the Mazarine in Paris, the British Museum, and the archives at Stuttgart, the Vatican, Modena, and Naples. I want to thank the Kentucky Research Foundation for its part in subsidizing my travels and researches. Finally, I am grateful to Librairie Droz for permission to quote from its splendid critical edition of the *Correspondance de Théodore de Bèze*, to Doubleday & Company, Inc., for permission to quote excerpts from *The Jerusalem Bible*, copyright © 1966 by Darton, Longman & Todd, Ltd. and Doubleday and Company, Inc. and to the editors of *The Historical Journal* for permitting my article, "The Cardinal of Lorraine and the Colloquy of Poissy," XII (No. 4, 1969), 596–605, to be presented in revised and enlarged form as my Chapter VIII, "The Case of the Cardinal of Lorraine."

Contents

Abbreviations

A.N.	Archives Nationales (Paris)
ARG	*Archiv für Reformationsgeschichte*
(Beza) *Correspondance*	*Correspondance de Théodore de Bèze.* Collected Hippolyte Aubert, ed. Henri Meylan and Alain Dufour *et al.* 6 vols. to date. Geneva: Droz, 1960–1970.
BHR	*Bibliothèque d'humanisme et renaissance*
B.N.	Bibliothèque Nationale (Paris)
BSHPF	*Bulletin de la Société de l'Histoire du Protestantisme Français*
(Calvin) *Opera*	*Joannis Calvini opera quae supersunt omnia* Ed. Guilielmus Baum, Eduardus Cunitz, and Eduardus Reuss. 59 vols. of *Corpus Reformatorum*. Brunswick and Berlin, 1863–1897.
CSP: Foreign	*Calendar of State Papers, Foreign Series, of the Reign of Elizabeth.* 23 vols. London: Public Record Office, 1863–1950.
CSP: Rome	*Calendar of State Papers, relating to English Affairs, Preserved Principally at Rome, in the Vatican Archives and Library.* 2 vols. London: Public Record Office, 1916–1926.
CSP: Spain	*Calendar of Letters and State Papers relating to English Affairs, Preserved Principally in the Archives of Simancas.* 4 vols. London: Public Record Office, 1892–1899.
CSP: Venice	*Calendar of State Papers and Manuscripts, relating to English Affairs, Existing in the Archives and Collections of Venice, and in Other Libraries of Northern Italy.* 38 vols. London: Public Record Office, 1864–1940.
CT	*Concilium Tridentinum: Diariorum, actorum, epistularum, tractatuum nova collectio.* Ed. Stephanus Ehses and Sebastianus Merkle. 10 vols. Freiburg-im-Breisgau: Görres-Gesellschaft, 1901–1919.

Diario	*Diario dell' assemblea de' vescovi à Poissy.* Ed. and prefaced Joseph Roserot de Melin. *Mélanges d'archéologie et d'histoire,* XXXIX (1921–1922), 47–151.
Discours	H. O. Evennett, "Claude d'Espence et son 'Discours' au Colloque de Poissy," *Revue historique,* CLXIV (1930), 40–78.
Haag	Eugène and Émile Haag. *La France Protestante.* 9 vols. Paris, 1846–1859. 2nd ed. (unfinished) 6 vols. Paris, 1877–1888.
HE	*Histoire ecclésiastique des églises réformées au royaume de France.* Ed. G. Baum and Ed. Cunitz. 3 vols. Paris, 1883–1889.
Institutes	John Calvin. *Institutes of the Christian Religion.* Ed. John T. McNeill. Tr. Ford Lewis Battles. 2 vols. Philadelphia: Westminster Press, 1960.
(Jedin) *CC*	*Crisis and Closure of the Council of Trent.* Tr. N. D. Smith. London and Melbourne: Sheed and Ward, 1967.
(Jedin) *CT*	*A History of the Council of Trent.* Tr. Dom Ernest Graf. 2 vols. to date. St. Louis, Mo.: Herder, 1957–1961.
(Jedin) *EC*	*Ecumenical Councils of the Catholic Church.* Tr. Dom Ernest Graf. New York: Herder and Herder, [1960].
Journal	*Le Colloque de Poissy* (of Claude d'Espence). Ed. Baron Alphonse de Ruble. *Mémoires de la Société de l'histoire de Paris et de l'Isle de France,* XVI (1889), 1–56.
MHSJ	*Monumenta historica societatis Jesu.* 93 vols. to date. Madrid: G. López del Horno, 1894–1965.
PG	J. P. Migne. *Patrologiae Cursus Completus. Series Graeca.* 162 vols. Paris, 1857–1912.
PL	J. P. Migne, *Patrologiae Cursus Completus. Series (Latina) prima.* 221 vols. Paris, 1844–1864.
(Romier) *C&H*	*Catholiques et Huguenots à la cour de Charles IX.* Paris: Perrin, 1924.
S.A.	Staatsarchiv (Stuttgart)
WA	*D. Martin Luthers Werke:* Kritische Gesamtausgabe. Weimar: Hermann Böhlau, 1883–.

Introduction

The first help given us by God, that is, the first step to beatitude, is that when we raise our eyes to the mountains.
  Erasmus of Rotterdam,
    De sarcienda ecclesiae concordia

There will come a time when three words uttered with charity and meekness shall receive a far more blessed reward than three thousand volumes written with disdainful sharpness of wit.
  Richard Hooker,
    Laws of Ecclesiastical Polity

An ecumenical age can appreciate, as probably none other, that the Reformation was a very complicated religious revival. Like all great movements in history, it was mixed in its effects. It was at once creative and disruptive, triumphant and tragic. The Christian commonwealth, already tottering, collapsed and was dismembered. If the desired substitute was Augustine's City of God—interestingly enough sometimes used as a code name for Geneva—by the seventeenth century the actual replacement, both Catholic and Protestant, sometimes looked disturbingly like Hobbes's Leviathan. And the sin of separation lingered.

The classical Reformers were themselves aware of the dilemma and cherished the ideal of a single Christian church. Martin Luther wrote, following the breach with the Zwinglians, that "it is a dangerous and terrible thing to hear or to believe something contrary to the one witness, faith and doctrine of the entire holy Christian Church, which has been maintained harmoniously from the beginning, that is, for more than fifteen hundred years, through the whole world."[1] John Calvin spoke movingly of the divisions of the church as

1. WA 30³ : 552.

1

the "horrible mutilations of Christ's body,"[2] and the Geneva Catechism made it quite plain that this body ought to be "one."[3] As the distinguished historian of Calvinism, John T. McNeill, summed it up, "With a considerable degree of insight, though not with logical consistency, the early Protestants attempted, in thought and organization, the recovery and promotion of catholicity in Christianity. It was partly through their own faults, partly through the faults of others, and partly through circumstances beyond all human control, that their efforts so largely failed of fulfillment."[4]

As regards "the faults of others," Roman Catholicism itself was not utterly free of responsibility for the chasm in Christendom. In 1522, the last non-Italian Pope, Adrian VI, candidly confessed that the religious upheaval was the consequence of sin, "especially of prelates and clergy." He was unequivocal: "We all, prelates and clergy, have gone astray from the right way, and for long there is none that has done good; no, not one."[5] And it is of interest that the first disciple of Ignatius Loyola, Pierre Favre, one of a society whose very name was tantamount to a challenge, expressed disquieting doubts about the rising tide of Catholic counterattack. He related that he prayed daily for the Reformers because he felt that "they were being judged harshly by many, and so a feeling of holy compassion for them" arose in his soul.[6] Needless to say, Adrian and Favre represent only a minority opinion.

2. *Calvini opera quae supersunt omnia*, ed. Guilielmus Baum, Eduardus Cunitz and Eduardus Reuss, in *Corpus Reformatorum* (59 vols., Brunswick and Berlin, 1863-1897), VII, 591. The citation is from Calvin's irenical tract: *Vera Christianae pacificationis et ecclesiae reformandae ratio* (1549), VII, 591-674.

3. *Ibid.*, VI, 39.

4. John T. McNeill, *Unitive Protestantism: The Ecumenical Spirit and Its Persistent Expression* (rev. ed., Richmond, Va., 1964), p. 87; see also his "Calvin as an Ecumenical Churchman," *Church History*, XXXII (Dec. 1963), 379-391.

5. Ludwig von Pastor, *The History of the Popes, from the Close of the Middle Ages* (34 vols., 5th ed., St. Louis, Mo., 1923-1941), IX, 134-135.

6. *Fabri monumenta*, p. 683, cited in James Brodrick, *Saint Ignatius Loyola* (New York: Ferrar, Strauss and Cudahy, 1956), p. 253, n. 2.

There was, nevertheless, a median between Luther and Loyola, Calvin and the Curia. This was a diverse group of men who are perhaps best designated irenicists—ecclesiastical peacemakers. They were not really a "third church" and only in a loose sense a "middle party," for they lacked formal organization. They were either Protestant or Catholic, though in sundry times occasionally both, but they generally intended these designations as only provisional. They sought a more perfect union; they were committed to Christendom as well as to Christ.

The foremost place among this group belongs to Erasmus of Rotterdam. While Erasmus had his impact upon both the Protestant and Catholic Reformations, his definitive thrust was toward a reconciliation of the two. He was the father of the Reformation quest for Christian unity. The Gospel according to Erasmus was an open-ended message rather than a closed system. His was a rare blend of theological reductionism and theological breadth, the explicit and the implicit, theology and the *Lebenswelt*. Erasmus was indeed involved, but on a scale broader than most of his contemporaries. His was neither reformation by ridicule nor merely reformation by education, but reformation by reeducation, and his philosophy of education was the *Philosophia Christi*. And in his last years, in the majestic and compelling *De sarcienda ecclesiae concordia* (1533), which has been considered his testament, he bequeathed to his heirs a program of reform, reconciliation, and reunion.

Erasmus was not only "the first and greatest irenical figure." He was also "the founder of a great irenical tradition" that survived for generations after his death.[7] Among the irenicists indebted to him were Philip Melanchthon,

7. *A History of the Ecumenical Movement 1517-1948*, ed. Ruth Rouse and Stephen Charles Neill (2nd ed., London, 1967), pp. 35, 37; see also Hubert Jedin, *A History of the Council of Trent*, tr. Dom Ernest Graf (2 vols. to date, St. Louis, Mo., 1957-1961), I, 358; Marcel Bataillon, *Érasme et l'Espagne* (Paris, 1937), 535; Robert Stupperich, *Der Humanismus und die Wiedervereinigung der Konfessionen*

Martin Bucer, Johann Gropper, Julius Pflug, George Witzel, Gasparo Contarini, George Cassander, Francis Baudouin, Michel de l'Hospital, and another great Dutchman, Hugo Grotius. These distinguished men became, in certain respects, the antiheroes of the Reformation.

The irenical ideal was, of course, far older than Erasmus: it had biblical roots, and it traced its descent through medieval Christendom. No doubt it owed something to lingering conciliarism and its unitive thrust. It was reinforced by the Renaissance stress upon the unity of the world—the *Pax philosophiae* and *Pax fidei*. The irenicist bent can be seen in the universalism of such quattrocento personalities as Nicholas of Cusa and Pico della Mirandola, who ardently, if perhaps sometimes naïvely, strove to embrace polarities. Humanism added a distinctive contribution, with its general preference for the dialogue form, the second person, and persuasion, in distinction to the rather ponderous school theologies. The Christian humanists, who sought a transformation of the old church from within, were generally committed to the inviolability of Christendom. Perhaps irenicism is the finest synthesis of Renaissance and Reformation. Religious unity as a value was simply part of the common stock of ideas received and generally accepted in the sixteenth century. Most people felt that unity was of the Spirit; division was of Satan.[8] Hence, there is less need to account for the presence of irenicism in the sixteenth century than there is to account for division, despite the irenical ideal.

(Leipzig, 1936), pp. 2, 19-20; Bruce E. Mansfield, "Erasmus and the Mediating School," *Journal of Religious History*, IV (Dec. 1967), 302-305; Roland Bainton, *Erasmus of Christendom* (New York: Charles Scribner's Sons, 1969), Donald Nugent, "The Erasmus Renaissance,"*Month*, CCXXIX (Jan. 1970), pp. 38-39. On the "third church," see Augustin Renaudet, *Érasme et l'Italie* (Geneva, 1954), p. 200. It is dubious whether this term should be understood literally.

8. See Conrad Russell, "Arguments for Religious Unity in England, 1530-1650," *Journal of Ecclesiastical History*, XVIII (Oct. 1967), 202-203.

There were essentially two vehicles by means of which the irenicists and all men of goodwill sought to realize the ideal of reunion: a general council and a national council. Protestantism was born in an anguished cry for a general council. The Protest of 1529, which gave Protestantism its very name, was essentially a call for a settlement of the religious crisis by means of a council.[9] From the very outset of his career as a Reformer, and for some twenty-four years thereafter, Luther had called for a "Free Christian Council in German Lands."[10] By "Free" he meant independent of papal control, by "Christian" he understood that judgments were to be based on the principle of Writ Alone and that laymen were to be enfranchised, and by "German Lands" he affirmed that the dispute should be settled where it began.[11] This was basically the sort of conciliarist council against which Rome had contended for a century. Given these mutually conflicting conceptions, it is not surprising that when an invitation was extended to the princes of the Schmalkaldic League in 1537 to attend what would be the Council of Trent the rejection was categorical.[12] The attitude of the Reformers was generally hostile.[13]

9. McNeill, *Unitive Protestantism*, pp. 106-107.
10. For such a call, see WA 54: 208. Jaroslav Pelikan, *Obedient Rebels: Catholic Substance and Protestant Principle in Luther's Reformation* (New York, 1964), pp. 56-57, points out that Luther's calls for a council could have been a simple strategy, and yet he was sincere in the matter as late as 1539. At one point he remarked: "Thank God . . . we are not so far gone that we would permit the Church to perish rather than compromise, even on weighty issues, so long as they are not against God." WA 50: 601, quoted in Pelikan, *Obedient Rebels*, p. 58. George Forell, *Faith Active in Love* (New York: American Press, 1954), pp. 39-41, is still more affirmative about the genuineness of Luther's calls for a council, but stresses that he was disillusioned by the time of Trent.
11. Hubert Jedin, *Ecumenical Councils in the Catholic Church*, tr. Dom Ernest Graf (New York: 1959), pp. 145-146, holds that these meanings were those generally given to the terms in question.
12. Robert Stupperich, "Die Reformation und das Tridentium," *ARG*, XLVII (1956), 31.
13. For Calvin, see his *Acta synodi Tridentinae cum antidoto* (1547), in *Opera*, XXXV, 365-506. Yet he could draw a moving conclusion: "Therefore, since the

The Protestant reaction was not without cause. The earlier sessions of Trent emphasized the highly delicate subject of dogma more than that of reform. The decrees on Holy Writ and original sin were published in 1546, the crucial decrees on justification in 1547, and those on the Eucharist in 1551. The decrees were too restrictive and the anathemas too stinging.

Still, it is possible to exaggerate the intractability of both sides. There were some Protestant representatives at Trent during the period of 1551-1552. It has recently been revealed that Calvin and his colleague, Pierre Viret, genuinely intended to attend and participate in the council at that time, but they were frustrated by circumstances.[14] There was at least nominal Lutheran attendance from the empire. Representatives of Brandenburg, Württemberg, Strasbourg, and Electoral Saxony were at Trent in 1551-1552. There was surprising goodwill on both sides, with the council postponing the publication of new decrees in order to gain the cooperation of the Protestants. The imperial party sought the concessions of the cup for the laity and the right of marriage for the clergy.[15] Any possible understanding was precluded, how-

churches are scattered . . . let us all contribute whatever we possess of counsel, of zeal, of talent, to build up the ruins of the church." *Ibid.*, 506. On Calvin and Trent, see also Robert M. Kingdon, "Some French Reactions to the Council of Trent," *Church History*, XXXIII (1964), 146-156. For the usually irenical Melanchthon, see *Opera quae supersunt omnia*, ed. Carolus Gottlieb Bretschneider, in *Corpus Reformatorum* (21 vols., Halle, 1834-1854), IX, 265-268.

14. See the fine essay of Robert P. Swierenga, "Calvin and the Council of Trent: A Reappraisal (III)" *Reformed Journal*, XVI (May-June 1966), 20-21, containing pertinent citations from the sources. My work in the following period compels me, however, to question Swierenga's statement that "The end of the second assembly of the Council of Trent also saw the end of Calvin's interest in reunifying Protestantism and Catholicism." *Ibid.*, 21. See *Opera*, XVIII, 285-287 and the discussion in Chapter II. Swierenga's work and this latter citation would seem to render untenable the statement of Jean Cadier, "Calvin and the Union of the Churches," *John Calvin*, ed. G.E. Duffield (Grand Rapids, Mich., 1966), p. 129, that Calvin would "abhor" Roman Catholic ecumenism.

15. Helmut Meyer, "Die deutschen Protestanten an der zweiten Tagungsperiode des Konzils von Trient, 1551-52," *ARG*, LVI (1965), 166-209.

ever, by the renewal of war, when the council was suspended indefinitely. This experience does at least suggest that mediation by way of a council was not, in principle (or despite principle), impossible.[16]

Even in the Catholic camp the reaction to Trent was often decidedly negative. In the first generation of the Reformation it was the empire that was shaken by the rising tide of Protestantism. Confronted with mass defection from the Roman church, the Holy Roman Emperor, Charles V, alternated between calling for a general council on the one hand and experimenting with conciliating the German Lutherans on the other. France had no serious problem with heresy. Its king, Francis I, given this situation, generally opposed the council lest his ancient enemy, Charles, should use it to placate his political and religious opponents within the empire and thus strengthen his hand against France. In fact, employing the maxim that "the enemy of my enemy is my friend," Francis supported the Lutheran rebels and initiated the anomaly of an alliance between Catholic France and the Lutherans of Germany. Though suspicious and obstructive, Francis was nominally represented by a few prelates at the council. His successor, Henry II, held even more aloof and refused to recognize the "convention" of Trent as a council.[17]

When Luther called for a general council, he judiciously allowed an alternative: a national council. While this may have represented a particular solution to a general problem, it could be, as Luther put it, a voice "heard from afar."[18] That is, it could have been more than regional implications. The

---

16. This was not really "the last and only attempt" to restore unity by a council (*ibid.*, 206), though it got farther than any other.

17. Jedin, *CT*, II, 183, and *EC*, p. 168, respectively, for Francis and Henry. Jedin affirms: "France, that citadel of conciliar theory, did more to prevent the Council of Trent than any other country." *CT*, I, 230.

18. Pelikan, *Obedient Rebels*, p. 73; WA 54: 208.

Reformation would witness, nevertheless, a quarrel of almost half a century between these two institutions.

It was the national council that became the characteristic vehicle of irenicism. The idea first seems to have appeared in 1523, when the Bavarian Estates pressed for a colloquy as an interim settlement, pending a general council. Rome opposed it, fearing national apostasy, and it was aborted when the young Charles V, still a "universal monarch," himself disapproved it, holding: "How dare one nation alter the Church's ordinances?"[19] But by 1530 and the Diet of Augsburg it was a different story. With much of Germany estranged and prospects of a remedial general council waning, Charles, under the influence of friends of Erasmus, became Europe's foremost hope for reunion.[20] At that diet, he sought a direct understanding with the Lutherans. The Catholic protagonists were, unfortunately, dominated by the uncompromising John Eck, while the Lutheran spokesman, the distinguished Melanchthon, was far more conciliatory than the rest of his party. Discussions centered upon Communion under both species, the sacrificial character of the Mass, the marriage of priests, and episcopacy. Even the attempt at a provisional settlement broke down when the Protestant Estates denied that the Confession of Augsburg was a complete statement of their doctrine. With that, "Luther triumphed over Melanchthon."[21] The Colloquy of Leipzig of 1539 featured Melanchthon again, as well as Martin Bucer, who has been called "the very incarnation of the irenic spirit,"[22] opposite Witzel. All were under the sway of Erasmus. But as their draft on reunion skirted controversy, it cannot be taken seriously. It was as much a private conference as a colloquy.

19. Jedin, *CT*, I, 217.
20. Bataillon, *Erasme*, pp. 246-249.
21. Jedin, *CT*, I, 261. The Colloquy of Marburg was not a Protestant-Catholic dialogue and need not be considered here.
22. McNeill, *Unitive Protestantism*, 146.

The high point of the concord movement in Germany was the Colloquy of Ratisbon (Regensburg) of 1541. Like so many others, it was not without political motivation. The Emperor was resolved to promote reunion in the face of a Turkish threat and an impending war with France, and at the same time to reduce the risk of civil war in the empire. The Protestants were led by Melanchthon and Bucer, with Calvin acting as observer and counselor. The Emperor prevailed upon Paul III to send the respected and conciliatory humanist, Gasparo Contarini, to lead the Catholics. The collocutors managed to reach agreement on free will, original sin, and even justification, but the rupture finally came on the Eucharist and, as it turned out, the colloquy's famous formula on justification, the *Iustitia duplex*, was rejected by both Wittenberg and Rome. The failure of Ratisbon pointed toward the Council of Trent. The Emperor's determined efforts to impose a settlement in the Augsburg Interim of 1548 obtained no consensus, and the Colloquy of Worms of 1557, inhibited by the decrees of Trent, found even Melanchthon no longer conciliatory and perhaps can be written off as anticlimactic. Irenicism in Germany became more and more a lost cause.

After the Peace of Augsburg (1555), Calvinism became the ascendant form of Protestantism, and France the terrain where the critical battle would be fought. Were "the eldest daughter of the Church" alienated from Rome, the prospects for Protestantism might be unlimited. And France, now rocked by the second wave of the Reformation, found itself in approximately the same position as Charles V at an earlier date. Though it could profit by the German experience, the German settlement, with its principle of *Cujus regio, ejus religio*, was unworkable in France. There was but a single prince. It was all or nothing.

Just as the ground of the Reformation was shifting toward France, so too was that of irenicism. Erasmus had had a wide impact on the country. The French enjoyed an old tradition of conciliarism and a more recent one of *réformisme*. The latter, both Catholic and evangelical, belonged to those gray but hopeful years when Renaissance shaded off into Reformation and was probably best exemplified in Jacques Lefèvre and Guillaume Briçonnet. And in 1534-1535 Francis I, ably assisted by Guillaume and Jean du Bellay, the latter the bishop of Paris, had invited Melanchthon to France in hope of effecting an accommodation in religion. Though both sides were responsive, the plan came to nothing, largely because political considerations worked against it.[23] In all events, there had been some prelude to the role that France was about to play.

The Colloquy of Poissy is more than a long-forgotten chapter in sixteenth-century ecumenism. Held on the eve of the French Religious Wars—to which it was a conceivable alternative—it might also be characterized as a sixteenth-century summit conference. The colloquy represented an attempt to establish peace and unity, and because men somehow ultimately preferred their opposites, a study of it necessarily brings out the unfinished and even tragic character of the Reformation.

The colloquy can be seen as the Reformation in miniature. It presented a synopsis of the dialectical complexities of sixteenth-century theology and provided a meeting place for religious idealism and political interest—and sometimes for the reverse. The Reformation was many things, but it was fundamentally a religious movement, and its language was theology. Poissy, as part of the Reformation, had its peculiar political, constitutional, and fiscal dimensions, but it was primarily a religious convention. Although theology was the medium of discourse, it was not an end in itself, but a means

---

23. *Ibid.*, 162-168. On *réformisme*, see Pierre Imbart de la Tour, *Les origines de la Réforme* (3 vols., Paris, 1905-1914), III; and Margaret Mann, *Érasme et les débuts de la Réforme française (1517-1536)* (Paris, 1934).

to a higher end: religious reconciliation. This is not, therefore, so much a study in the abstractions of theology as a study in ecumenism. Poissy is not an island, and the colloquy must be seen against a larger historical background, and an estimate must be made of what chances of unity then existed. Within this larger context it will be argued that the colloquy represented the final crossroads for the crisis of the sixteenth century. With it, the Reformation was sealed and the Counter-Reformation signaled. This assessment involves some revision of the conventional view of both.

The colloquy has been studied before, but not from quite this perspective. Two works on the subject appeared in the nineteenth century. The better is that by Henri Klipffel, *Le Colloque de Poissy* (Paris, 1867), though Klipffel had a limited appetite for theology and really approached the colloquy from the perspective of a *politique*. The other, Napoléon Peyrat, *Le Colloque de Poissy* (Paris, 1868), is little more than a short whig polemic (98 pages to Klipffel's 207) and warrants no serious consideration as history. Neither exploited the available sources, and both are now out of date. Our century has seen several works dealing with the colloquy, notably Lucien Romier, *Catholiques et Huguenots à la cour de Charles IX* (Paris, 1924), and H. Outram Evennett, *The Cardinal of Lorraine and the Council of Trent* (Cambridge, Eng., 1930). The former treated the colloquy sparingly, and while the latter considered it at greater length, he did not really appreciate it as a serious dialogue. Both men wrote in what was almost a different world, one that presumed schism as normative. Neither treated the conference on images at Saint-Germain, intimately related to Poissy, and neither elaborated upon the full implications of the colloquy vis-à-vis the Council of Trent or the special significance, which will be argued here, of the new pontificate of Pius IV. In a letter to me in 1962 Evennett encouraged my own endeavors before his death. The late Paul

F. Geisendorf's *Théodore de Bèze* (Geneva, 1949) and several more recent essays by other writers show that the critical role of the enigmatic cardinal of Lorraine has never been resolved. With the appearance of the relevant volumes of the critical edition of the *Correspondance de Théodore de Bèze* all the major sources have now been published. The publication of Beza's correspondence and the growing volume of work in sixteenth-century ecumenism, not the least of which is that of Hubert Jedin, make this an appropriate time for a new investigation of the colloquy in its wider context. For it may be that an ecumenical age best understands ecumenism.

I / Two Medici and Two Overtures

Ostons ces mots diaboliques, noms de parts, factions et séditions: luthériens, huguenots, papistes, ne changeons le nom de Chrestien.

Michel de L'Hospital[1]

Sainct Augustin, instruisant une dame,
Dit que l'amour est l'âme de nostre âme,
Et que la foy, tant soit constante et forte,
Sans vraye amour est inutile et morte.

Chanson pendant le Colloque de Poissy[2]

Twin events make 1559 a good year to open our story. That year marked an arresting but apparently unobserved coincidence of occurrences on opposite sides of the Alps, in Rome and in the North. They can be intriguingly related.

We can begin in the North. In 1559 the Treaty of Cateau-Cambrésis—often seen as signaling the emergence of the Counter-Reformation—concluded the long and extravagant Italian wars between the Hapsburg and Valois monarchies. Both Philip II and Henry II were financially exhausted, and neither could afford the luxury of a dynastic rivalry in the face of the advance of Protestantism. Needless to say, their swords were not converted into plowshares, but they were prepared for the chastisement of heresy. The festive games accompanying the treaty ended suddenly, however, in a funeral dirge when the lance of a nobleman accidentally opened and entered the French King's visor. The blow that killed Henry ultimately effected a revolution in

1. *Oeuvres complètes de Michel de l'Hospital, Chancelier de France*, ed. P.J.S. Dufey (3 vols., Paris, 1824-1825), I, 402.
2. Lancelot de Carle *et al.*, in V.L. Saulnier, "Autour du Colloque de Poissy: Les avatars d'une chanson de Saint-Gelais à Ronsard et Théophile," *BHR*, XX (1958), 57.

French policy and brought the magnificent Valois monarchy to the point of dissolution.

The King's heir and successor, Francis II, was but fifteen years of age, a fact likely to encourage dissident elements. Moreover, the new King, with persuasion from his engaging young wife, Mary Stuart, bypassed the princes of the blood, the Protestant Bourbons, and delegated the administration of the realm to her uncles, the Catholic Guises.[3] This brought into a new prominence the permanent party of the Counter-Reformation in France. But the triumph of the Guises had the compensating effect of uniting Bourbon and Huguenot in a common cause against their rule. The Bourbon-Guise rivalry must not be underestimated: the Florentine ambassador went so far as to characterize the whole religious contest as a variation on their contentions.[4] Though this is undoubtedly an exaggeration, it compels a brief review of the political background, which has been fully treated by others.

The Guise family was at this time led by Francis, duke of Guise, a war hero and the most admired warrior in France, and his thirty-four-year-old brother, Charles, the cardinal of Lorraine. His biographer described Lorraine as "optimistic, forceful and mercurial," and the Florentine ambassador spoke of him as "Pope and King in France."[5] There was no immediate change of policy after the death of Henry. The Guises not only continued but intensified his repression. But martyrdom only multiplied conversions, in this, the Huguenots' finest hour. It is held, for example, that there were sixty-two Reformed congregations in France at the

3. H. Outram Evennett, *The Cardinal of Lorraine and the Council of Trent* (Cambridge, Eng., 1930), p. 66; *Négociations diplomatiques de la France avec la Toscane*, ed. Abel Desjardins (6 vols., Paris, 1859-1886), III, 401-402.

4. *Négociations*, ed. Desjardins, III, 464.

5. Evennett, *Lorraine*, 23; *Négociations*, ed. Desjardins, III, 404. For a general and rather inadequate study on the Guises, see Henri Forneron, *Les Ducs de Guise et leurs époque: Étude historique sur le seizième siècle* (2 vols., Paris, 1877).

death of Henry II;[6] two years later there were an estimated 2,150.[7] At the latter date the total Huguenot population was put variously as above 600,000,[8] and once even as high as 4,000,000.[9] In May 1959 the dauntless Huguenots held their First National Synod in the capital itself. Everywhere the sacraments were administered à la mode de Genève.

The number of the Huguenots was probably not as significant as their quality. After the Treaty of Cateau-Cambrésis the unsettled and unemployed nobility found that they could enhance their position by becoming patrons of the new churches. Within a few years of the peace an estimated half of the nobility were of the Reformed party.[10] This both fortified and diluted the Huguenot churches, which could at times be used as a vehicle of protest against the rule of the *parvenu* Guises.

6. Félix Rocquain, *La France et Rome pendant les guerres de religion* (Paris, 1924), p. 22. Unfortunately, the author does not give the source of his information.

7. *Histoire ecclésiastique des églises réformées au royaume de France*, ed. Johann Baum and Edward Cunitz (3 vols., Paris, 1883-1889), I, 669. Following custom, I shall cite the pagination of the original edition of 1580, provided in the margins by the present editors. Modern writers consider these figures reliable: see Robert M. Kingdon, *Geneva and the Coming of the Wars of Religion, 1555-1563* (Geneva, 1956), p. 79. For a recent study on the *HE*, one of the foremost sources for Poissy, see E. Droz, "L'Imprimeur de l'*Histoire Ecclésiastique* (1580)," *BHR*, XXII (1960), 371-376. The exact place of the first printing is unknown; it was given as Antwerp to facilitate circulation. The author notes that Beza himself took the initiative in the compilation of the work; Simon Goulart was more of an editor.

8. This figure was given by the Venetian ambassador. *CSP: Foreign*, Mar. 14, 1562, No. 935 (4).

9. Four million was the, undoubtedly grossly inflated, figure noted in the remonstrance of Charles IX to the Pope. *Mémoires de Condé, Ou Recueil pour servir à l'histoire de France, contenant ce que s'est passé de plus mémorables dans le royaume, sous le regne de François II, et sous une partie de celui de Charles IX, où trouvera des preuves de l'histoire de M. de Thou* (6 vols., London, 1743-1745), II, 812. In a moment of exasperation the cardinal of Lorraine declared that Protestants constituted two-thirds of the kingdom, a comparable exaggeration. Evennett, *Lorraine*, p. 661.

10. Lucien Romier, *Le royaume de Catherine de Médicis: La France à la veille des guerres de religion* (2 vols., Paris, 1922), II, 258-259.

Poised against the Guises were some of the highest ranking families of the realm. Foremost among them was, of course, the House of Bourbon. Anthony of Vendôme, king of Navarre, was the nominal head of the family. Vacillating but ambitious, he sought to replace the Guise ministry with his own and even dreamed of inheriting the crown of Charlemagne himself,[11] as well as recovering Spanish Navarre, lost in the course of the Hapsburg-Valois duel. Anthony's wife was the famous Jeanne d'Albret, higher principled, more Protestant, and certainly more faithful than her husband. His brother, Louis, prince of Condé, was bolder than Anthony and equally ambitious.[12] Another great house aligned against the Guises was that of Châtillon. The most eminent member of the family was Gaspard de Coligny, admiral of France. Coligny, a devout Calvinist and a Protestant hero even if he could view religion from a political point of view, would be the effective leader of the Huguenots until his martyrdom on St. Bartholomew's Day.[13] His brother Odet, cardinal-archbishop of Beauvais, was a heterodox prelate privately affiliated with the Reformed Church.

The Huguenots, then, were no longer a minority to be persecuted but a power to be reckoned with. This boded ill for the Guises because the Huguenots, whether religious or *politiques*, had a common interest: the subversion of Guise

11. Baron Alphonse de Ruble, *Antoine de Bourbon et Jeanne d'Albret* (4 vols., Paris, 1881-1886), III, 263-264. Lucien Romier, *Catholiques et Huguenots à la cour de Charles IX*(Paris, 1924), judges this work severely. He is especially critical of Volume II. See also his *La conjuration d'Amboise* (Paris, 1923).

12. See Duke Henri d'Aumale, *History of the Princes of Condé in the XVI and XVII Centuries*, tr. Robert B. Berthwick (2 vols., London, 1872), I, 50. The cardinal of Bourbon, who remained with the old faith, is an exception to most of the statements made about the Bourbons collectively. On Jeanne d'Albret, see Nancy Lyman Roelker, *Queen of Navarre, Jeanne d'Albret* (Cambridge, Mass., 1968).

13. See the vast biography of Jules Delaborde, *Gaspard de Coligny, amiral de France* (3 vols., Paris, 1879-1882). See also J. Shimizu, *Conflict of Loyalties: Politics and Religion in the Career of Gaspard de Coligny, Admiral of France, 1519-1572* (Geneva, 1970).

rule. The explosive possibilities of the situation were realized when religious and political interests came together—heresy allied with treason—in an abortive, Bourbon-inspired coup in March 1560 known as the Conspiracy of Amboise.[14] The conspiracy had contrasting and paradoxical effects. The initial result was a horrible vengeance wreaked upon the conspirators by the redoubtable Duke of Guise, although Condé, the mastermind of the plot, feigned innocence and was spared. The ultimate effect was more striking: the very occurrence of the conspiracy marked the failure of force and proved the imperative need for a change in policy.

The key figure in this new turn of affairs was Catherine de' Medici, "the merchant's daughter" of Florence, now Queen Mother, who thus made her debut in the profession of statecraft. This was an indirect consequence of the Guise ascendancy. The conspiracy, and the attendant criticism of the Guises, provided Catherine with the incentive to enlarge her hitherto passive role in affairs. In effect, she compensated for the loss of her husband by a new passion for politics. She was encouraged in this by the Huguenots and particularly by Coligny, with whom she developed a kind of working arrangement. He attached himself to the royal cause, in return for which she threw her weight on the side of toleration. This bore fruit in the form of several royal edicts, as a consequence of which persecution finally relented.

This was an impressive beginning to what might almost be termed a *volte-face* in royal policy. An act of equal significance was the sudden call by the cardinal of Lorraine for a national council of the Gallican Church, a project to which

14. Amboise has generated several important studies. In addition to the works of Romier, see Henri Naef, *La conjuration d'Amboise et Genève* (Geneva, 1922). Two months before the conspiracy, and as though in anticipation of it, the circumspect Hubert Languet, Calvinist observer of August of Saxony, surveyed the situation and remarked that it was "impossible that things could continue in this manner any longer." *Arcana seculi decimi sexti* (3 vols. in 1, Halle, 1699), III, 32.

he held tenaciously throughout the heated and multifarious correspondence that it generated in the year following.

It was perhaps as inevitable as it was ironic that Lorraine's acquiescence in the new tolerance rebounded upon him. The Huguenots, exhilarated by the first taste of royal indulgence after the long repression, erupted into iconoclasm, the Guises being not the least of the idols to crack. On Easter Sunday Lorraine was hanged in effigy in Paris. The confidence of the Guises was shaken by an outpouring of Calvinist invective, the most notable piece being Francis Hotman's famous *Epître au tigre de la France*.[15] Criticism of the Guises only strengthened Catherine's hand. It was against this setting that the Queen Mother summoned an Assembly of Notables where, among other things, the Guises might render an account of their stewardship.

Known as the Assembly of Fontainebleau, the meeting convened in August 1560. Fontainebleau is less important for the defense of the past by the Guises than for the new personalities whom it introduced. Foremost among them was the new Chancellor, Michel de l'Hospital, one of the finest products of the French Renaissance. Legist, orator, and poet, he was above all an Erasmian humanist, temperate and reformist.[16] Another important personality who became a moderating voice at court was the maverick prelate, Jean de Montluc, bishop of Valence. Tolerant and irenic, he was suspected of heresy, but was more probably a spirit in advance of his time. Montluc delivered the boldest speech at Fontainebleau. He spoke sharply of the indolence of the French

---

15. On Hotman, see R. Dareste, "François Hotman, sa vie et correspondance," *Revue historique*, II (1876), 1-59, 367-435.

16. The best recent study on the Chancellor is Albert Buisson, *Michel de l'Hospital* (Paris, 1950), who stresses his Erasmian background and feels he was a Huguenot at heart. He remained a Catholic, but his wife and children were of the Reformed faith. See Henri Amphoux, *Michel de l'Hospital et la liberté de conscience au XVIe siècle* (Paris, 1900), p. 192. See also the Chancellor's letter to the Pope, Aug. 1561, *Oeuvres*, II, 478-479.

clergy, contrasting the luxury of their lives with the zeal of the Huguenot ministry. He passionately opposed persecution, the remembrance of which made his "hair stand up on his head." And he confirmed that "punishment has profited nothing, but to the contrary, the patience of those who have endured these things has inspired more to favor their cause." His remedy was a general or a national council, preferably the latter, based on the example of Charlemagne. Montluc was among the first to suggest that Calvinist leaders be invited to such an assembly, in the hope of reaching an accord. It is small wonder that he was suspect.[17]

The assembly resolved upon a convocation of the Estates General for December and, a month later, in default of a general council, on an Assembly of Prelates. Meanwhile, leniency would be shown to all Protestants not involved in treason. It is ironic that a new equation of Protestantism and treason promptly occurred.[18] The conspiracy was that of Lyon; the conspirators, the Bourbons. And, as before, the scheme misfired. This time the Bourbons were in complete disgrace, and Condé was under sentence of execution. But chance saved him. On December 5, after a short illness,

17. Montluc was especially suspected by the militantly orthodox Spanish ambassador, Thomas de Perrenot, count of Chantonnay. *Condé*, II, 20, 22. The dean of his own chapter denounced him as a heretic. J. Plèche, "L'Évêque Jean de Montluc et la réforme à Valence (1560)," *BSHPF*, LXXVII (1928), 22, n. 2. Evennett, *Lorraine*, pp. 146, 242, denies that he left the Catholic Church, but considers him "a loose living, sceptical and secularized Dominican," an exaggerated view. Montluc himself advanced the spectacular claim of having reconciled 40,000 souls in his diocese by allowing Communion under both kinds, which was illicit. George Cassander (Cassandri), *Opera que reperiri potuerunt omnia* (Paris, 1616), p. 1132. See Montluc's *Apologie contre certaines calomnies mises sus à la desfaveur et desavantage de ce roiaume* (n.p., 1562), a later defense of Catherine's policies, where he sounded like a liberal Catholic. For his speech, see *Condé*, I, 555-568, especially 567, for the quoted passages.

18. Pierre de la Place, *Commentaires de l'estat de la religion et république sous roys Henry et François seconds et Charles neufviesme (1565)*, ed. J.A.C. Buchon, *Choix de chroniques et mémoires sur l'histoire de France* (Paris, 1836), p. 68; *Négociations lettres et pièces diverses relatives au règne de François II*, ed. Louis Paris (Paris, 1841), pp. 486-490; Ruble, *Bourbon*, II, 315-316; Romier, *Amboise*, p. 219; Paul F. Geisendorf, *Théodore de Bèze* (Geneva, 1949).

young Francis II died—and with him the claims of the Guises
to rule. The Huguenots were understandably jubilant and
praised God for what seemed a miraculous deliverance.

These events were the prelude to a quiet revolution at
court, which was as significant in effect as the contrived
seditions of the Bourbons had been in design. The new King,
aged ten, was Catherine's second son, Charles IX. By custom
the regency belonged to Navarre, but he had forfeited his
position by his recent intrigues. This provided the opportunity for the Queen Mother, who was forty-one and free of
compromising commitment to either Bourbon or Guise, to
consolidate her power by assuming the regency herself.

Catherine's Protestant-oriented policies were based less on
conviction than circumstance. Her pervading desire was to
preserve the independence of the throne; to achieve this she
strove to maintain a fine, if uneasy, balance between the
great families, favoring at one time the Bourbon at another
the Guise. Because the latter had dominated the realm in the
recent past and still had a majority on the Council, Catherine
first turned to the Bourbons to establish equilibrium.[19]

The new policies were soon put into effect. The Estates
General convened without result at Orléans in December.
Because it followed so closely the death of the King and the
change at court, there was a prevailing mood of uncertainty.[20] When the Estates proved reluctant to approve

19. Paul Van Dyke, *Catherine de Médicis* (2 vols., New York, 1928), I, 243.

20. For the Estates, see J. Russell Major, *The Estates General of 1560*
(Princeton, N.J., 1951). One cause for uncertainty was that the Huguenots were
not invited to the Estates since they were in poor repute at the time of its
announcement, which followed shortly on the recent conspiracy. See Letter for
Assembly of the Estates General, Nov. 1560, Paris, *Négociations*, 636-639. They
did, nevertheless, present a petition to the Estates requesting "a free and holy
Synod" where they might be heard, the liberation of prisoners held for religion or
sedition, and toleration. Coligny, who had been a deputy of Catherine at Orléans,
presented the petition to the Council, but it failed to obtain a majority.
Delaborde, *Coligny*, I, 499-500. In his *Mémoire sur le Concile*, written about the
same time, Calvin made an oblique appeal for a national council. See his *Opera*,
XVIII, 287. This will be considered in Chapter II, below. For another Huguenot

Catherine's regency, they were prorogued so that they could consult their constituents. When they reconvened in the new year, at Pontoise, they reflected the spirit of the new government. The provincial estates meanwhile displayed aggressive anticlericalism, called for the expulsion of the Guises from court, and even envisaged a Protestant France.[21] Condé and Coligny soon took seats in the Council, and though Catherine was too politic to rout the Guises completely, she vented her resentment against "those who are accustomed to be King" in letters to her daughter, the wife of Philip II.[22] Her wrath was formalized in a private agreement with Anthony. He waived his rights to the regency, in return for which she appointed him lieutenant general of the kingdom— an office only recently held by the Duke of Guise—thus making Anthony second-in-command. The pendulum had gone full swing.

The advances of the Huguenots at court were paralleled by expansion throughout the realm, in what has been called "The Huguenot Lent."[23] Feeling that the court was on their side, Calvinist pastors abandoned restraint. Popular passions were unleashed, and the realm was rent by riots and disorders, with excesses committed on both sides. Catherine herself scandalized the Catholics by conducting the King and her other children to a Calvinist sermon at the admiral's château. It was the year of the high tide of French Calvinism.

The Huguenot Lent, however, was only the prelude to a resurrection of Catholic power on Easter Sunday. If Catherine was tardy to balance the weight of the Huguenots within

---

appeal for a national council, associated with the Estates of Orléans, see *Condé*, II, 649-655.

21. For details, see Noël Valois, "Les Estats de Pontoise," *Revue d'histoire de l'église de France*, XXIX (1943), 237-256.

22. *Lettres de Catherine de Médicis*, ed. Hector de la Ferrière (10 vols., Paris, 1880-1909), I, 581, 592-593.

23. Romier, *C&H*, pp. 71-87. Meat was being sold freely in Paris. La Place, *Commentaires*, p. 122.

the government, it should be done without. The Constable, Anne de Montmorency, had hitherto been attached to his nephews, the Châtillons. But he was a militant Catholic and was now induced by circumstances to abandon his long-standing rivalry with the Duke of Guise. On Easter Sunday 1561 they, along with the marshal, Jacques d'Albon de Saint-André, struck an alliance known as the "Triumvirate." The three men of arms pledged themselves to ensure the orthodoxy of the royal house and the defense of the Catholic faith. The promoter of the Triumvirate was the old-guard prelate, the Cardinal Francis de Tournon, archbishop of Lyon and, as such, primate of Gaul.[24] It is not without irony that Tournon, who had counseled Catherine to assume the regency, hoping thereby to diminish the authority of his rival, the cardinal of Lorraine, now set a watchdog over her. It was essentially a defensive action, but it also held a threat.

Catherine reacted to the Triumvirate by becoming even more dependent upon Navarre and the Reformed party. On April 19 she indirectly established religious toleration within private homes. Within a few days Tournon and the Spanish ambassador, Thomas de Chantonnay, made one of their many remonstrances.[25] But the cleavage went deeper than the matter of toleration, and turmoil continued. Far off in Geneva, Theodore Beza surveyed the situation in France: the churches swelling but Paris in tumult; the confusion following the promulgation of new and contradictory edicts;[26] and

---

24. Michel François, *Le Cardinal François de Tournon: Homme d'état, diplomate, mecéne et humaniste, 1489-1562* (Paris, 1951), pp. 406-407. Evennett, *Lorraine*, p. 230, stresses Lorraine's independence of the alliance. For the triumvirs other than Guise, see Francis Decrue, *Anne de Montmorency, grand maître et connétable et pair de France sous les rois Henri II, François II, et Charles IX* (Paris, 1889); and Lucien Romier, *La carrière d'un favori: Jacques d'Albon de Saint-André, Maréchal de France (1512-1562)* (Paris, 1909).

25. *Condé*, II, 6-10; François, Tournon, p. 405.

26. In July a joint session of the King's Council and the staunchly orthodox Parlement of Paris brought about a new edict, the Edict of July, theoretically proscribing Huguenot worship. See *Condé*, I, 42-45. It remained a dead letter.

the formation of the Triumvirate. Seeing all this, he reflected darkly of the future: "it looks like civil war or wretched servitude."[27]

Catherine had three choices at this point. First, she could return to a repression of the Huguenots. This course had not only been tried and found wanting, but the Huguenots were simply too numerous for maternal corrections. Second, she could join the Huguenots and throw the weight of the crown on their side. In view of St. Bartholomew's Day, there is, paradoxically, evidence that this possibility did enter into Catherine's calculations, and the young King was reported to have promised to become a Protestant upon reaching his majority.[28] But this alternative meant a confrontation with the Triumvirate. Either solution promised a civil war. In this dilemma, religious reunion seemed to furnish a third possibility, and this the court tried to achieve.

The irenicist George Cassander wrote in 1561: "All Gaul is divided into three factions." One was the "Papists," headed by Tournon; another was the "Huguenots." Both were implicitly extremists. But there was another group that he called "the third party," which was moderate and pacific. This included Catherine, l'Hospital, Montluc, the cardinal of Lorraine, and the king of Navarre.[29] The Colloquy of Poissy was, in the main, the work of this third group.

The foremost role must be accorded the Regent, the affairs of the realm being ultimately her responsibility. Catherine was far from a theologian; in fact, the Venetian ambassador commented that she "did not understand what the word

27. *Correspondance de Théodore de Bèze*, collected Hippolyte Aubert, ed. Henri Meyland and Alain Dufour *et al.* (6 vols. to date, Geneva, 1960-1970), III, 113.

28. See Beza, *Correspondance*, III, 226, 242. The young Charles IX reportedly told his aunt, Jeanne d'Albret: "Assuredly, aunt, when I am my master I shall quit the Mass." Jules Delaborde, "Les Protestants à la Cour de Saint-Germain lors du Colloque de Poissy," *BSHPF*, XXII, 504; Roelker, *Queen of Navarre*, p. 171.

29. Cassander, *Opera*, p. 1131.

dogma meant."[30] She was a mother, and she wanted peace. She sought national reform, provisional toleration, and "sweet reconciliation."[31] Her irenicism may have been expedient, but it was nonetheless real.

The attitude of l'Hospital and Montluc has already been described. The Chancellor's ideal is summed up in the stirring address at the opening of the Estates at Orléans wherein he made a celebrated and unique appeal for one faith. "Let us remove these diabolical words, names of parties, factions and seditions: Lutherans, Huguenots, Papists; let us not change the name of Christian."[32] As regards Montluc, he was among the first to suggest that the Huguenots be invited to the projected national council. Both were high in Catherine's counsels and outspoken irenicists. They were to prove their words with deeds. Lorraine is included in the middle party. But the cardinal was a many-sided and controversial man, and his role at Poissy cannot be summarized at this point.

Another important member of the circle was the King of Navarre, who played a prominent role in setting up the colloquy; to this Catherine herself attested.[33] Anthony is important not only for his personal efforts, but because he helped connect the national council with the mainstream of European irenicism.

The two remaining personalities were Cassander himself and Francis Baudouin. Cassander was heir of Erasmus as perhaps the foremost irenicist of his day. He held that the key to reunion was a wide, liturgically rather than dogmatically centered, reform, modeled on Christian practice in the

---

30. *Despatches of Michele Suriano and Marc' Antonio Barbaro, Venetian Ambassadors at the Court of France, 1560-1563*, ed. Sir Henry Layard, Huguenot Society of London, VI (Lymington, 1891), 42.

31. Romier, *C&H*, 177. Jean Héritier, *Catherine de Medici*, tr. Charlotte Haldane (New York, 1963), p. 181, who says that *Salus populi suprema lex esto* was Catherine's principle, also says that "Ecumenism was the fundamental basis of her religious views."

32. *Oeuvres*, I, 402.

33. *Lettres de Catherine de Médicis*, I, 190-192, 607.

first five or six centuries. Baudouin, Cassander's prophet,[34] was a historian-legist. Though he was formally a Calvinist, his religious orientation was one of moderation, and his religious professions were various.[35] He had been banished from France for heresy some fifteen years earlier, spent some time in the company of Calvin at Geneva, and was now in the service of the Elector Palatine at Heidelberg. As early as 1558 Anthony, though titular head of the Huguenot party, had shown definite interest in the counsels of moderation, as giving best hope of a settlement for France and had ever since been in contact with Baudouin.[36] It is not surprising that the latter, hearing of the developments in France, scurried off to the French court. Baudouin conferred with Navarre, Catherine, and Lorraine about the Cassandrian ideals[37] and entered the service of Anthony as something like his agent on ecumenical affairs. One of his assignments was to seek Cassander's presence at the colloquy, or at least his advice. By July Baudouin was on his way to Cologne.[38] And by this

---

34. Both were Belgians, though Cassander normally resided at Cologne. On Cassander, see A. Fritzen, *De Cassandri ejusque sociorum studiis irenicis* (Munster, 1865). Jacques-Auguste de Thou, *Histoire universelle* (11 vols., The Hague, 1740), III, 489, eulogized him thus: "He spent his entire life obtaining instruction in the fundamental controversies of the century, seeking ways to calm the passions lest there be greater divisions in the church." On Baudouin, see J. Duquesne, "François Baudouin et la Réforme," *Bulletin de l'Académie Delphinale* (1917) pp. 55-106.

35. The rather uncomplimentary article in *La France Protestante*, ed. Eugène and Émile Haag (6 vols., 2nd ed., Paris, 1877-1878), I, 994-1066, holds that he changed his religion seven times. The more sympathetic treatment of Duquesne emphasizes the continuity in Baudouin's religious thinking and maintains that he always managed to reconcile his conscience in external acquiescence to local practice wherever he happened to be. In the period 1561-1563 he began drifting back to Catholicism, but he did not formally profess the Roman faith until 1563. Duquesne, "François Baudouin," pp. 73, 95-96. Haag, 2nd ed. I, 997.

36. Duquesne, "François Baudouin," pp. 62-63. Anthony's own religious predilections changed with chameleon-like ease throughout the year 1561.

37. Cassander, *Opera*, pp. 1161-1162.

38. Duquesne, "François Baudouin," p. 65. Ill health prevented Cassander's attendance, but he held forth the promise of an appropriate theology for the national council. Cassander, *Opera*, pp. 1123-1125.

time the ship of the middle party had been launched, and the course set.

The decision to hold the colloquy had been made in council by April 22. At that time Catherine mentioned to the imperial ambassador her plans for what she described vaguely as an assembly of a great number of learned and virtuous men. The object of the convention was to be reform and reunion.[39] On June 12, 1561, a convocation of the Gallican Church was formally announced. It remained only to issue specific invitations.

A national solution to the religious troubles in France represented a convergence of the religious fervor of the Huguenots, power politics among the nobility, and the desire for a religious reconciliation to avoid a military reckoning. Religion and politics, irenical idealism and common sense, perhaps even God and mammon, joined hands. The Gallican Church, which meant different things, but stood especially for a certain administrative autonomy, was not itself a direct issue. It undoubtedly had helped produce the cast of mind that turned to a French colloquy at this juncture. But the originators of the colloquy invoked not Gallican principles but historical necessity. They followed precedents and were faithful to patterns set earlier in the Reformation. One of the most striking of these precedents was that which related the failure of the Colloquy of Ratisbon to the first assembly of a critical general council. In just the same way, the Colloquy of Poissy was intimately related to the final assembly of the same council.

What was happening south of the Alps? In the summer of 1559, when Henry II died, with the results discussed, a potentially similar situation had arisen in Rome with the death of Pope Paul IV. Paul, like Henry, had been a violent

39. *Lettres de Catherine de Médicis*, I, 190-192.

persecutor. His successor, like Catherine, was a moderate, and curiously enough, was also surnamed Medici. His succession might well augur a new order in Rome, and hence throughout Europe: perhaps a breakthrough of the religious impasse. It was not impossible, at all events, that this new and relatively inconspicuous Pope would prove the most important one of the century.

Gian Angelo de' Medici was born on Easter Sunday, 1499, and was elected Pope as Pius IV on Christmas Day, 1559. This curious coincidence did not make him a man of destiny. He was a compromise candidate of a troubled, venal, and, above all, locked conclave that had lasted four months. He was perhaps best known for what he was not, and in particular he was not a Paul IV, against whom his election represented a reaction.[40] This negative quality meant doubt as to the kind of Pope he would be and the direction in which he would steer the Church. Perhaps he only personified the Italy of his time. At any rate, implicit within him was a curious mixture of qualities that pointed to three disparate possibilities: Renaissance, Counter-Reformation, and religious reconciliation. The critical question was which of the three would become explicit and set the dominant theme of his reign.

In the first place, there was the possibility that Pius would represent a return to the more relaxed spirit of the Renaissance. He bore the significant name of Medici. Though he was unrelated to the more illustrious Florentine family, being of a lesser Milanese patrician stock, yet, like the two Medici popes before him, he had been something of a humanist-prelate, and it was not impossible that the muses would return to San Pietro once again. Poets were his familiars. He was by training and temper a statesman rather than a theologian, a calm

---

40. Theodor Müller, *Das Konklave Pius IV* (Gotha, 1888), esp. pp. 236-242, 252-256; and Pastor, *History of the Popes*, XV, 6-63.

diplomat rather than an ardent reformer. In 1558 he had left
Rome and the Curia disgusted with the severity of his
fervent, but fanatic, predecessor. His earlier background was
not without blemish. In what was, for the Renaissance,
almost time-honored tradition, he had fathered three illegiti-
mate children before taking major orders. His later piety
seems of a solid if temperate sort. He was a nepotist,
appointing some dozen of his relatives to remunerative
positions, including three to the cardinalate. In the case of St.
Charles Borromeo, a twenty-one-year-old nephew raised to
the cardinalate and appointed the Pope's Secretary of State,
the appointment was amply justified. Apart from Borromeo,
who would be perhaps the greatest Catholic churchman of
the dawning generation,[41] the Renaissance pattern is pain-
fully familiar.

If the Renaissance had not yet completely run its course, a
case can be made that the second alternative, the Counter-
Reformation, had hardly begun, and any concerted Franco-
Spanish war on heresy was prevented by the lance that felled
Henry II. It would probably be more proper to speak of
Catholic Reform at this juncture. Though the fierce Paul IV
breathed the spirit of both Catholic Reform and Counter-
Reformation, he was an individual rather than an institution,
a moralist rather than the architect of a reform movement.
Paul's pontificate was too personal and divisive. His temper
was such that he chose to work without the Council of Trent,
and his intransigence such that he held the new Society of
Jesus suspect. He severed diplomatic relations with the Holy
Roman Emperor, whose office had been the secular cham-

41. Pastor, *History of the Popes*, XVI, 403, wrote of Borromeo as "the good
genius" of Pius. On Borromeo, later archbishop of Milan, see Giuseppe Alberigo,
"Carlo Borromeo come modello di vescovo nella chiesa post-tridentina," *Rivista
storica italiana*, LXXIX (1967), 1031-1052; and André Deroo, *Saint Charles
Borromée, Cardinal réformateur, docteur de la pastorale* (Paris, 1963). On Pius in
general, see Pastor, *History of the Popes*, XV-XVI. Pastor summarizes Josef Šusta,
Pius IV před pontifikatén a nu pocátku pontifikátu (Prague, 1900).

pion of Catholicism in the previous generation, and declared war on Philip of Spain, who would be that champion in the next. Only a legal technicality prevented Paul from excommunicating Philip and pronouncing his deposition.[42] He had isolated the court of Rome and alienated almost every Catholic power.

Paul's pontificate was a reign of terror rather than a reformation. Paul had been the chief inspiration of the Roman Inquisition and employed it not only ruthlessly but recklessly. He put the distinguished liberal, Cardinal Giovanni Morone, to rot in the dungeons of St. Angelo. He revoked the legatine authority of Reginald Pole, archbishop of Canterbury and chief architect of the Marian Restoration, and summoned him to Rome to be tried for heresy, an ordeal he was spared only by death. There was the possibility that he would even consign the Grand Inquisitor himself to the prisons of the Inquisition.[43] Given all this, one can hardly insist that Paul IV launched the Counter-Reformation without allowing at the same time that he was destroying the Catholic Church. Earlier, Paul III may have finally convoked the Council of Trent, but in many respects he continued the ways of the Renaissance. And if Adrian VI failed to launch the Counter-Reformation because his pontificate was too short, Paul IV failed because his pontificate was too violent.[44] In sum, Catholic energies were dissipated, and the religious scene unsettled.

42. Pastor, *History of the Popes*, XIV, 158.
43. *Ibid.*, 317.
44. Hubert Jedin, *Crisis and Closure of the Council of Trent*, tr. N.D. Smith (London and Melbourne, 1967), p. 2, states that Paul's severity brought the reforming party into "disrepute." For some recent views of the Counter-Reformation, see H. Outram Evennett, *The Spirit of the Counter-Reformation* (Cambridge, Eng., 1968), esp. Chapter 1, and the "Editor's Postscript" of John Bossy; Giuseppe Alberigo, "The Council of Trent: New Views on the Occasion of its 4th Centenary," *Concilium*, VII (Sept. 1965), 38-48; A. Dupront, "Du Concile de Trente: Réflections autour d'un IVᵉ centenaire," *Revue historique*, CCVI (1951), 262-280; and Hubert Jedin, *Katholische Reformation oder Gegenreformation* (Lucerne, 1946). I myself am more concerned with the timing than the term.

Paul IV would not be mourned. His passing would, in fact, be greeted in Italy much as the death of Henry II was among the Huguenots. There was a general sense of relief, and there were riots in Rome in which the buildings of the Inquisition were demolished. The dismembering of a statue of the late pope was symbolic of the attitude toward much he had represented. With creative leadership, there was an opportunity for a fresh approach and perhaps some kind of breakthrough in the religious crisis of the Reformation.

The third choice before the new Pope was religious reconciliation. It was impossible to be sanguine about prospects for a general reunion, at this or any other time. But the dream had not been discarded by contemporaries. And Pius was undoubtedly interested in reconciliation and possessed some of the qualities required to fulfill such a formidable ambition. This Pope was by nature accessible, tactful, pacific, and unceremonious. He was the opposite of Paul, making a "complete break" with his rigorism.[45] Pius mitigated the severity of the Inquisition.[46] He restored the surviving representatives of the older "Catholic Evangelism"—the Italian counterpart of réformisme—to positions of dignity in the Church. Cardinal Morone, relegated to the dungeons of the Inquisition by Paul IV, was vindicated and became a close adviser to Pius. The gentle Morone was the ablest diplomat in Italy and the one most familiar with conditions in Germany—homeland of the Reformation.[47] Ercole Gonzaga, cardinal of Mantua, who had earlier also been suspected of heresy and who had reformed Mantua along the lines of Contarini, was to play a vital role in the new administration. He himself had almost been elected at the conclave of 1559,[48] further evidence that there was a genuine desire for

45. Jedin, *EC*, p. 3; Müller, *Das Konklave Pius IV*, pp. 236-42.
46. Pastor, *History of the Popes*, XV, 126.
47. Jedin, *EC*, 3, 102; Jedin, *CT*, I, 333-34.
48. Pastor, *History of the Popes*, XV, 22, 49. There was some preference for a man like Contarini, Pole, or Morone. Müller, *Das Konklave Pius IV.*, p. 155.

change. Finally, much of Italy marveled when the distinguished Augustinian, Girolamo Seripando, who had been deprived of influence during the pontificate of Paul IV, was raised to the cardinalate by Pius. As has been said recently: "It is enough to reflect on the wave of expectation and, on the other hand, the anxiety aroused by Seripando's nomination as Cardinal in 1560."[49] Liberal Catholicism in Italy may have been declining after 1542, and faced by the Roman Inquisition, but it was not dead.[50] Pius was renewing the faith of Italian religious reformers in the possibilities of the Papacy.

There is firm evidence that the new Pope's irenicism was more than a mere façade. He could reveal suggestively liberal tendencies and, in his own words, had even been "reputed a Lutheran" at the conclave of 1559 because he was disposed to permit wives to the clergy and the cup to the laity.[51] This

Gonzaga earlier wrote: "I am a Catholic and should like to be a good Catholic. If I am not a member of the brotherhood of the rosary, then have patience—it is sufficient for me to belong to the brotherhood of Christ." Jedin, *EC*, p. 24. His distinguished sister, Giulia Gonzaga, was still alive and was still faithful to the principles of Juan de Valdés, who might be described as the fountainhead of Catholic Evangelism in Italy. Another member of the same circle, Pietro Carnesecchi, who was summoned to Rome by the Inquisition under Paul IV, secured a vindication under Pius IV, only to be executed under his successor. Oddone Ortolani, *Pietro Carnesecchi* (Florence, 1963).

49. Oddone Ortolani, "The Hopes of the Italian Reformers in Roman Action," *Italian Reformation Studies in Honor of Laelius Socinus*, ed. John A. Tedeschi (Florence, 1965), p. 17. The author insists they had high hopes for the Papacy into the reign of Pius IV. *Ibid.*, 19. On Seripando, see Hubert Jedin, *Papal Legate at the Council of Trent: Cardinal Seripando*, tr. F.C. Eckhoff (St. Louis: B. Herder Book Co., 1947).

50. On this problem, see the first chapter of Philip McNair, *Peter Martyr in Italy* (Oxford, 1967), although the author is sometimes too categorical and makes some untenable statements about Erasmus (p. 4). Delio Cantimori, *Prospettive di storia ereticale Italiana del cinquecento* (Bari, 1960), p. 28, describes four phases: that until the Roman Inquisition in 1542, which he calls the period of Evangelism; the time of crisis from 1542 to 1560, the debacle of liberalism between 1560 and 1580; and the time of utopias from 1580 to 1624.

51. This was what Pius told the French ambassador in 1561. *Instructions et lettres des rois très-chrestiens, et de leurs ambassadeurs, et autres actes concernant le concile de Trente*, ed. P. Dupuy (Paris, 1654), p. 110. He had said the same as early as 1552: Wilhelm Voss, *Die Verhandlungen Pius IV. mit den katholischen*

was not a fortuitous slip of the tongue: he had said the same things many times over the years. These concessions were designed to encourage the reconciliation of the largely Protestant German Empire. They had been part and parcel of the imperial program of reunion for a generation, and Medici had visited Germany.[52] It is true that Paul III was willing to accept similar concessions, pending a council, at the time of the Augsburg Interim. But as these concessions were more or less extorted from him by imperial *Diktat*,[53] the two cases are hardly comparable. Pius volunteered the concessions, despite whispers of heresy. All of this associates the new Pope with the irenical tradition.

It would be easy to dismiss the concessions and their implications as inconsequential. It should also be possible to exaggerate the nature of the theological differences separating the churches. Perhaps the theologians protested too much. Theology is not above the divinization of historical traditions and the rationalization of shifting circumstances. The queen of sciences will be given more than her hour later in this study. For the moment, it should be stressed that disciplinary matters, products of positive law, were the more familiar terrain of the Reformation. The people (not to mention some of the theologians) did not understand the subtleties of justification; they were impressed by externals— by sensible things. Foremost among them were the chalice, celibacy, and a vernacular liturgy. For the people, these were

---

Mächten über die Neuberufung des Tridentiner Konzils im Jahre 1560 (Leipzig, 1887), p. 8. See also Theodor von Sickel, *Zur Geschichte des Concils von Trient: Actenstücke aus österreichischen archiven von Trient* (Vienna, 1870), pp. 18-20, Müller, *Das Konklave Pius IV.*, p. 152; and Gustave Constant, *Concession à l'Allemagne de la communion sous les deux espèces: Études sur les débuts de la réforme Catholique en Allemagne (1548-1621)* (2 vols., Paris, 1923), I, 162-163. With reference to the "heresy" of Pius, it appears that he was obliged to make some kind of retraction in conclave. It would have little effect: "Son sentiment ne varia point." Constant, *Concession*, I, 163. Pastor, *History of the Popes*, XV, 58.

52. Pastor, *History of the Popes*, XV, 76-77; also see Constant, *Concession*, I, 161.

53. Constant, *Concession*, I, 36-37; Pastor, *History of the Popes*, XII, 440-441.

the most conspicuous differences between Rome and the Reformation. Philip Melanchthon understood this and urged upon friend and foe that there could be no accord until, above all, there was an understanding on celibacy and the chalice.[54] Of the two, mandatory clerical celibacy was no doubt the more important. Its relaxation and the consolations of marital love would have the effect of reconciling dissident and conscientious clergy toward a moderate reform within the institutional Church. It could help to remove the feeling that there is no middle way between all and nothing. And the reception of the cup by the laity could also help to soften the overly sharp distinction drawn between laymen and clergy. Both would break down the inordinate stratification in the Church, encourage theological assimilation, and stimulate mutual rediscovery. Both Melanchthon and Medici knew what they were about.

The Pope's potential role as a conciliator depended upon one critical matter. In conclave Medici was pledged to convene a general council of the Church. Although he indicated variously that the concessions might be granted by himself or by a council, his considered view was probably that this should be done by a concurrence of the two.[55] This means that for him a council represented the way to conciliation.

The matter of a council needs to be considered further. Though Pius had been pledged to a general council in conclave, this was little more than a formality.[56] Conciliar

54. Constant, *Concession*, I, 86-88. For an exploration of some of these general problems, see Donald Nugent, "The Historical Dimension in Reformation Theology," *Journal of Ecumenical Studies*, V (Summer 1968), 555-571.

55. Constant, *Concession*, I, 163; Sickel, *Zur Geschichte des Concils von Trient*, 18; and Pastor, *History of the Popes*, XV, 32-33.

56. Müller, *Das Konklave Pius IV.*, 100-105. In September 1559 a convention of cardinals, in conclave, enjoined upon the future Pope various things, but especially the calling of an ecumenical council for the elimination of heresy, the restoration of morals, and the promotion of peace. *CT*, VIII, 1. For Pius' confirmation of the pledge, see *CT*, VIII, 1-3. It does appear that the old irenicist, Jean du Bellay, dean of the sacred college, may have played an important role in

morale was low. The old Council of Trent was "no more than a torso," and one that few, either among its former participants or present supporters, had much heart for completing. Cardinal Pole had resigned his legatine authority in 1546 because he questioned the propriety of defining the central question of the Reformation, justification, in a council of such an unequal and limited composition. The council had had little discernible effect of a positive nature. Its decrees had been neither officially published nor confirmed by the Pope. They might well become a dead letter.[57]

These facts support the argument that the Counter-Reformation had hardly started. Equally, there was a distinct possibility that it might not start at all. The new council could follow the old path of Trent, pursuing it to its conclusion, or it might conceivably be an instrument of confessional reconciliation. It might be a more or less "closed," Roman Catholic council, or an "open" council of truly ecumenical dimensions and broader aspirations.

The new Pope carried, consequently, an enormous responsibility upon his shoulders. Pius' fundamental inclinations were probably known at this point only to himself. At his first consistory on January 10, 1560, he confirmed his pledge to hold a council and expressed a readiness to acknowledge the earlier decrees of the Council of Trent, especially those on reform.[58] And, however unrealistic he may have been, this

the capitulations. Jean Lulvès, "Päpstliche Wahlkapitulationen. Ein Beitrag zur Entwickelungsgeschichte des Kardinalats," *Quellen und Forschungen aus Italienischen Archiven und Bibliotheken herausgegeben vom Koenigl. Preussischen Historischen Institut in Rom*, XII (1909), 226. This, however, may have been only a formality, as he was dean of the cardinals.

57. Jedin, *CC*, p. 13; Jedin, *CT*, II, 314-316. On Pole, see Jedin, *CT*, II, 279. This was his primary reason.

58. Stephan Ehses, "Die letzte Berufung des Trienter Konzils durch Pius IV," *Festschrift G. von Hertling* (Kempten, 1913), p. 140. Ehses, an editor of the *CT*, used the *Acta* of the consistory, and his account is probably better balanced than that in Cardinal de Siguenza to Philip II, Jan. 18, 1560, in *Beiträge zur politischen Kirchlichen und Kulturgeschichte den sechs letzten Jahrhunderten* ed. J.J. Döllinger (3 vols., Ratisbon and Vienna, 1863-1882), I, 328.

did not stop him from urging the hope that the council would end the schism in Christendom. It was clear that there would be overtures to the Protestant world, and Pius believed that at least some of the Lutheran princes would be represented.[59] At one point the Pope told the new and ultra-Catholic Spanish ambassador, Francisco de Vargas, that he was contemplating a council, not in Rome, but in some suitable place where Protestants might come; thus, the burden of guilt would be theirs should they refuse.[60] This might sound equivocal, but Charles V had earlier said much the same.[61] The irenicism of the Pope should be neither exaggerated nor ignored.[62] At this time he might best be described as moderate and conciliatory, and both Protestant and Catholic of similar humor hoped with him that the council would be a bridge to reunite separated Christians.[63]

59. *CT*, VIII, 30, 140-141.

60. Voss, *Die Verhandlungen Pius IV.*, 16.

61. R.B. Merriman, *The Rise of the Spanish Empire in the Old World and the New* (4 vols., New York, 1918-1934), III, 353.

62. In the past the Pope's irenicism has most often been ignored; for example, Pastor, *History of the Popes*, XV, 89, glosses over Pius' attitude toward concessions as an indiscretion that "must be attributed to the want on his part of a thorough theological training." This cannot be taken seriously. The concessions involve no theological subleties. Moreover, Pastor himself elsewhere *History of the Popes*, (XV, 78) allows that Pius was "respected among his colleagues on account of his intimate acquaintance with Canon Law," and it is precisely canon law that the concessions involve. Evennett, *Lorraine*, p. 135, seems to follow Pastor, but is not disposed to develop the point. Jedin, *CC*, makes no mention of the concessions. The concessions, it need hardly be said, encourage one to take the mediatory potentialities of the council seriously.

63. Voss, *Die Verhandlungen Pius IV.*, pp. 8-14; B. Dembinski, *Rzym i Europa przed rozpoczeciem trzeciego okresu soboku trydenckiego* (Krakow, 1890), résumé in *Bulletin International de l'Académie des Sciences de Cracovie* (1890), pp. 235-251, speaks of this as the period when "Rome made its last efforts to restore and consolidate by means of a Council the unity of the Church." C.G. Bayne, in his fine study, *Anglo-Roman Relations, 1558-1565* (Oxford, 1913), p. 46, paints Pius as conciliatory and moderate, but says that while he "desired to offer an olive branch" he "held a sword in reserve." He stresses, however, that Pius intended the council to be one of reunion. Constant, *Concession*, I, 89, notes a revival of the hopes of the party of moderation in Germany at this time; see his Chapter II. The "moderate party" or "party of conciliation" included Pius IV, the Emperor, and many others. The "intransigent party" included most of the sacred college, the Jesuits, and Philip II.

The council was to be the real test of Gian Angelo de' Medici's quality as Pope.

The events of 1559 show that, however elusive the ideal of reunion may have been, some considered it possible, and many had high hopes. There is little reason to consider either Poissy or the Pope's new council a mere gesture. Although in the case of France, irenical zeal arose from mixed motives, it would be improper to speak of the two suits of France and of Rome as inspired, respectively, by politics and religion. There were genuine irenicists in France.

There are interesting but limited parallels between the two Medici. Both sought religious reconciliation. The Medici Queen's own objective was perhaps primarily political, but she used a religious means to the end. The Medici Pope's objective was no doubt religious, but his articulation of it varied according to political expediency. He would speak in slightly different accents with the Spanish and imperial ambassadors. Again, neither Medici was a great theologian, and both were practical people. In both of them there was potential for personal development. In the end, though Catherine and Pius may initially have shared a common purpose, their differences at the instrumental level—general council versus national council—put them at cross-purposes.

II / National Council or General Council?

All Catholics believe that the salvation of the whole Church depends on this Council.
                    Polish delegate on arrival at Trent[1]

Open your eyes, fathers, brothers, sons: Open your eyes, and see how Christ Jesus, redeemer of the world, converted the imprudent. Never in all the Scriptures did He anathemize those coming to Him.
                    Guillaume Postel, irenicist[2]

Contention between the two Medici was predictable. Their overtures show that the dissolution of Christendom was not yet an accepted fact. France was not an island, but part of a larger community, and particular solutions could be held suspect. This was especially the view of Rome. To the new Pope, Catherine's projected royal wedding of Calvinist and Catholic looked more like an elopement than holy matrimony, and he was to insist that only he could officiate at such a union. For him, the danger of a Gallican settlement was theological compromise and national schism. For the French court, elopement was the part of discretion. The French remembered the earlier Tridentine decrees and the rejection of them by the Reformers; they felt that the danger of this kind of Roman solution was theological triumphalism and irrevocable general division. The French court was loath to put its future in the hands of others. The one overture, then, inhibited the other.

1. *Annales ecclesiastici ab anno MCXCVIII., ubi desinit cardinalis Baronius, auctore Odorico Raynaldo . . . accedunt in hac editione notae chronologicae, criticae, historicae . . . auctore Joanne Dominico Mansi . . .* (15 vols., Luca, 1747-1756), (1562), No. 121.
2. *De nativitate ultima,* cited from William J. Bouwsma, *Concordia Mundi: The Career and Thought of Guillaume Postel (1510-1581)* (Cambridge, Mass., 1957), pp. 198-199.

All would depend upon the responses. Curiously, and contrary to general knowledge, the national council inspired almost as much interest as the general council. Christendom made itself a party to Poissy. To show how a French colloquy became a European event, it is necessary to revert to the situation in 1559, beginning with the way it appeared in Spain.

Spain was not only an interested third party in the events already described, but was the other signatory of the Treaty of Cateau-Cambrésis. Events there bear out the theory that the period around 1559 represents some kind of turning point in the sixteenth century. A certain heightening of religious intensity was combined with a combativeness on the part of Catholicism suggestive of a second and critical phase of the religious crisis: the rise of the Counter-Reformation. This seems particularly true for Spain, which was to provide the Catholic antithesis to the two irenical theses advanced.

Spain had not always played this role. In the age of Charles V, Erasmianism, with its mixture of irony and fervor so congenial to the Spanish spirit, flourished more brilliantly there than elsewhere.[3] The Emperor had in his service and entourage a host of Spanish moderates like his Chancellor, Alfonso de Valdés, brother of the more famous Juan, Francisco de Toledo, Bartolomé de Carranza, and Agustín Cazalla. During the second period of the Council of Trent (1551-1552), the Imperial-Spanish party was the champion of concessions and compromise, being often in advance even of the Emperor. At one point, the harried Pope, Julius III, complained: "People here say the Council of Trent is the Council of Toledo."[4] Though this was probably not a direct reference to the city but to the ambassador, Francisco de

---

3. This is well shown in the outstanding study by Marcel Bataillon, *Érasme et l'Espagne* (Paris, 1937), pp. 846-848.

4. *CT*, XI, 776, cited in Helmut Meyer, "Die deutschen Protestanten an der Zweiten Tagundsperiode des Konzils von Trient 1551-52," *ARG*, LVI (1965), 183; also see Igino Rogger, *Le nazione al Concilio di Trento durante la sua epoca imperiale 1542-52* (Rome, 1952).

Toledo, the effect is the same. Charles was a cosmopolitan King, and Spain was generally responsive to the larger needs of Europe.

Things changed about the time that Charles retired. He divided his estates between his brother, Ferdinand, who assumed the imperial dignity, and his son, Philip II, who was heir to Spain, the Netherlands, and the Mediterranean territories. Effective leadership of the Hapsburgs and a position in the center of the stage passed from the Emperor, who ruled lands of mixed religious loyalties, to Spain, monolithically Catholic. Philip would, of course, be encouraged to keep Spain that way. The loss of a unified command meant that imperial needs could no longer swing Spanish policy. The situation led in effect to a breakdown of communications between Spain and the German Protestant territories. The general transition was from a cosmopolitan to a Castilian orientation. Philip was every inch a Spanish monarch, and 1559, when he departed from the Netherlands and Cateau-Cambrésis for the peninsula that he would never leave again, has been properly seen as signaling "the real dividing line between the era of the Hapsburg-Valois wars and that of the Counter-Reformation."[5] During this period the relatively "open" Spain of the Renaissance was superseded by the relatively "closed" Spain of the Counter-Reformation.

This change was one of times more than persons. For

5. Merriman, *Rise of the Spanish Empire* IV, 16. This proposition has considerable general support. Bataillon, *Érasme* p. 743, states that "the spiritual climate of Spain changes very quickly and very profoundly" between 1556, year of the retirement of Charles, and 1563, year of the closure of Trent. J.H. Elliott, *Imperial Spain 1469-1716* (New York, 1966), pp. 213, 221, confirms Bataillon's dates, with the distinction between an "open" and "closed" Spain. Fernand Braudel, *La méditerranée et le monde méditerranéen à l'époque de Philippe II* (2 vols., 2nd ed., Paris, 1966), II, 269-270, seems noncommittal. John Lynch, *Spain under the Hapsburgs* (2 vols., Oxford: Basil Blackwell, 1964-1969), I, 90, 239, is somewhat inclined to revisionism. This tendency is developed systematically in Manuel Fernández Álvarez, *Político mundial de Carlos V y Felipe II* (Madrid, 1966), who argues ardently for the continuity between Charles and Philip. This kind of revisionism would seem to go too far. It breaks down on such things as concessions, the council, and Carranza. (See Fernández Álvarez, *Político mundial*, pp. 236, 238-239.)

example, Charles V's policy of conciliation had not been successful, and, especially in the disillusionment of his later days, he was uncompromising about the prosecution of heresy. There is definite continuity between Charles and Philip, but it is a continuity with a difference. Taken broadly, their reigns do in fact reveal some notable contrasts. This is especially conspicuous if one is investigating irenical rather than political trends. Charles was a student of Erasmus; in 1559 the Spanish Index proscribed much of Erasmus, including the *Enchiridion*. Charles was the great proponent of concessions to Protestants; Philip would be their greatest royal opponent. Charles often obstructed papal policy in the general council; Philip would be its "strongest supporter."[6] Charles was surrounded by men of an Erasmian mold; Philip's most trusted religious adviser was Melchior Cano, the Dominican counselor to the Inquisition. And when Cano announced the principle that "There are propositions which, without overturning the edifice of the faith, shake it,"[7] we seem to be passing from something analogous to a doctrine of a "clear and present danger" to one of merely a "bad tendency." The Inquisition was reinforced in 1559, and applied. The first great auto-da-fé was directed against "Protestants," or heterodox Christians of an Illuminist variety. The year 1559 also saw the scandalous proceedings against Cardinal Bartolomé de Carranza, archbishop of Toledo and primate of Spain, which has been called perhaps "the most important affair during the career of the Inquisition."[8] The same Carranza had attended the Emperor on his deathbed, and the passing of Charles deprived him of the one man who might have saved him the indignity of seventeen years of imprisonment.[9] Philip could allow his power to be identified with the

6. Jedin, *CC*, p. 106.
7. Bataillon, *Érasme*, p. 768, and, in general, Chapter XII.
8. Henry Charles Lea, *A History of the Spanish Inquisition* (4 vols., New York: Macmillan Co., 1906-1907), II, 45, and 45-87 for the entire case.
9. *Ibid.*, 57-58; Karl Brandi, *The Emperor Charles V*, tr. C.V. Wedgwood (London: Johathan Cape, 1965), p. 643.

Inquisition in a way that Charles had never done, and in this extraordinary case he enjoyed the incidental benefit of seventeen years of Carranza's sequestered revenues.[10]

There is one final consideration concerning Spain. The juridical base of the Inquisition's first auto-da-fé against Protestantism was the Tridentine decrees on justification of 1547.[11] Philip himself was in the royal gallery at the great auto-de-fé at Valladolid on October 8, 1559, which meant that these decrees had been confirmed by fire. Whereas Charles had done what he could to obstruct the decrees,[12] Philip would be one of their most vocal exponents. More than orthodoxy was now involved: the honor of the Inquisition was concerned as well as that of the Catholic King himself.[13] Spain was now irrevocably committed to the Council of Trent.

This is by no means to suggest that the grotesque portrait of Philip of the black legend has not been properly discredited. He enjoyed no particular monopoly on intolerance. This period witnessed a new and heightened phase in the religious struggle; this involved personalities as well as incommensurables. Philip's ambassador to Rome, the irascible Francisco de Vargas, summed it up. During the conclave of 1559 Vargas was found climbing through windows and breaches in the walls in order to cajole the cardinals. At one point he shouted to those inside that they were deceiving themselves if they thought they were living in the times of Charles V; it was now "another world."[14]

Spain, the major Catholic power, played a critical part in

10. Elliott, *Imperial Spain*, p. 226; Lea, *Spanish Inquisition*, II, 86.
11. Fidel García Cuéllar, "Política de Felipe II en torno a la convocación de la tercera etapa del Concilio de Trento," *Miscelánea conmemorativa del Concilio de Trento (1563-1963)* (Madrid and Barcelona, 1965), p. 58.
12. For example, Jedin, *CT*, II, 312-313, 280-282, 265.
13. García Cuéllar, "Política de Felipe II," pp. 57-59. On Philip and the auto-da-fé, see Merriman, *Rise of the Spanish Empire*, IV, 17.
14. *Beiträge*, ed. Döllinger, I, 306. Pastor, *History of the Popes*, XV, 26, 63-64. Vargas held quite different principles from Charles's envoy to Trent of the same name. See, e.g., Jedin, *CT*, II, 282.

determining what kind of world this would be. Its role is best revealed in the labyrinthine diplomacy that pitted France against Rome.

The clash began under the ministry of the cardinal of Lorraine. In January 1560, shortly after the conclave and a year before Catherine undertook the regency, Lorraine sent a diplomatic feeler to the emerging champion of Catholicism, Philip of Spain, soliciting support for a general council.[15] France was previously uninterested and even scornful toward the council; its interest now was a telling comment on the effectiveness of the Huguenot apostolate. Lorraine had some cause to expect the concurrence of Philip. A council was not only written into the capitulations of the recent conclave: in the negotiations for the Treaty of Cateau-Cambrésis, Philip and Henry II had agreed to a renewed general council as soon as possible.[16] Philip was, nevertheless, evasive and reluctant to cooperate. At this point he feared that a council might trouble the European peace and that it might not be well received in Germany.[17] It is ironic, then, that Spain justified the French in consulting their own interests.

This was done without delay. On March 22 Lorraine took the matter directly to Rome. Grieving that France was rent and *in extremis*, he pleaded that the projected general council would require precious time to prepare, especially the obtaining of the necessary consensus of the Christian monarchs. He prayed that the Pontiff would send the trusted Cardinal de Tournon—still in Rome with faltering health following the conclave—as legate *a latere* with powers to convoke an assembly of the Gallican Church. While Lorraine pledged that the requested assembly would not replace the general coun-

15. *Négociations*, ed. Paris, pp. 206-207.
16. This council was to obtain "a true union and concord." Lucien Romier, *Les origines politiques des guerres de religion* (2 vols., Paris, 1913-1914), II, 343.
17. *Négociations*, ed. Paris, pp. 278-279.

cil, he was obscure about its precise nature.[18] There was no indication at this point that he intended an interconfessional colloquy. The French court was in a hurry and on March 31 issued the first formal announcement of a convention of the Gallican Church. Its purpose was not only reform, but reconciliation.[19] This could involve compromise—and danger.

The Pope reacted with concern to what can only be called an accomplished fact. On May 12 he wrote to Lorraine, complaining that a certain indulgence was being shown to heresy, but especially against the notion of an assembly of the Gallican Church which, to employ the dreaded word, "manifests schism," particularly in view of a declared general council.[20] He followed this up by appointing a new nuncio to France, Sebastian Gualterio, bishop of Viterbo. The bishop's lengthy instruction can be reduced to two points: to prevent the Gallican convention; to present the case for the general council.[21]

It was soon apparent that a vigorous pursuit of the latter might best serve to frustrate the former. On first hearing of the proposed meeting in France, Pius informed the brother of the French ambassador that he had desired to call a general council since the beginning of his reign; now he planned to convoke it at an early date.[22] What was more emphatic, the Secretary of State, Borromeo, contacted the court of Spain about the desired general council and the dreaded national council, affirming that the Pope "has resolved to use every possible diligence, in order to prevent the said National

18. The Latin text of the missive is published in Evennett, *Lorraine*, appendix I, 471-472. For Evennett's treatment of Poissy against Trent, see Chapters IV-VIII; for Pastor, *History of the Popes*, see XV, Chapters V-VII.
19. *CT*, VIII, 14-15; also see Evennett, *Lorraine*, pp. 475-480.
20. *CT*, VIII, 19-20.
21. *Ibid.*, 20-22.
22. *Ibid.*, 16; *Annales ecclesiastici*, 1560, No. 24.

Council with his universal Council."[2 3] It was not inconceivable, therefore, that the general council might be turned into a mere instrument to obviate the national council.

Pius still revealed both plasticity and sincerity about the possibilities of the council. He was willing to consider various sites and, if the normally judicious Venetian ambassador can be believed, he was prepared not only to accept, but even himself to attend, a general council in the heart of Germany.[2 4]

But the Pope's attitude hardened inopportunely. Forced to action by France and fearful of losing time, he held several weeks later a critical consistory and, on June 3, announced its resolution to the ambassadors assembled in Rome. To avoid interminable delays over the matter of site, as well as the manner of procedure, he would lift the suspension of the Council of Trent. The council would convene at Trent; later, should it so decide, it could move to a more suitable location. He expressed the hope that the Protestant princes would be represented. It was stressed that time was extremely important, "for every day things get worse, as in Germany, or in France, where they are said to be preparing a National Council."[2 5] The "open" council that Pius still sought now seemed more confining.

The Pontiff began to reveal a distinct tough-mindedness in other ways. In following up Lorraine's request of March, Pius now named both Lorraine and Tournon legates *a latere* and inquisitors-general. The former appointment empowered them to summon a small advisory body of bishops, and the

23. Borromeo to the nuncio in Spain, May 25, 1560, *CT*, VIII, 27: His Holiness "ha resoluto di usare ogni possibile diligenza, per previnure il detta concilio nationale con il suo universale." For further confirmation, see *ibid.*, VIII, 28-30. and *CSP: Venice*, June 17, 1560, No. 172.

24. Giovanni Michiel to the doge, May 21, 1560, *CSP: Venice*, No. 161. This was, of course, secondhand information, obtained from the French ambassador in Rome.

25. *CT*, VIII, 30-31.

inclusion of Lorraine was probably a politic gesture to wean him away from a genuine national council; the latter was directed toward a more determined prosecution of heresy.[26] In this same month of June, Pius lent his support to a proposal of the Duke of Savoy for crushing the seat of Calvinism, Geneva, which was suspected of participating in the Conspiracy of Amboise.[27] In the sixteenth century, there was apparently nothing incompatible between gestures of conciliation and measures of coercion. They were both means to a common end.

Philip of Spain responded to Pius' announcement first. He had originally been cool to the suggestion of a council, wary lest it upset the precarious peace or compromise his special relationship with England. But the sands of circumstance change. Philip grew increasingly anxious as he watched the rapid advance of heresy north of the Pyrenees and south of the Spanish Netherlands, and listened to what seemed the reckless talk of a national council. Such inducements stimulated reconsideration. Within weeks, he was conveying his approval to Rome, conditional upon that of the Emperor and of France.[28] It is significant that he not only wanted this to be a council *at* Trent, but *of* Trent. It should be a continuation of the old, rather than a new, council. And this relates to the incendiary question of justification.[29]

The positions of France and Spain can be readily contrasted. The French could not be enthusiastic about the continuation of a general council to which Protestants had

26. *Ibid.*, 28, no. 2, and 34-35; François, *Tournon*, p. 388.

27. François, *Tournon*, pp. 394-395; Naef, *Amboise*, pp. 422-423, 513-517. The proposal was dropped owing to the opposition of both France and Spain. François, *Tournon*, pp. 394-395; Lucien Romier, *La conjuration d'Amboise*, (Paris, 1923), pp. 160-161. Perhaps it should be pointed out that both parties to the religious upheaval mused over such projects at this period. See Intelligence from the court, *CSP: Foreign*, June 1, 1560, No. 149, for a Protestant equivalent.

28. Voss, *Die Verhandlungen Pius IV.*, pp. 49-50.˜ ed., *Beiträge*, ed. Döllinger, I, 37-39.

29. *CT*, VIII, 78-79.

shown such animosity and which had produced such censures. France wanted a fresh start. In July 1560 the government wrote several long appeals to Spain, urging the support
of Philip for a general council, but not the one Pius seemed
to have in mind. Anything less than a new council would be
"in vain" and would lead to "terrible extremities." Using
frank and compelling language, the French insisted that "the
errors of Trent" must not be repeated.[30] Philip offered his
own characteristic rebuttal: a just repression of the heretics
would be of more value than the kind of council the French
had in view, and to this end he volunteered 7,000 or 8,000
men, as well as his gendarmerie.[31] There would be no
meeting of minds.

The Emperor was in a position to break the deadlock. As
has been indicated, Philip's acceptance was contingent on
that not only of France but of the Emperor, and a general
council that did not enjoy some kind of imperial participation would be no more than a tinkling cymbal. For this
reason, all eyes turned to Vienna. There the pious and liberal
Ferdinand I, brother of the late Charles V, was himself
surrounded by an entourage of irenicists,[32] and far beyond
that, what seemed a sea of heresy. Ferdinand understandably
did not want to see these waters disturbed. Germany rested
in the uneasy modus vivendi of the Peace of Augsburg, and
the Emperor was wary lest a council—and, what is more, one
without Lutheran representation—would be hostile toward
his Protestant subjects, incite strife, and perhaps bring back
the horrors of the Schmalkaldic Wars. Because of all these
factors, his view was closer to that of the French.

Ferdinand went even beyond the French. The Pope was to

30. *Négociations*, ed. Paris, pp. 431-435, 442.
31. *Ibid.*, p. 553.
32. For some particulars on this circle, see Constant, *Concession*, I, 102-36; see
also O.H. Hopfen, *Kaiser Maximilian II und der Kompromiskatholizismus*
(Munich, 1895). Constant, *Concession*, I, 89, n. 3, speaks of German Catholicism
as being profoundly penetrated by a sentiment for unity at this time.

see that Protestants, including those of England, Denmark, and Sweden, were represented in the council. Liberal safe-conducts would be necessary, and the Protestants must have ample opportunity to address the assembly. It should be a new council, not a continuation of that at Trent, to which Constance and Ratisbon were preferable locations. It was also proposed that the Pope have recourse to other means of restoring religion, such as a thorough moral reform, Communion under both species, and permission for priests to marry.[33] Furthermore, the Emperor sought a reconsideration of the crucial decrees on justification.[34]

The Pope replied as diplomatically as possible. Germany was ruled out as a site because the powerful Protestant majority might force the Emperor's hand. Protestants were, nevertheless, to be guaranteed a liberal safe-conduct. The Pope dealt obliquely with the status of the old council, suggesting that it was only the wars of Ferdinand's brother, the late Charles V, that had caused its suspension in the first place. A discreet silence was observed on the issue of justification, for Philip was importuning for its solemn confirmation.[35] The requested concessions, toward which the Pope was seemingly amenable, were shrewdly converted into an argument for the council. Pius submitted them to the Congregation of Cardinals, who declared that they could be decided only by the council itself.[36] This was an inducement

33. Hosius to Borromeo, June 21, 1560, *Nuntiaturberichte aus Deutschland 1560-1572 nebst Ergänzenden Actenstücken*, ed. Stefan Steinherz, (2 vols., Vienna, 1897-1903), I, 53-56.
34. Vargas to Philip, June 19, 1560, *Beiträge*, ed. Döllinger, I, 364-65.
35. *CT*, VIII, 78; *Nuntiaturberichte*, ed. Steinherz, I, 99-109.
36. *CT*, VIII, 78-79. Constant, *Concession*, I, 196, characterized Pius as "very irresolute" and says this was a means "to evade the question." Most of the cardinals were opposed, particularly those created by Paul IV, whose influence was not terminated by the grave. Morone and Gonzaga were among the minority in favor. Constant, *Concession*, I, 174. The arguments of the opposition were scarcely respectable or edifying. Constant, *Concession*, I, 173-176. Pius was to some extent becoming captive to this group.

to get Ferdinand's acceptance of the council. In another important respect, however, it was a tactical miscalculation, for it made the Pope dependent upon the more conservative sacred college. This would inhibit creative leadership.

By autumn 1560 Ferdinand had made something of a reassessment. The key here seems to be that although France and the Emperor could make common cause on the general council, Ferdinand, like Philip, was frightened by prospects of a French national council. Such assemblies can be contagious, and should the French example inspire one in Germany, it would be dominated by the Protestant princes, thus serving neither the Emperor nor his faith. Though he expressed his preference for Innsbruck as the site for the council, his acceptance was qualified by two conditions: special approaches were to be made to the Lutheran Princes; and it was not to be considered a continuation of the prior Council of Trent. The requested concessions would be set before the council.[37]

The Emperor also acceded to a suggestion that he use his good offices to encourage French concurrence. His fervent missive to France was not without effect, for by November the French had acquiesced in the general council.[38] But surrender was not unconditional. France followed the Emperor and the King of Spain in accepting Trent, but contrary to the wishes of the latter and in accordance with

37. *Nuntiaturberichte*, ed. Steinherz, I, 132-140; *CT*, VIII, 79-85.

38. Another consideration that softened France for acceptance was a remarkable letter from the cardinal of Ferrara to Francis II and Lorraine. This letter, no longer extant, alleged that Pius considered several new locations acceptable, including the Savoyard town of Vercelli, which Lorraine had earlier approved. In France a new site sounded like a new council. Perhaps Ferrara was repeating loose talk in Rome about the possible transference of the council once it had been convened in Rome; perhaps he was attempting a crafty stroke to end a deadlock. In any event, Lorraine acceded. See cardinal of Lorraine to cardinal of Ferrara, Oct. 31, 1560, Evennett, *Lorraine*, appendix V, p. 482; Francis II to cardinal of Ferrara, Oct. 31, 1560, *CT*, VIII, 91-92; Vincenzo Pacifici, *Ippolito II d'Este, Cardinale de Ferrara* (Tivoli, 1920), pp. 294-295; see also *Négociations*, ed. Paris, p. 619, for Pius' earlier treatment of Vercelli and Besançon.

the view of the former, this was to be, in effect, a new council, not a continuation. It might be announced with or without mention of this. Time was dear, and, if the Pope acted without delay, "all the other particular assemblies and congregations will cease and the memory of them will be extinguished." The important thing was that there be a "good Council free and general."[39] But this expression could sound in Rome like the familiar Protestant formula.

The summer and fall of 1560 was a long and trying season for the Pope. The conditional concurrence of France and the Emperor resolved nothing. He could not meet their conditions for a new council without risking a rupture with Philip: there was no mean between starting a new council and continuing an old one. In this dilemma, circumstances disposed the Pope toward Spain. First, Spain was the most positive of the "big three" Catholic powers. Philip had demonstrated his goodwill by dispatching to France a special envoy, Don Antonio de Toledo, to argue the case for his construction of a general council and aversion toward a national council—only to exercise his good offices in vain.[40] Second, not only were the French and imperial reactions similar, they were received in court about the same time, thus inclining the Pope to detect some kind of Franco imperial cooperation against his own purposes.[41] This compounded the Pope's fear of a schism.[42] Beyond this, it may well have had the dual effect of inducing the Pope to associate concessions and colloquies, so that his horror of the latter

39. Francis II to the Pope, Nov. 5, 1560, *CT*, VIII, 95-97.
40. *Ibid.*, 63-65; *Négociations*, ed. Paris, pp. 616, 622.
41. *Correspondance de Philibert Babou de la Bourdaisière, Évêque d'Angoulême, depuis cardinal, ambassadeur de France à Rome*, ed. E. Henry and C. Loriquet, *Travaux de l'Académie Impériale de Reims* (Reims, 1859), pp. 12, 16-18. These fears were not without foundation. There had been some Franco-imperial efforts at coordination. *Nuntiaturberichte*, ed. Steinherz, I, 84, 89-91, 127-128.
42. La Bourdaisière, *Correspondance* p. 34.

prompted a timidity about the former,[43] and of rendering him generally more defensive. Finally, of the three powers, the Pope was beginning to despair of France. He considered Ferdinand "of good will but weak." He reportedly told the French ambassador that Ferdinand was so weak he was "little obeyed by his own children."[44] The rivalry of the one power and the reserve of the other were enough to drive the Pope into the arms of Spain.

The Pope seems to have been inclined toward Spain even before he went into a second critical consistory on October 3, 1560.[45] The worst was presumed about France, which it was held might soon be alienated from the Holy See. The Pontiff attacked the Guises and declared that Tournon was "the only good Catholic in France."[46] It was agreed that the general council would be opened by the removal of the suspension of the former Council of Trent.[47]

The next week, Pius sent a poignant message to the Catholic King, acknowledging the failure of the Toledo mission and gravely remarking that most of France seemed to be turning to "Lutheranism." He then went on to affirm his resolution: "So much the more are we resolved presently to open the Council of Trent, even if we have only the assistance of Your Majesty, knowing that all Italy and many princes outside Italy will follow this holy proposal; and we will hope that the Emperor, now beset with great difficulties . . . may at last defer to our wills . . . and if this will happen, then the Emperor will know how to influence France to do the same. Thus we will begin happily and we will prevent this National Council, may God help us."[48] All

43. *Ibid.*, p. 13.
44. This is a reference to Ferdinand's son, Maximilian, who was as close to the Lutherans as he was to the Catholics. *Ibid.*, pp. 20-21.
45. *Ibid.*, pp. 13, 57-58.
46. These extravagant statements were probably based on a report from Toledo. *CT*, VIII, 63-65.
47. A secret dispatch from Amulius to the doge, Oct. 13, 1560, *ibid.*, 88.
48. Pius to Philip, *manu propria*, Oct. 11, 1560, *ibid.*, 86.

this suggests that the kind of council Christendom would get was determined by a paradoxical combination of Spanish support and Franco-imperial dissent.

The bull formally convoking the general council, *Ad ecclesiae regimen*, was drawn up and published on November 29, 1560. Because of the contradictory positions of France and Spain, it need hardly be said that the text of the bull severely taxed the diplomatic finesse of the Pontiff. He tried to be all things to all men. Pius reviewed the history and travails of Trent in such a way as to do no more than imply the validity of its earlier decrees. The council would open at Trent on Easter Sunday, 1561, and all Christian princes would be invited. The key words were that it was convened "sublata suspensione quacumque" (each and every suspension being lifted). The phrase meant that the suspension of the Council of Trent was to cease, and while it was implied, it was not explicitly stated that this entailed a continuation of the earlier assembly.[49] In an effort to please the French and the Emperor, the word "continue" was conspicuously absent from the bull, though it was included in the proclamation of indulgences preceding it; to satisfy the King of Spain, a "new" council was not mentioned. It remained to be seen whether such ingenious ambiguity would satisfy the great powers.

In France a new government hopefully awaited the bull. It

49. *Ibid.*, 104-107. It should be noted that one of the chief theological consultants assisting the committee that drew up the bull was Diego Lainez, general of the Jesuits. He was a strong "continuationist" and an important figure at Poissy. See Hartmann Grisar, *Jacobi Lainez disputationes Tridentinae* (2 vols., Innsbruck, 1884), II, 1-17. The references of Lainez to the possible presence of "heretics" suggest this must have been a serious concern in the counsels of the committee. *Ibid.*, II, 3ff. A final remark on Poissy as a cause of Trent is irresistible. When the bull had been at consistory on November 29, Pius turned to the cardinal of Ferrara and asked: "Nonne, putatis, concilium nationale Franciae hac via sublatum iri?" Ferrara answered: "Concilium illud jam extinctum est". *Acta consistorialia, CT,* VIII, 103-104. Ferrara would soon be on his way to oversee this "extinct" French council.

will be recalled that on December 5 the young Francis II had died, and an even younger Charles IX ascended the throne. Lorraine had been dislodged from power, and Catherine de' Medici was ready for her beginner's lesson in politics. Not one to tarry, the day after her elder son's death Catherine wrote to the bishop of Rennes, her ambassador in Vienna, indicating her approval of a general council. But this was predicated upon the expectation that there would be a new convocation rather than a simple continuation of the old Council of Trent.[50] The bull was presented to the court on December 17. The cardinal of Lorraine seems to have cooled the initially warm reaction when he pointed out that the *sublata* clause implied continuation and not a new convocation. The court apparently followed his lead when he indicated that his own personal acceptance or rejection would depend upon the reaction of the Emperor.[51] A week later Catherine sent a message to Rennes, urging him to persuade the Emperor to press the Pope for a revision of the bull. Otherwise, "we will be forced, to my great regret and in despite of what I have done up to now, to bring about the National Council."[52]

50. *Lettres de Catherine de Médicis*, I. 156-57.
51. *CT*, VIII, 139.
52. ". . . et contre ce que j'ay faict jusques icy en ceste affaire." *Lettres de Catherine de Médicis*, I. 159. This, incidentally, offers some corroboration of the view that Lorraine had led the government's conciliar policy up to this time. Romier, *Amboise*, p. 157, despite a certain ambivalence, holds that Catherine took the initiative in summoning the national council. His proof is, however, unconvincing. He bases his argument on Lorraine's request that the cardinal of Tournon, his *rival* and someone whom Catherine trusted implicitly, should preside over the projected assembly. (See also his *Le royaume de Catherine de Médicis* [2 vols., Paris, 1922], II, 143-145.) Evennett, *Lorraine* pp. 95-96, on the other hand, credits Lorraine with the leadership, arguing forcefully that Tournon was requested because a non-French presiding officer would be unpopular. It must be borne in mind that this was an ecclesiastical matter and one on which Catherine would be unlikely to have bold views, at least at this time. On the efforts of the English to dissuade the French from accepting the bull, see *CSP: Foreign*, Dec. 31, 1560, No. 832(7), Jan. 15, 1561, No. 883(3), Feb. 26, 1561, No. 1030(5-7, 21), Apr. 29, 1561, No. 151(4). These attempts were principally the work of William Cecil.

Meanwhile, on January 4, 1561, the crown sent an appropriately ambiguous message to the bishops of the realm. While the summons to Trent was announced, it was also stated that Easter would hardly allow adequate time. Then the national council was postponed, and the bishops were instructed to remain in their dioceses until further notice, praying God that the Pope might find "more convenient" ways to bring about the general council and that all Christians might be united in a common faith.[53]

The French reaction to the bull placed added weight upon the already weary shoulders of the Emperor. While Ferdinand was disheartened by the phrasing of the bull, he was realistically inclined to doubt that the mere removal of offensive terms would conciliate the Lutherans. His caution about the council was moreover, probably balanced by his fear of a French national council.[54] Wary of commitment, he opted to make no formal statement until he might consult the Protestant princes.[55] They were themselves about to convene at Naumburg to consider the council and their own lack of unity in the face of it.

Protestants would obviously play an important role in determining what kind of council this would be, for they were, fundamentally, what the council was about. There had already been something of a preliminary sounding of Protestant Germany in the summer of 1560. This was done, curiously, through the agent of the bishop of Rennes, French ambassador to Vienna. Rennes sent his agent, a Dr. Beier, into Germany, apparently with instructions to make discreet inquiries from the princes about the Conspiracy of Amboise.

53. *CT*, VIII, 122-123.
54. *Die Römische Kurie und das Konzil von Trient unter Pius IV. Actenstücke zur Geschichte des Konzils von Trient*, ed. Josef Šusta, (4 vols., Vienna, 1904-1914), I, 183.
55. Hosius to Borromeo, Jan. 22, 1561, *Nuntiaturberichte*, ed. Steinherz, I, 195-199.

In the process, Beier managed to explore their attitudes toward the general council and to intimate to them the views of the French government. The answers varied. Philip of Hesse was vague, but indicated favor for a council based on the model of the early Church. Frederick, duke of Saxony, and Wolfgang, count palatine, concurred with France.[56] The Duke of Württemberg, recalling the fruitless presence of his theologians at Trent in 1552, said a council called by the Pope had little hope of success.[57] Beier reported the mission to Heinrich Bullinger, who, in turn, described it to Calvin.[58]

Calvin himself was closely attuned to conciliar developments. Sometime during this period Calvin conceived and wrote a remarkable memorandum in which he revealed his own conciliar thinking and, particularly in view of the polarity between Geneva and Rome, an encouraging penchant for conciliation. He announced that "a free and universal" council was essential to end the divisions in Christendom. He dealt with locale, safe-conducts, voting, the Papacy (to which he might permit a kind of first rank but which would be subject to, and not above, the assembly), procedure, and an extensive enumeration of the pertinent theology to be discussed. He declared, however, that if a truly universal council could not be held, a prince could remedy his own troubles with a national council. This seemed a gesture toward France. Finally, he stated that if a "partial Council" claimed universality, it would only increase discord.[59] This was a warning directed at Trent. In sum, the

56. Arthur Heidenhain, *Die Unionspolitik Landgraf Philipps von Hessen* (Halle, 1890), pp. 173-174, 192.

57. Bernhard Kugler, *Christoph, Herzog zu Wirtemberg* (2 vols., Stuttgart, 1872), II, 138ff.

58. Aug. 30, 1560, Calvin, *Opera*, XVIII, 171-173. It might be added that in the spring of the next year Catherine sent the Marshal de Vieilleville on a "goodwill mission" to Germany concerning conciliar developments. Abbé Charles Marchand. *Le maréchal François de Scépeaux de Vieilleville et ses mémoires* (Paris, 1893), pp. 183-190, 344-349.

59. "Mémoire sur le concile," Calvin, *Opera*, XVIII, 285-287. Jaques Cour-

work seems ambivalent, but reveals Calvin's genuine concern for the unity of Christendom.

The effective Lutheran answer to Trent was given at Naumburg. There the princes of the Confession of Augsburg gathered in January 1561 to consider the council and the problems it presented. They included the electors of Saxony and of the palatinate; Philip, landgrave of Hesse; the dukes of Saxony, Pomerania, Württemberg, Deux-Ponts, Brunswick, Lüneburg, Mecklenburg, Holstein, and Anhalt; the marquis of Baden; and the count palatine.[60] It is no wonder the Emperor was careful of Protestant sensitivities.

Before the end of January the papal nuncios Zaccaria Delfino and Giovanni Commendone appeared before the Naumburg Convention. They presented special invitations, offered safe-conducts, and provided assurances that the Protestants, addressed as "Beloved son," would be given fair hearing. The announced goal of the council was nothing less than the restoration of religious unity.[61] But there was now, conspicuously, no mention of concessions. The reaction was one of disappointment, but given circumstances and precedents, perhaps it was predictable. The princes affirmed their own secure unity under the Confession of Augsburg[62] and

voisier, "La dialectique dans l'ecclésiologie de Calvin," *Regards contemporains sur Jean Calvin, Actes du Colloque Calvin, Strasbourg, 1964* (Paris, 1965), p. 100, supports, at least by implication, the view that Calvin took the irenical possibilities of the general council seriously. See also the comments of McNeill, *Unitive Protestantism*, p. 213. This *Mémoire* has been dated December 1560 and March 1562. For particulars, see Beza, *Correspondance*, IV, 50, n. 5, 58, n. 22, and Chapter VII, n. 78.

60. Calvin, *Opera*, XVIII, 293. That this ensemble was a European concern, see for England, *CSP: Foreign*, Dec. 31, 1560, No. 832 (7); for Spain, *Correspondance de Marguerite d'Autriche, Duchesse de Parme*, ed. Louis Gachard (3 vols., Brussels, 1867-1881), I, 446; and for France, *Lettres de Catherine de Médicis*, I, 579.

61. *CT* VIII, 142-143; see also Robert Calinich, *Der Naumburger Fürstentag 1561* (Gotha, 1870), pp. 188-208.

62. It was not exactly true that the princes were united. Naumburg fanned the flames of the old Flaccian-Philippist controversy. See, e.g., Bullinger to Calvin and Beza, May 26, 1561, Beza, *Correspondance*, III, 105-106; Heinrich Heppe,

responded to the nuncios with a resounding *nein.*[63] Commendone spent much of the year canvassing the empire from Brandenburg to Denmark on behalf of the council, but in vain.[64]

The first decade of Elizabeth I's reign was the definitive period for the Reformation in England, Europe's historic balancer. There are some interesting reasons for arguing that, in 1561, England's religious future had not been definitively decided. Certainly the Pope had great hopes for a reconciliation. Although the Act of Supremacy of 1559 had renounced allegiance to Rome, the personal religion of the young Elizabeth was a will-o'-the-wisp. Her occasional protests of Catholicism were undoubtedly politic, but she did hint that she wished to be represented at the council and declared herself anxious for reunion.[65] The ambitious and unpredictable Robert Dudley, Elizabeth's favorite and suitor, was a curious element in her calculations. Dudley has been described as "the most important single individual in the political world of the new reign."[66] A politician, Dudley claimed to have Catholic sympathies at this time and solemnly affirmed that Elizabeth and he were determined to restore Catholicism by means of the general council.[67] Moreover,

Geschichte des Deutschen Protestantismus in dem Jahren 1555-1581 (4 vols., Marburg, 1852-1859), I, 364ff.

63. *CT*, VIII, 151-152. There had earlier been indications that the old attitude had not altered. *CSP: Foreign*, Dec. 12, 1560, No. 781 (14).

64. *CT*, VIII, 162-169. For an invitation to an oriental church, see Raffaele de Simone, "L'invito di Pio IV ad Ivan IV Zar di Russia per la partecipazione al Concilio di Trento," *Unitas*, IV (1962), 342. I could find no indication, however, that an invitation was expressly delivered to Geneva. This may be because relations between Geneva and its former overlord, the Duke of Savoy, were completely ruptured.

65. *CSP: Spain*, Apr. 27, 1561, No. 127; C.G. Bayne, *Anglo-Roman Relations 1558-1565* (Oxford, 1913), pp. 93-94, and appendix, pp. 259-260.

66. W.T. MacCaffrey, "Elizabethan Politics: The First Decade, 1558-1568," *Past & Present*, XXIV (Apr. 1963), p. 30; see also his *Shaping of the Elizabethan Regime* (Princeton, N.J., 1968), esp. Chapter V.

67. Quadra to Philip II, Jan. 22, 1561, *CSP: Spain*, No. 122. See MacCaffrey, "Elizabethan Politics," p. 38; and N.M. Sutherland, "The Origins of Queen

Elizabeth was strong in her indignation "against the Protestant preachers who, in the pulpit, had not concealed their disapproval of her behaviour" toward Dudley.[68] This might render her receptive to the advances of Rome.[69]

So encouraged, Pius prepared his overtures, but from the beginning everything went amiss. Philip grew restive lest the project end in fiasco and result in the total alienation of Elizabeth, thereby damaging his special relationship with England. Elizabeth herself became equivocal, fearing political undertones. Her Secretary of State, William Cecil, more Protestant than the Queen, fabricated a "priest scare" which, coupled with the threat of rebellion in Ireland, disposed Elizabeth to listen to his blandishments. The final blow came when the Knights of the Garter pronounced against the Elizabeth-Dudley match. The papal nuncio, Abbot Girolamo Martinengo, was denied admission to the realm.[70] From this point England grew ever more fixed in the Protestant orbit, and a future emissary from Rome would be the Armada.

Pius' promise of "fatherly mildness," made in consistory prior to the issue of the bull of convocation,[71] was far from enough to lure the Protestants to Trent. In accordance with a request from the Emperor, notices of safe-conduct were later posted on the doors of the cathedral there, with the normal designation "heretic" replaced by the expression "those who do not agree with us in faith, and believe otherwise than the

Elizabeth's Relations with the Huguenots," *Proceedings of the Huguenot Society of London* XX (1966), 639-640, for their various reactions.

68. Conyers Read, *Mr. Secretary Cecil and Queen Elizabeth* (London: 1955), p. 203; he holds it "doubtful" whether Elizabeth really contemplated a return to Rome. Doubt, however, implies the existence of a certain possibility. We should be wary of reading history backward. There would have been, moreover, some material advantages to Elizabeth in a restoration, such as the securing of her throne against Mary Stuart, and a Spanish alliance.

69. *Ibid.*, p. 203.

70. *CSP: Rome*, "News Letter" of July 24, 1561, No. 89; Read, *Mr. Secretary Cecil*, p. 209.

71. Voss, *Die Verhandlungen Pius IV.*, p. 127.

Holy Roman Church teaches."[72] There were no Protestants
inside. Circumstances were such that the council would be
more Catholic than catholic.

One cause of this was France. As has been seen, the threat
of a French national council had caused Pius to react harshly,
without giving mature consideration to the problems posed
by a general council. It diminished the choices, narrowed
possibilities, and accelerated, or, perhaps, precipitated, the
papal decision for the ill-starred, and ominous location of
Trent. A Tridentine council was *a fortiori* an unacceptable
general council to Protestants. A French dialogue reduced
the possibility of holding a genuinely European dialogue,
and, conversely, the failure of a European solution inspired
national remedies.

There was, at the same time, the paradox that while an
international council was allowed to become largely national,
a national council showed promise of becoming international.
For example, Jean Sturm, the humanist and irenicist of
Strasbourg, reacted to the announcement of a council with
his own proposals. He urged a synod of European Protestants
to effect Protestant unity; failing that, he advocated the
internationalization of the national council in France, so that
it would include Germans and Englishmen as well as the
French. The ambitious and ubiquitous Anthony of Navarre,
lieutenant-general of France, was central to Sturm's plans.[73]

72. *Annales ecclesiastici* (1562), No. 17.
73. Sturm to the Elector Palatine, Jan. 1561, Calvin, *Opera*, XVIII, 320-326. It
is worth noting that such a synod was advanced at the Diet of Augsburg in 1559.
There Philip of Hesse advocated a synod of all evangelical Christians to effect
Protestant unity. Arthur Heidenhain, *Die Unionspolitik Landgraf Philipps von
Hessen* (Halle, 1890), pp. 58 ff, 86 ff. The call was perhaps prompted by
Cateau-Cambrésis and the latent threat of a concerted Catholic attack upon
heresy. Melanchthon, who had earlier been such a champion of unity, referred to
the proposal as "only a Platonic idea" and dismissed it, asking, among other
questions, who would convoke it, preside over it, and so forth. *De synodo
theologorum*, Melanchton's *Opera quae supersunt omnia*, ed. Carolus Gottlieb
Bretschneider, in *Corpus Reformatorum* (21 vols., Halle, 1834-1854), IX,
989-993.

Anthony had long cultivated his relationship with the German princes;[74] they now wanted to reciprocate.

The princes who were assembled at Naumburg, viewing with curiosity the developments in France, sent a message to the French court, urging the rejection of the Pope's council. At the same time, undoubtedly with one eye on the national council, they promised their readiness to assist "with all their best means in advancing religion."[75] The Duke of Württemberg, a militant Lutheran, was more explicit. On June 12, responding to a call from Anthony for political support for the persecuted Huguenots, he urged a Gallican council upon Anthony—with learned representatives from Germany. And he enclosed a copy of the Confession of Augsburg, soliciting its serious consideration.[76] Navarre sought political support and received the Confession of Augsburg! Christopher Mundt, Elizabeth's observer at Naumburg, noted that the Germans wanted the adoption of this confession in France, but he pointed out that this would cause "some difficulty" with the Calvinists.[77] Nevertheless, the English, responding to the suggestions of Navarre[78] and Coligny,[79] showed a keen interest in the national council.[80] Interest in a French council, then, seems to complement lack of interest in Trent.

74. Henri Hauser, "Antoine de Bourbon et l'Allemagne," *Revue historique*, XLV (1891), 54-61. Ruble says: "The relations of the King of Navarre during the Colloquy of Poissy were only an incident of the great negotiations that the Prince directed secretly against the King of Spain." *Bourbon*, III, 264.

75. *CSP: Foreign*, May 9, 1561, No. 189(1).

76. Kugler, *Christoph*, II, 291-293, 303-304. At the same time the Duke of Guise had been in communication with the Duke of Württemberg, a complication treated later. Their correspondence will be found in the S.A., Frankreich, A 115, Büschel 15, 18, 19 and 20. The relevant pieces are published in the *BSHPF*, XXIV (1875), 71-83, 113-122, 209-221, 499-511.

77. Mundt to Cecil, *CSP: Foreign*, July 15, 1561, No. 319(1).

78. Navarre told the English ambassador that if there were no accord on a general council they would arrange a national council in France and that if Elizabeth would "send some learned personages thither it would do great good." Throckmorton to Elizabeth, *ibid.*, Dec. 31, 1560, No. 832(7).

79. Throckmorton to Elizabeth, *ibid.*, Apr. 29, 1561, No. 151(4,9).

80. Throckmorton to Cecil, *ibid.*, May 31, 1561, No. 218.

Needless to say, European interest in a national council could be a hazardous thing. It is mentioned here to show the connection among Trent, the Protestant world, and Poissy.

As the year 1561 progressed, Rome observed developments in France with increasing anxiety; the concern was not without some basis. The Estates at Orléans had shown extreme anticlericalism. And on January 31, 1561, the Ordinance of Orléans undertook to legislate a part of the *cahiers*, forbidding Annates and Preventions and abolishing any power of the Pope to confer benefices in France.[81] Earlier there had been fears in Rome that Lorraine aspired to a French "patriarchate." In January 1561 an alarmed Pope told the Spanish ambassador that Lorraine was a "heretic."[82] Cursed by the Huguenot as persecutor and maligned by Rome as heterodox, Lorraine was at this time "universally hated."[83]

Authority now rested in the hands of Catherine de' Medici. It will be recalled that her reaction to the bull of convocation was made contingent upon that of the Emperor. Though Catherine was anxious for news from Naumburg, she was apparently at this time ill informed about events in Vienna. Rome, or Viterbo, put a wide interpretation on the Emperor's reluctance to reject the announcement and encouraged Catherine to believe that the Emperor had, in effect, accepted the bull of convocation. Catherine therefore felt compelled to keep her word, and she accepted. She instructed the cardinal of Lorraine to make the necessary preparations for the Gallican Church.[84]

Events proved that this acceptance was of little moment. Easter Sunday, April 6, 1561, the appointed day for the

81. *Die Römische Kurie*, ed. Šusta, I, 88.
82. *Beiträge*, ed. Döllinger, I, 349; *CT*, VIII, 65, 1, 139, n. 5.
83. *Suriano, Despatches*, p. 14.
84. *Die Römische Kurie*, ed. Šusta, I, 169.

opening of the Council at Trent, arrived at last—and so had four bishops. There were not even any papal legates at Trent.[85] This, joined with other considerations, led to the revival of the national council and its actual convocation. A number of factors assisted in this decision: the nature of the general council and the council's delay;[86] Protestant rejection of the council at Naumburg; renewed violence and religious strife during "the Huguenot Lent"; and the influence of the advisers to the French court.[87]

The order for the convocation of the national council was issued on June 12. The Gallican Church was to assemble on July 20 at Poissy and to meet concomitantly with the Estates General at Pontoise. The stated objectives suggested nothing extraordinary: the choice of prelates for Trent; discussion of the role of the Gallican Church at Trent; measures that must be considered for the securing of the flocks during the absence of their pastors; and deliberations on "several things of great importance" about which the Queen desired to consult the prelates.[88] This was an oblique call for a national solution of the religious troubles of France.

Rome was soon aware of the facts. The French ambassador there, Sieur de Lisle, was soon emphasizing to the Pontiff that France needed "a stronger medicine" than other countries since it was "more sick." This could be "a free and general council" and a "new convocation." He stressed the responsibility of the King to his subjects and the danger of a

85. Pastor, *History of the Popes*, XV, 252.

86. The Pope prorogued it for six months, or as some cynics said, "ad Calendas Graecas." *CSP: Foreign*, Apr. 26, 1561, No. 147(3).

87. For example, l'Hospital argued that a general council without Lutherans would be superfluous. *Die Römische Kurie*, ed. Susta, I, 181, 184. On Chantonnay's reports of these events to Margaret of Parma, see *Ibid,.*, 183-184, 202-203.

88. *Instructions et lettres des rois-très chrestiens, et de leurs ambassadeurs, et autres actes concernant le concile de Trente* ed. P. Dupuy (Paris, 1654), pp. 79-80.

permanent division of Christendom through an ill-conceived general council. The pope reportedly considered France "lost and abandoned."[89] Nevertheless, Pius took action. He immediately dispatched instructions to Viterbo to do all that was possible to postpone the Gallican council and, failing that, to restrict its discussions to secondary matters.[90] At the same time the Pontiff obtained reinforcements—or prepared to administer an "extreme unction." Rome felt that the crisis called for spokesmen more perceptive and astute than Viterbo. This brought forth Ippolito d'Este, cardinal of Ferrara, a man of broad political experience, who was appointed legate *a latere* to France.[91] The Pope selected Diego Lainez, general of the Jesuits, as a theological counterpart. Lainez had been an adviser to popes from Paul III to Paul IV and had played a decisive role in the earlier deliberations at Trent, where he had been the foe of theological compromise and the friend of conservatism.[92] Ferrara and Lainez would serve the Pope well. Finally, Pius sent a moving exhortation to the French court hoping, among other things, to delay affairs in France pending the arrival of his reinforcements.[93]

The Pope was, meanwhile, compensated elsewhere for his agonies over France. In May the Emperor resigned himself to the council, declaring that he had done what he could to obtain Protestant participation. He even affirmed that he would go to Trent himself, if the Pope would do likewise.[94]

89. Lisle to the King, June 26, 1561, *ibid.*, 82-84.

90. June 26, 1561, *Die Römische Kurie,* ed. Šusta, I. 214-215, 203.

91. Pacifici, *Ippolito II d'Este*, p. 292; Evennett, *Lorraine*, pp. 259-260. Viterbo would be replaced in October. Both he and Tournon had been duped by the subtlety of Catherine's summons and her assurances that the Gallican Council would deal only with moral reform. Viterbo could not believe "the boasts of these Huguenots" that they would participate in the assembly. *Die Römische Kurie,* ed. Šusta, I, 200-201, 207-208, 217.

92. Feliciano Cereceda, *Diego Lainez: En la Europa religiosa de su tiempo 1512-1565* (2 vols., Madrid, 1945-1946); Jedin, *CT,* II, 256, 383.

93. *Die Römische Kurie,* ed. Šusta, I, 219; Noël Valois, "Les Estats de Pontoise," *Revue d'histoire de l'église de France,* XXIX (1943), 240.

94. *Nuntiaturberichte,* ed. Steinherz, I, 248-252. Ferdinand, then, finally turned a deaf ear to what Delfino called "the bad offices" of France. *CT,* VIII, 113, n. 1.

Spain shortly rendered its formal concurrence. Philip accepted on June 5, promising that his prelates would leave for Trent no later than September 1.[95] Philip sought and obtained assurances—though in private form—that the bull of November 29, 1560, did not call a new council but rather continued the old.[96] By September 1561 Viterbo was entertaining Philip with thoughts of a league, headed by Spain, to ensure the maintenance of Catholicism in France.[97] And as early as January, the Legate Tournon, ever loyal to Rome, addressed Philip as one of "the principal pillars of the faith," saying that it was in the Catholic King that he "put all his confidence."[98] All this was part of a larger development whereby Spain and Rome, so estranged under Paul IV, seemed to be tying their fortunes together under Pius IV. To many, Spain and Roman Catholicism became almost interchangeable loyalties. This was, obviously, the period when Spain was emerging as the leading champion of the Counter-Reformation.[99]

95. Bologna to Borromeo, *Die Römische Kurie*, ed. Šusta, I, 193-194. Philip's thinking on the council had matured even earlier. See Philip II to the Duchess of Parma, Mar. 16, 1561, *Correspondance*, ed., Gachard, I, 448.

96. *CT*, VIII, 279-280. Vargas was stressing, meanwhile, that the council ought not take up the question of Justification. *Instructions*, ed. Dupuy, p. 85. The Pope had long equivocated. *Beitrage*, ed. Döllinger, I, 364-365.

97. *Die Römische Kurie*, ed. Šusta, I, 250-254.

98. François, *Tournon*, pp. 404-405.

99. This is a matter of subsidiary controversy, especially insofar as it predicates religious idealism (in the formal sense) on the part of Philip. The earlier study by Marcelino Menéndez y Pelayo, *Historia de los heterodoxos españoles*, celebrated Philip's Spain as "the scourge of heretics, the light of Trent, the sword of Rome, the cradle of St. Ignatius." Quoted in Lynch, *Spain under the Hapsburgs*, I, 236. This is a view to which Lynch, pp. 257-270, takes sharp exception. He stresses Philip's political realism and his quarrels with the popes and denies emphatically that Philip was "the secular arm of the Counter-Reformation." This seems to be a healthy corrective that has gone too far. A strained alliance is still an alliance, and to deny that Philip and the papacy were allied is comparable to denying that the U.S.A. and the U.S.S.R. were allied in World War II. Bataillon, *Érasme*, p. 746, puts it well: "Philip II assumes, by a sort or external necessity rather than by an intimate vocation, the role of champion of the Counter-Reformation." See also Merriman, *Rise of the Spanish Empire*, IV, 55; Fernández Alvarez, *Politico mundial*, pp. 240, 244, 282; and De Lamar Jensen, *Diplomacy and Dogmatism: Bernardino de Mendoza and the French Catholic League* (Cambridge, Mass., 1964), p. 224. N.M. Sutherland, "The Foreign Policy of Philip II and the French

Philip early saw his responsibilities (and interests) as transcending frontiers. In February 1561 he made an effort comparable to the Toledo mission of 1560, sending another special ambassador to the French court, Don Juan Manriquez. The ostensible purpose of the visit was to tender condolences over the death of Francis II and congratulations to Charles IX. In the course of his visit he was received in secret council and spoke of weightier concerns. He made it clear that if any new sect were introduced into the realm, Philip would be "compelled to take up arms to suppress it." This was expedient not merely to preserve the dominions of his brother-in-law, but to protect his own kingdom from "being infected by this pest."[100] Finally, on June 23, the Spanish ambassador, Thomas de Chantonnay, informed Catherine of his master's decision to accept Trent. At the suggestion that she do likewise, Catherine skillfully expressed pleasure at Spain's action—"I thank God"—while parrying the proposal with the argument that, in effect, Poissy was the way to Trent.[101] She later told Rennes that Philip's move was simply an "artifice" to break up the Gallican council.[102] Philip's efforts were still luckless.

Catherine was capable of employing artifices of her own. While she blandly argued that the national council was not intended to prejudice the general council or to innovate, but was merely a preparation for Trent, she confided to Rennes, "We proceed to the fact of the General Council only by mien and appearances, and with infinite tediousness and disguises."[103] And while protesting the innocuous nature of the

Catholic League," *History*, LI (1966), 323-331, takes issue with Jensen within this context. It should also be brought out, as it is by Lynch, that Philip was a Caesaropapist and often had the initiative. For Pius IV, see Bayne, *Anglo-Roman Relations*, pp. 73-78, 85ff. Lea, *Spanish Inquisition*, II, 76, wrote: "Pius IV had carried to an extreme his subservience to Philip."

100. As put by *Suriano, Despatches*, pp. 14-15.

101. Viterbo reported Chantonnay's conversation to Borromeo, *Die Römische Kurie*, ed. Susta, I, 210-11; *Lettres de Catherine de Médicis*, I, 209.

102. June 30, 1561, *Lettres de Catherine de Médicis*, I, 209.

103. *Ibid.*; *Instructions*, ed. Dupuy, p. 88.

Gallican council, she had been privately negotiating, through Coligny, to obtain representatives from the Reformed Church.[104] She revealed her hand as late as possible, allowing a minimum time for a damaging confrontation with Rome. It was only on July 25, less than a week before the first meeting of the French council, that she clarified the cryptic announcement of June 12. She now made it clear that the assembly was not to be one of prelates alone, but "all subjects" who desired to be heard were welcome. That safe-conducts were guaranteed was even more suggestive.[105] And in August, on a suspicion that Viterbo and Chantonnay were in league against her, Catherine had the courier of the nuncio intercepted and his papers violated.[106] Jedin holds that Catherine's "seesaw politics" brought the defection of the eldest daughter of the Church within "the range of possibility."[107]

It did not take Rome long to learn of these events and to divine Catherine's real intentions. An embittered Pius IV was urging in the late summer that heretics be met by "fire and the sword."[108] Viterbo disconsolately reported on Septem-

104. Marlorat to Calvin, July 11, 1561, Calvin, *Opera*, XVIII, 548-549.

105. *Condé*, I, 41-42. A few days earlier, l'Hospital announced to the Parlement of Paris that Protestants were to be invited to the convocation, but without disclosing that there would be a colloquy. Geisendorf, *Théodore de Bèze*, p. 128. Catherine supported her case by reference to the divine right of monarchy. Edward M. Beame, "The Development of Politique Thought during the French Religious Wars (1560-95)," unpub. diss., University of Illinois, 1959, p. 211-215.

106. He ̮was intercepted at Turin and imprisoned four days. *Die Römische Kurie*, ed. Šusta, I, 237; Pastor, *History of the Popes*, XVI, 168-169, for Rome's reaction.

107. Jedin, *EC*, p. 172.

108. *Die Römische Kurie*, ed. Šusta, I, 139. Jodoci le Plat, *Monumentorum ad historiam Concilii Tridentini* (7 vols., Louvain, 1781-1787), IV, 714. Pius had employed this time-honored formula in September 1560; as far as I have been able to discover, this was his first use of it. La Bourdaisière, *Correspondance*, pp. 31-32. All this must be understood against the heightened tension, the plots, and counterplots, not excluding that of Geneva. La Bourdaisière, *Correspondance*, p. 23; *CSP: Foreign*, June 1, 1560, No. 149; Archivio Nazionale di Napoli, Registro di lettere di S. Carlo Borromeo, MS XI, G.3, fol. 80.

ber 8 that the French prelates were no closer to Trent than
before. Indeed, they were now at Poissy, as were also "the
heresiarchs of Geneva."[109] The next day the Colloquy of
Poissy began. The Medici of Florence had not bowed to the
Medici of Milan.

Both Medici seem to have been educated by events between
1559 and 1561. Catherine had progressed from being an alien
unversed in government to the regency and expedient irenicism. She had proved more than adequate in bringing to
fruition a scheme originally propounded by the cardinal of
Lorraine. In the process she showed promise of becoming a
master of dissimulation and a disciple of Machiavelli, which
made her the equal of most contemporary princes. The
development of the Pope is subtler and more critical. It
would be premature at this point to delineate the character
of his reign, but certain trends can be divined. He had
developed from a relatively obscure but agreeable prelate of
the Renaissance into a Pope of the gathering Counter-Reformation. His fundamentally moderate and conciliatory nature
had been overtaken and changed by events. He was himself a
compromise candidate at his election, a circumstance likely
to inhibit bold and imaginative leadership. He lacked the
dynamism or charisma, and perhaps even the conviction,
necessary to reverse the tide then enveloping Christendom.
No doubt it was easier to be liberal outside the Curia than
within, and the shadow of Paul IV still haunted the sacred
college. By the following year, 1562, he was more or less the
captive of "the zealots" who exaggerated the perils of
moderation.[110] Already he had demonstrated goodwill
toward the Jesuits and a proclivity for strong measures. And
he had made his choice between the Spanish option and the

109. *Die Römische Kurie*, ed. Šusta, I, 248-249; Archivio di Vaticano, *Concilio*,
Registro 150, fol. 123, for a comparable letter of the same to Borromeo.
110. Jedin, *CC*, pp. 90-92.

Franco-imperial, the familiar and the unknown. It was now predictable that his universal council would be largely a meeting of the Mediterranean world. Protestants who would not take the road to Trent had, meanwhile, taken the path to Poissy.

III / Heresiarch and Inquisitor-General: A Court Divided

Here are the dogs of Geneva!
                Cardinal de Tournon

It is necessary that there be dogs in the flock of the Lord, in order to guard against the wolves.
                Theodore Beza[1]

Geneva responded to a royal invitation with Theodore Beza, and on August 23, a week after departure, he was present at court and prepared to plead the case for Reformed Christianity. In mid-life, Beza had a varied past behind him, was now second-in-command and heir apparent to Calvin, and would succeed him as international leader of the Reformed Churches.

Beza was born of a distinguished Burgundian family in 1519. His family was steeped in the law, and Beza, like Luther and Calvin before him, was destined for a place in this auspicious and lucrative profession. In the years 1535-1539 he studied at Orléans under some of the finest legal minds of the day. Thereafter he was to be found in Paris, where his first love was not law, but classical literature—and leisure. Although he obtained a benefice by relatives who engaged to set him up well in the law, these were his bohemian years. During this period he produced the *Juvenilia*, a collection of amorous verses and a source of later embarrassment. Perhaps he would have subscribed to the contemporary dictum: "Extra Parisium nulla esse Paridisum."

1. "Questions et Réponses—Correspondance," *BSHPF*, XIII (1864), 284; Henri Hauser, *La preponderance espagnole* (Paris, Félix Alcan, 1933), p. 57.

In 1548 a grave illness brought him to a spiritual crisis and the frontier of a new life. He turned against his past and toward God; as he tells us: "I renewed my vow to serve Him openly in His true Church. In short, to give myself totally to Him."[2] Thereupon he volunteered for Geneva, where he was warmly greeted by Calvin, whom he had met in his student days at Orléans. Then began his new career as Reformer.

At first, employment was found for him as professor of Greek at Lausanne. In 1554 he wrote a tract defending the burning of Servetus, and in the years that followed he traveled extensively throughout Europe in behalf of the Reformed cause. He attended the Colloquy of Worms in 1557. During these years he gained a reputation in Europe. In 1558 he returned to Geneva (Villedieu, as he sometimes called it), taking the chair of Greek and, after Calvin's death in 1564, the chair of theology. There he became one of Europe's leading educators and an eminent biblical scholar and exegete who influenced students for some two centuries after. He made two chief modifications in Calvin's doctrines: he elaborated and heightened the doctrine of predestination, and he extended Calvin's political theories with reference to resistance to tyrants.[3] Both a fine Latin poet and a formidable theological polemicist, he was an ecclesiastical statesman, teacher, orator, and gentleman. Now, at forty three, he was called to carry the scepter of Protestantism before the princes and prelates of France.

There was some feeling that Geneva should be represented

2. Paul F. Geisendorf, *Théodore de Bèze* (Geneva, 1949), p. 27 (the best work on Beza). For Beza's Parisian days, see E. Droz, "Notes sur Théodore de Bèze," *BHR*, XXIV (1962), 392-412; for Beza's humanist background and conversion period, see Natalie Zemon Davis, "Peletier and Beza Part Company," *Studies in the Renaissance*, VI (1964), 188-222; Henri Meylan, "La conversion de Bèze ou les longues hésitations d'un humaniste Chrétien," *Genava*, VII (May 1959).

3. McNeill, *Unitive Protestantism*, pp. 204-205. For some particulars on Beza as rebel, see Robert M. Kingdon, "The Political Resistance of the Calvinists in France and in the Low Countries," *Church History*, XXVII (Sept. 1958), 220-233.

at the colloquy by Calvin himself.[4] But the consensus was for
Beza, and by mid-July his presence was being implored in
separate letters from Coligny, Condé, and Jean Le Maçon,
spokesman for the Reformed Church of Paris.[5] Actually
Calvin was never seriously considered. The city council of
Geneva was unwilling to risk the loss of the commander in
chief and forbade his going. Calvin was a risk in two senses.
Apart from his chronically poor health, he was known to be
choleric and uncompromising, and his presence might mili-
tate against concord and even irritate the Queen. Coligny
thus considered it inadvisable for him to attend.[6] Beza, on
the other hand, was a skillful diplomat and a polished orator,
and, as a nobleman, would be equal to the exacting demands
of court protocol. While he was as firm in the faith as Calvin,
he was more conciliatory on matters of form.[7] In this
respect, he was a fine complement to Calvin and an attractive
choice.

Beza reached Paris on August 22 and the next day went to
Saint-Germain-en-Laye, a quiet village some fourteen miles
west, where the court had taken up residence the month
before. The stately royal château sits on a bluff at the edge of
the winding Seine, providing a view that surveys the stretch
of land to Paris and a position that defies assault. As he
approached the château, Beza may have felt some apprehen-
sion, especially in view of the recent and punitive edict of

4. Church of Paris to the ministers of Geneva, July 14, 1561, Calvin, *Opera*,
XVIII, 553-554; Marlorat to Calvin, July 11, 1561, *ibid.*, 547-549.

5. Beza, *Correspondence*, III, 119-123. As early as May, moreover, Beza
referred to a correspondence with Navarre, which may have represented secret
negotiations. *Ibid.*, 102. This correspondence is apparently lost. *Ibid.*, 104, n. 18.

6. Geisendorf, *Théodore de Bèze*, considers the whole matter, pp. 128-129. Le
Maçon (La Rivière) to Calvin, *Opera*, XVIII, 578, warns that "the enemy rages
against us" and points out the difficulties in getting a safe conduct for Calvin. It is
strange that the Huguenot gentleman, Ruble, *Bourbon*, III, 156, held that the
"illustrious" Calvin was reluctant to commit his reputation before the bishops, an
unwarranted opinion.

7. Geisendorf, *Théodore de Bèze*, pp. 128-129.

July. But Le Maçon had sent him assurances that this ordinance was only a screen to placate Spain and a means of extracting money from the prelates.[8] In any event, doubt was soon dispelled, for the royal invitation was matched with a royal welcome.

The Chancellor greeted him cordially and immediately introduced him to the other personages at court. He was amiably received by Coligny, whom he found "marvellously well disposed," and by his brother, Odet, cardinal of Châtillon, who had recently professed the Reformed faith. The Bourbons—Anthony and Condé—literally "threw themselves" on him, though Beza had private reservations about Anthony's constancy.[9] Even the cardinal of Bourbon expressed a desire for better understanding. And the next night he was to meet the Queen.

Beza's presence was reinforced by a formidable array of French Calvinists, who had been about court for several months.[10] Their company included François de Morel,

8. Beza's concern is implicit in Le Maçon's communication, August 10, 1561. Beza, *Correspondance*, III, 128. See also Calvin, *Opera*, XVIII, 606-607.

9. When Beza recounted this reception to Calvin on August 25, he expressed doubt that Anthony would be so happy to see him later, implying that he planned a long talk with Navarre about his sagging morals and shifting faith. Beza, *Correspondance*, III, 134. Anthony had a weakness for the "dangerous sirens" about court, and throughout the spring and summer he ostensibly vacillated between Catholicism and Protestantism. Ruble, *Bourbon*, III, 131-133. The likely explanation is that Anthony, through Catherine, was entreating Spain at this time for a settlement on Lower Navarre. Occasional protests of Catholicism were politic. Ruble wrote: "Fervent Calvinist or Lutheran before the German and English Ambassadors, Anthony was known to deceive the Italian envoys by his Catholic protestation." *Bourbon*, III, 282.

10. This was because the National Synod at Poitiers during the previous March had resolved that twelve delegates, who were to represent the provinces, should petition the crown for "temples." This was accomplished on June 11 and may well have been an incentive toward the court's announcement of a national council the following day. Romier, *C&H*, p. 144. For the text of the petition, see *Condé*, II, 370-372. It has already been indicated that Catherine negotiated with the Huguenots by way of Coligny. Coligny, his chaplain Merlin, and various Huguenot delegates drew up the definitive roster for the Reformed (Calvin,

moderator of the First National Synod, now attached to the
court of the Duchess of Ferrara, widowed daughter of Louis
XII; Jean Raimond Merlin, of Geneva, then chaplain to
Coligny; Augustin Marlorat, pastor of Rouen, a former
Augustinian and a Scripture scholar;[11] Jean Malot, a Parisian
minister, then attached to the House of Condé; Nicolas des
Gallars, Parisian born and formerly a minister at Geneva, now
head of the French Reformed Church in London, who had
been invited by Coligny and the Parisian ministers;[12] François de Saint Paul, deputy from Dieppe; Nicolas Folion,
minister at Orléans; Claude de la Boissière, a gentleman of
Dauphiné who had studied at Geneva, now minister at
Saintonge; Jean Boquin, pastor at Oléron; Jean de la Tour, an
elderly minister of Béarn; Jean de l'Espine, a scholar of
Touraine, whose Calvinist sympathies matured into formal
allegiance on the eve of the colloquy;[13] and Jean Virel,
formerly chaplain to Condé, now a minister at Paris.[14] Even
without Calvin the group boasted some of the finest talent of
French Calvinism. They also enjoyed the support of some
sixteen Huguenot laymen, who would be passive at Poissy,
but nevertheless provided additional moral support for their
side.[15]

Opera, XVIII, 548-549) but no details are provided. The list of the ministers is
taken from HE, I, 490.

11. Marlorat was fated to be executed in October 1562, following the siege of
Rouen. H. Dannreuther, "Le Martyr Augustin Marlorat et son frère Martin,"
BSHPF, XL (1891), 2-22.

12. Fernand de Schickler, Les églises du refuge en Angleterre (3 vols., Paris,
1892), I, 128.

13. Beza, Correspondance, III, 151-152. On l'Espine, see Louis L. Hogu, Jean
de l'Espine (Paris, 1913), p. 25.

14. Jules Delaborde, "Les Protestants à la cour de Saint-Germain lors du
Colloque de Poissy," BSHPF, XXII (1873), 392.

15. The laymen included Barbanson, Battier, Bléreau, de Chamon, de Falme,
Dubois, Dumas, Gabert, Bervault, Laroche, Lebarbier, Moineville, de Pienne,
Précréan, Raguier, Raucout (ibid., 393). The manuscript sources do not entirely
agree about the laymen involved: for example, see B.N., Dupuy Collection, ms.
10331. Correspondance of Chantonnay, A.N., K 1494, No. 95; and A.N., G8*
591, fol. 249.

Beza's warm welcome only echoed the treatment that the ministers received. The exasperated Roman Catholic, Claude Haton, complained that they were better received at court than "would have been the Pope of Rome."[16] Cardinal Châtillon constituted himself their host, and provided them with chaplaincies. They were lodged with the great families of France. Beza entered the service of Jeanne d'Albret, who arrived shortly afterward, and Condé and the Châtillons took in the others. The court at Saint-Germain appeared almost Protestantized. The ministers availed themselves of a fairly general liberty of preaching, and even Haton related that Beza's "beautiful and becoming French . . . his appearance and gestures attracted the hearts and wills of his hearers."[17] The indignant Spanish ambassador felt he might as well be in Geneva.[18]

In general, then, Calvinist spirits were high and brimming with *joie du combat.* As early as July, Merlin wrote Calvin in a state of "marvelous perplexity" about the zeal, even impetuosity, of the ministers, in their eagerness to do battle with the Catholics for the Gospel. He was afraid that the Catholics might not want to dispute, save under conditions that assured them the victory. But he noted that Lorraine was gathering savants who were "incessantly after the study in order to surprise us."[19] Lorraine was now in fact at Poissy, for the Assembly of Prelates had already convened.

Poissy is a town three miles to the west of Saint-Germain. Its name apparently derives from *poisson,* after a fishpond that was once there. From such humble origins, it became celebrated as the birthplace of St. Louis. The fine Gothic church and even the baptismal font, whose waters baptized

16. *Mémoires de Claude Haton, contenant le récit des évenéments accomplis de 1553 à 1582,* ed. Félix Bourquelot (2 vols., Paris, 1857), I, 155.
17. *Ibid.,* 156.
18. *Condé,* II, 17.
19. Calvin, *Opera,* XVIII, 551-553.

him, still stand. His later successor, Philip the Fair, gave an old castle there to the Dominican nuns, who made it into one of the most distinguished convents in France. There were good reasons for selecting this convent as the site of the colloquy. One of the participants explained them: the convent was just on the outskirts of town, where it would provide privacy and discourage curiosity seekers; the commodious refectory would be well suited for such a large assembly; the prelates could be lodged close enough together to communicate readily with each other; the convent church was ample in size and conducive to prayer; Poissy was near the court, being a short and pleasant ride from Saint-Germain, the favorite residence of the Valois; and the place was generously endowed by nature, the air was salubrious, and the woods invited a relaxing promenade after a day of grave deliberations.[20]

Some fifty prelates of the realm—out of 113—responded to

20. *Le Colloque de Poissy*, ed. Baron Alphonse de Ruble, *Mémoires de la société de l'histoire de Paris et de l'isle de France*, XVI (1889), 11-12. This journal, which is highly trustworthy, is one of the basic sources for Poissy. Twenty years after the colloquy, Cardinal Armagnac wrote that upon reading it he seemed to have what had passed at Poissy before his eyes again. *Collection des procès-verbaux des assemblées générales du clergé de France*, ed. Antoine Duranthon (9 vols., Paris, 1767-1768), I, 23, n. There has been some question concerning the authorship of the journal. The editor, Ruble, attributed it to Claude d'Espence, a Catholic theologian who played an important role in events at Poissy. H. Outram Evennett discussed the matter, and the general bibliographical questions involved, in "Claude d'Espence et son 'Discours' du Colloque de Poissy," *Revue historique*, CLXIII-CLXIV (1930), esp. 55-59. Evennett not only criticized the editing of Ruble, but suggested that d'Espence was probably not the author, since he failed to find the name of d'Espence in the journal. D'Espence's name does, however, appear in the copy of the Bibliothèque at Nimês, Nouveau Fonds, 257. Many identical passages can, moreover, be found in the journal and in the "Discours," which is carefully edited by Evennett, "Claude d'Espence," pp. 60-78. In sum, I believe that the journal is reliable and that d'Espence probably was its author. It will be cited as *Journal*, in distinction to *Discours*. A beautiful copy of the Journal is in B.N., Fonds français 5812, where there is also a copy of the *Discours*. Numerous copies of both are in the *Procès-verbaux des assemblées générales du clergé* at the A.N., e.g., G⁸* 588, G⁸* 589ᵃ. For the town of Poissy, see Edmond Bories, *Histoire de la ville de Poissy* (Paris, 1901). The convent itself was razed in the nineteenth century.

Catherine's summons. On hand were six cardinals (Tournon, Lorraine, Armagnac, Bourbon, Châtillon, and Guise) and three archbishops (Bordeaux, Tours, and Embrun). There were over forty bishops: Chartres, Uzès, Évreux, Saint-Malo, Sisteron, Lantriguet, Bayeaux, Nantes, Riez, Mans, Troyes, Paris, Orléans, Amiens, Meaux, Saint-Brieuc, Castres, Pamiers, Châlons, Autun, Lavaur, Soissons, Mâçon, Vannes, Nevers, Lisieux, Vence, Tulle, Auxerre, Saint-Papoul, Cornouailles, Mirepoix, Toulon, Aleth, Luçon, Poitiers, Dol, Coutances, Aire, Comminges, Séez, and Valence.[21] In addition, there was a group of canonists, including the Chancellor of Paris, the dean of Sens, the dean of Amiens, and the "Officials" of Tours, Reims, Évreux, and Uzès.[22] Finally, there was a group of theologians or *periti*: Jean de Salignac, Jean Bouteiller, Claude d'Espence, Cotignon, Simon Vigor, Jacques du Pré, Coquier, Brochot, Sénéchal, Ciry, Claude de Sainctes, and Toussaint Gibou.[23] The company counted some men of real learning. It included some who were prepared to consider a rapprochement with the Protestants, but the great majority, at least of the prelates, were unbendingly loyal to Rome, suspicious of the designs of the crown and hypersensitive to heresy.

The King, on the last day of July 1561, opened what might best be called a synod of the Gallican Church. The colloquy was to be a later part of a larger meeting. The Chancellor delivered the brief for the crown. He spoke in French, the official language of the assembly, in deference to the royal family and the princes. L'Hospital justified the convention, alluding to the divine inspiration that had moved the King—a

21. *Journal*, p. 12; Henri Klipffel, *Le Colloque de Poissy* (Paris, 1867), pp. 50-51.

22. *Journal*, p. 16; Klipffel, *Le Colloque*, p. 51.

23. *Journal*, p. 16. In April the government sought assistance from the Faculty of Theology of the University of Paris. The Sorbonne refused the request, but the chancellor intervened quietly and obtained some doctors from the Sorbonne and elsewhere. Pierre Feret, *La faculté de théologie de Paris: Époque moderne* (5 vols., Paris, 1900-1907), I, 352.

child who was probably puzzled by these proceedings—to convoke it. Its object was to forge tranquility and unity out of the religious disorders of the realm. He minimized its novelty, noting that the late Francis II had made many appeals for a "good council." A national council was expedient on account of "the infirmity" of France and the fact that "brothers" could find and prescribe a medicine more salutary than could "a foreign doctor." He implored the prelates to rise above passion and private interest, and then, referring to Protestants, asked the prelates to conduct themselves as fathers and pastors, admonishing, teaching, and drawing them gently, forgoing the rigor of the past, which had served only to multiply heresy. This seemed a broad hint of future Huguenot participation. Finally, the Chancellor remarked that if the prelates shrank from calling the meeting a "council," they might prefer to term it an "assembly." He assured them that all proceedings would be sent to the general council or submitted to the scrutiny of Rome.[24]

This was not quite satisfactory to Cardinal Tournon, the aged warrior who would be the vital center of conservative dissent. After the customary civilities, he indicated that the prelates would bear themselves as fathers and pastors toward

24. *Diario dell'assemblea de' vescovi à Poissy*, prefaced by a study of the sources by Joseph Roserot de Melin, "Rome et Poissy (1560-61)," *Mélanges d'archéologie et d'histoire*, XXXIX (1921-1922), 47-151. This is an important anonymous source, not used in the older studies of Klipffel and Peyrat. Along with such works as the *HE*, it is one of the basic sources for Poissy and supplements the Catholic accounts found in the *Journal* and the *Discours*. It is generally trustworthy, but written with the pronounced bias of a conservative Catholic. Melin, the editor, feels that the author was probably an eyewitness, an Italian, and more than likely an agent of the nuncio. H.O. Evennett, "The Cardinal of Lorraine and the Colloquy of Poissy," *Cambridge Historical Journal*, II (1927), 133, n. 1, inclines to accept this view. François, *Tournon*, p. 413, sees the hand of Chantonnay in it, since part of it is duplicated in the Spanish ambassador's report to Philip of September 17. A.N., K 1494, No. 103. He likewise thinks that it emanated from the nunciature in Paris. I would myself see proof of Chantonnay's involvement in the fact that certain errors appear in both his correspondence and the *Diario*. Cf. Chantonnay to Philip, A.N., K 1495, No. 81, Oct. 2, 1561, and the *Diario*, pp. 125, 133, where both speak of the events of September 24 as occurring on October 25, and confuse September 26 and 27.

those of "the new religion," provided the latter were willing to receive instruction rather than give it. When he sought a copy of the Chancellor's address, l'Hospital alleged that the speech had been given extemporaneously.[25] Perhaps the latter was reluctant to have it scrutinized for heterodoxy. In any event, the opening proceedings showed characteristic intransigence on the part of the prelates, and there were suggestions of a certain lack of frankness on the part of the crown. Neither augured well for the future of such a grand design.

The next day, August 1, the first regular session of the Assembly of Prelates convened. The bishops, taking Tournon's lead, reacted to the Chancellor's address in the expected way: there were a declaration of loyalty to the Pope and an affirmation that the prelates would confine their consultations to the morals, not the faith, of the Gallican Church. All would be remitted to the Pope for final approval. They were happy to concur with at least one suggestion of l'Hospital: the meeting would be a simple "assembly," not a "National Council."[26] On these subjects the bishops spoke as one.

When this was achieved, the necessary organization was effected. Tournon, dean of the college of cardinals, and primate of Gaul, served as president. Lorraine himself arrived in a litter on July 29, having taken ill a short distance from Poissy. Young and indomitable, he was soon on his feet; articulate and politic, he was immediately elected speaker or floor manager of the assembly. Particulars for the procedure

25. *Diario*, p. 94; *Journal*, p. 17. This extemporaneousness, real or asserted may be why P.J.S. Dufey, editor of Michel de l'Hospital, *Oeuvres Complètes* (3 vols., Paris, 1824), failed to include the Chancellor's address in his *Oeuvres*. But another reason may be a textual problem, treated below.

26. *Diario*, p. 95; *Journal*, p. 15. Other reports on the assembly, treated only cursorily here, will be found in *Die Römische Kurie*, ed. Šusta, I, 227-230, 235-236, 239-241; Chantonnay's correspondence, A.N., K 1494, Nos. 89-98; and Bruslart's record in *Condé, I, 48-50*. See also the study of J. Laferrière, *Le contrat de Poissy* (Paris, 1905), and Evennett, *Lorraine*, pp. 283-295.

of the meeting were settled in good order. They were originally to meet twice weekly, but later opted for daily sessions. Lorraine drew up a list of articles for deliberation. The theologians then were summoned to assist the bishops. Some of them, especially Claude d'Espence, Jean de Salignac, Jean Bouteiller, and Toussaint Gibou, were decidedly liberal in orientation. It may be noteworthy that Lorraine sought to enfranchise the theological consultants, but was overridden by the prelates.[27] As at Trent, only bishops could vote, and there would be no proxies. On August 4 Tournon proposed that the assembly devote itself to four principal concerns: a subvention or subsidy for the King, reformation of the Gallican Church, election of prelates for the general council, and means to effect the pacification of the realm.[28] This agenda was to be inhibited from the beginning by forces both within and without the assembly.

That same day the prelates evinced considerable concern over rumors that the crown had ready an edict to provide for the popular election of the parish clergy; they were also disquieted by reports of a projected spoliation of Church property. The assembly delegated several prelates to make inquiry at court about these matters. Catherine denied the first; she was equivocal concerning the second. She stated that she had never dreamed of appropriating ecclesiastical property; it would be sufficient if the prelates could find some means of acquitting the debts of the government.[29] But implicit here was a threat of spoliation in order to make the prelates more obliging. Menaced thus, the prelates were moved to action and by the end of the month had given a preliminary decision in favor of the subvention.

There were equivalent troubles within the assembly itself. On August 3 several bishops and theologians absented them-

27. *Die Römische, Kurie*, ed. Šusta, I, 229.
28. *Journal*, p. 17.
29. *Ibid.*, pp. 17-18; Klipffel, *Le Colloque*, p. 68.

selves from what was to be a general Communion, and communicated elsewhere "à leur mode," that is to say, under both species. The group consisted of Châtillon, Montluc, and Jean de Saint-Gelais, bishop of Uzès, with the theologians Salignac, Bouteiller, and Gibou. Uzès preached, paradoxically, on the text: *De coena Domini sacramento concordiae et caritate.* If the action of the mavericks attested a lack of concord, they received sparse charity from the orthodox. The scandalized and incensed prelates wanted them expelled from the assembly. That was not done, but they were thereafter held suspect.[30] When Catherine revealed these happenings to Chantonnay, Lorraine casually remarked that Communion under a single species was not a question of divine law.[31]

Confidence within the assembly was further disturbed by the fact that the proceedings, supposedly secret, were being divulged to the Queen. When the question of a remonstrance came up, Lorraine curiously remarked that it would be useless; one of them, he said, was a "devil." All eyes reportedly turned on Montluc.[32] Whether or not he was guilty—it has been suggested that the target of the remark was really the radical prelate, Antonio Caraccioli, bishop of Troyes[33]—the incident undoubtedly further alienated the liberal minority, militating against their playing a creative role in the succeeding events and adding justification to the worst premonitions of the intransigent majority.

There was another difficulty. Many of the prelates apparently preferred the attractions of Paris to the exactions of Poissy. When some of the prelates were spending whole days sightseeing in Paris, the assembly's work could scarcely

30. *Journal,* pp. 16-17; *Diario,* pp. 96-97.
31. *Die Römische, Kurie,* ed. Susta, I, 230. Lorraine's remark is some evidence of moderation on his part.
32. *Condé,* I, 50; *Journal,* p. 25, n. 1. One reason for the suspicion of Montluc was undoubtedly that he had just that month been censured by the Faculty of Theology of Paris. Feret, *La faculté,* I, 270.
33. *Négociations,* ed. Desjardins, III, 462.

proceed expeditiously. This occasioned a complaint from the nuncio, Viterbo, about the waste of precious time while Trent beckoned forward, and a similar refrain from Chantonnay. Catherine tried to placate them by ordering that no prelate leave Poissy without her permission.[34]

Despite all these frustrations, the month of August witnessed a vigorous discussion of reform. Points treated included the duties of bishops and the question of dispensations, which it was agreed Rome had granted too readily, occasioning many abuses. Some theologians espoused the popular election of curates, but it was decided best to take this up with Rome. There was acid criticism of the monasteries, and salutary suggestions were made for their reform. Montluc advanced the idea that the laity should receive the cup four to six times a year, which scarcely increased his popularity with the conservatives. Several of the theologians, especially Salignac and Cotignon, expressed approval of the use of the vernacular in some of the priestly administrations. The bishop of Troyes, who would later defect, made an extraordinary speech in which, among other things, he equated the authority of bishops and priests and suggested that poor priests might learn a useful trade, as did Paul and John. The bishop of Paris countered by reprimanding him for his alleged irrelevancies. Châtillon shocked the prelates by his occasionally radical opinions. This perhaps emboldened Bouteiller to deliver one of the most daring speeches of the assembly. He not only inveighed against organs in the churches, but questioned the superiority of bishops to priests and implicitly challenged the primacy of the Roman Church.[35] Lorraine felt compelled to excuse him before an irate nuncio, but shrewdly observed that some theologians considered Annates and Preventions just as abominable as

34. The events were related by Viterbo to Borromeo, Aug. 18, 1561, *Die Römische Kurie*, ed. Šusta, I, 235-236; *Journal*, p. 20.
35. For these speeches, see *Diario*, pp. 102-118; *Journal*, pp. 18-19.

Bouteiller's outburst.[36] By August 21 the assembly had dealt with half the proposed articles and suspended deliberations for a few days.

But for the crown, the affair had scarcely begun. The prelates were on stage, the champions of the Huguenots in the wings, and the court was now prepared to raise the curtain. On August 25 the government finally and formally announced, through Cardinal Armagnac, that the Huguenots were to be heard in the assembly. It was now clear that the synod was as much the preparation for an interconfessional colloquy as it was for a general council. The *fait accompli* was softened by the court's request that the prelates recommend the form that the Calvinist representation should take.[37] The prevailing view of the prelates was that the Huguenots should, at the most, be given a hearing, the report of which would be transmitted to Rome; only five bishops were categorically opposed.[38] Lorraine suggested that one of the Huguenots be given responsibility to appear before the assembly and to present the views of his colleagues. He preferred that the prelates occupy themselves with reform before advising on matters concerning the delegation.[39] Thus, Lorraine did not exude enthusiasm, at least not before the prelates. It was finally decided that Lorraine would continue as speaker in the colloquy, but he solemnly affirmed that he would not enter into discussion with the heretics, but only allow them to present their proposals, be it in written or oral form.[40] At this point little more could be guaranteed.

Lorraine's conduct in the assembly reveals a characteristic

36. *Die Römische Kurie*, ed. Šusta, I, 236.
37. *Journal*, p. 24, gives the date as August 26, as against the *Diario*, p. 109, and *Die Römische Kurie*, ed. Šusta, I, 241.
38. *Die Römische Kurie*, ed. Šusta, I, 241.
39. *Diario*, p. 109.
40. As reported by Chantonnay to Viterbo, *Die Römische Kurie*, ed. Šusta, I, 242.

ambivalence. He implicitly justified the meeting on the grounds that the Pope had only given lip service to a general council.[41] And about August 21 he even confessed, speaking for all the bishops, that "they had failed to feed their flocks, and that it was God's just punishment that they were molested by the heretics." He was even reported to favor the abolition of images and the elimination of Latin in sermons and prayers.[42] This was his liberal side. Yet he reacted with cool orthodoxy and prelatic propriety when the court announced its decision for the colloquy. Lucien Romier suggests that the ostensible return to orthodoxy was to ensure that the bishops would designate him as their speaker.[43] The cynical Chantonnay remarked that Lorraine supported the colloquy for the purpose of displaying his erudition.[44] In any case, at this point the work of the Assembly of Prelates was well under way.

The month of August in fact featured two distinct assemblies at which Catherine's plans were unraveled. Besides the ecclesiastical assembly at Poissy, there was a parallel lay assembly of the Estates General at Pontoise, just to the north. In constituting the latter, Catherine had encouraged the Reformed element, contriving to use it as a means to make the prelates, sitting apart at Poissy, more amenable to her designs. As the desired consequence, the "new sects" obtained an uncontestable majority in the Second and Third

41. This was related by the later nuncio, Santa Croce, to Borromeo, Nov. 15, 1561, *Archives curieuses de l'histore de France depuis Louis XI jusqu'à Louis XVIII*, ed. M.L. Cimber and F. Danjou (1st series, 15 vols.; 2nd series, 8 vols., Paris, 1834-1839), VI, 7.

42. As recounted by Morel to Calvin, Aug. 25, 1561, Calvin, *Opera*, XVIII, 642-643, who added, "but I do not hold this for an article of faith." He referred to Lorraine's *mea culpa* as "the penitence of foxes."

43. Romier, *C&H*, p. 209.

44. *Die Römische Kurie*, ed. Šusta, I, 242.

Estates.[45] Instructions to the Protestant delegates, which perhaps emanated ultimately from Geneva,[46] heralded the national council. There was, meanwhile, to be freedom of worship for all except Anabaptists, libertines, and atheists; all ecclesiastical jurisdictions were to be abolished; no money was to be sent to Rome; no holder of an ecclesiastical benefice was to fill a royal office; and priests were not to carry the Blessed Sacrament in the streets in an ostentatious way.[47] The *cahiers* were themselves understandably less militant, though equally hostile to the clergy and reflective of the Reformed Churches. Both Second and Third Estates were agreed that the colloquy was not to be interrupted under any pretext. All decisions were to be impartial. As the last resort, it was allowed that problems could be resolved by the next "holy and free" ecumenical council, but it was specified that Trent did not satisfy these qualifications.[48] There were complaints about the thorny question of taxation. It is notable that the Third Estate pleaded that it "could offer your Majesty nothing but good will" and suggested the seizure of ecclesiastical property and the taxation of clerical benefices.[49] The last proposals help account for the anxieties of the prelates and their pliability in taking up the subvention for the crown.

This anxiety was scarcely mollified by the events of a joint session of the two assemblies—the prelates from Poissy and

45. As reported by Chantonnay Aug. 26, 1561, A.N., K 1494, No. 91. It was confirmed by the well-documented account of Noël Valois, "Les états de Pontoise (August, 1561)," *Revue d'histoire de l'église de France*, XXIX (1943), 237-247, which details the technicalities of Catherine's maneuver. On the Estates, see also Paul Van Dyke, "The Estates of Pontoise," *English Historical Review*, XXVII (1913), pp. 472-495; and Russell Major, *The Estates General of 1560* (Princeton, N.J., 1951), pp. 107-113.
46. Valois, "Pontoise," p. 241.
47. *Ibid.*
48. *Ibid.*, p. 249.
49. Van Dyke, "Pontoise," p. 492.

the Estates from Pontoise—on August 27 at St. Germain. The Chancellor, speaking for Catherine, voiced another earnest appeal for peace between the religious factions. He propounded that it was not a question "of constituting a religion, but of constituting a republic; and some can be citizens without being Christians: even the excommunicate do not cease to be citizens."[50] A novel distinction between politics and religion was made, and there was a noteworthy suggestion that l'Hospital was veering toward toleration and away from the "one faith" position that he had announced at Orléans the previous year. The hope was still for concord, but the meeting obtained little. There was early contention between the princes of the blood and the cardinals over the proprieties of precedence. The princes prevailed, and Lorraine and Tournon stormed out of the assembly in protest. The Calvinist delegates were jubilant.[51] This perhaps encouraged the strongest speech of the day. Jacques Bretagne, speaker of the Third Estate and mayor of Autun, stood before the prelates and delivered a scathing assault upon the clergy. Beyond violently attacking their avarice, he particularly wounded them by comparing the young King to Josias, being careful to provide him competent instruction, and then parried the standard objection of the antiquity of Roman Catholicism in France by announcing that the purity of the Gospel was at last being revealed, after having been hidden since the time of Christ.[52] The constable was so provoked that he wanted the scoundrel "hanged on the spot." Catherine had to help calm him, but the irascible Montmorency went to bed with "the colic and the gout."[53] The inflamed protests of the prelates were countered by Catherine's bland astonishment at the insignificance of the incident and by the

50. *Oeuvres de l'Hospital*, ed. Dufey, I, 452.
51. *Die Römische Kurie*, ed. Šusta, I, 240.
52. *Condé*, II, 437-454; Valois, "Pontoise," p. 251.
53. *Suriano, Despatches*, p. 40; A.N., K 1494, No. 94.

Chancellor's ingenuous pretense that he had not heard the remarks. It should by now have been clear that the crown would not throw its support to the prelates, but, if anything, sustained the Reformed, probably with the hope of equalizing power and forcing the prelates to make a sober reappraisal of the virtues of compromise at the future conference table.

In the meantime, dividends accrued to Catherine. Thanks partially to the good offices of Coligny, the Estates General finally tendered its formal acceptance of Catherine's regency. For this, she reciprocated by putting through the antipapal Ordinance of Orléans, finally registered on September 12.[54]

Thus, the Estates had been more a royal success than a Roman triumph, and what had begun on the first day of August dissolved *sine die* on the last.

Catherine's hopes were also heightened by a signal meeting several days before, which served as an effective prologue to the colloquy. This was on August 24, the day after Beza's arrival at Saint-Germain. That evening he was called into the chambers of the King of Navarre, where he found not only Anthony, but Catherine herself, Condé, the cardinals of Lorraine and Bourbon, and several ladies of the court. The Queen received him cordially, expressing the hope that his presence might bring some happy repose to the kingdom. But there was a moment of tension when Beza and Lorraine, the stalwarts of their respective communions, confronted each other. As a prelude, their dialogue is worth recounting at some length.

Lorraine, as it were measuring Beza, started on a rather chilly note: "Formerly you have been known to me by your writings, which in your absence have incited discord in this

54. Major, *Estates General*, p. 110; Evennett, *Lorraine*, p. 340; Van Dyke, "Pontoise," 493. But the Guisard president of the Parlement of Paris protested so strongly against the ordinance that Catherine had to confine him to his home. *CSP: Foreign*, Aug. 30, 1561, No. 461(4).

kingdom. Let us hope that your presence here will be a means to pacify these disturbances."[55] Beza replied tactfully that he was too diminutive a personage to trouble such a powerful kingdom, nor had he the will to do so, as would his writings attest and he demonstrate at the forthcoming colloquy.[56] After this initial exchange, Lorraine steered the conversation directly into some theological particulars. He referred to a work, attributed to Beza, in which there were some peculiar passages. For example, Beza was alleged to have written somewhere that "Christ is no more in the Eucharist than in mud"[57] —words offensive to the Queen and the rest of the company. Beza responded that he could speak with greater certitude if the alleged treatise were at hand, but nevertheless provided an impromptu reply. He denied categorically that such an expression could be found in his writings and dismissed the notion as "absurd and full of blasphemy."[58]

Lorraine then posed the crucial question of how Beza understood the words "This is my body," noting the lack of agreement on this fundamental point. Beza lamented with him that there was not better concord on this doctrine, but concurred at once as to the Real Presence itself. The problem was in the modality of this presence. Beza proceeded to advance an extended argument for the orthodox Calvinist interpretation: he held for a real, but spiritual and sacramental, presence, an interpretation that mediated between

55. On this meeting, see La Place, *Commentaires*, pp. 155-157; *HE*, I, 492-497; Geisendorf, *Théodore de Bèze*, pp. 136-140; Evennett, *Lorraine*, pp. 295-299.

56. La Place, *Commentaires*, p. 155.

57. A play on words: "Christus non magis est in coena quam in coeno." Beza, *Correspondance,* III, 135. Jacques-Auguste de Thou, *Histoire universelle* (11 vols., The Hague, 1740), III, 64, attributed the expression to Melanchthon, but this is denied by the editors of *HE*, I, 493, n. 1. As regards the treatise to which *HE* refers, the only pertinent one written by that date, *Summa doctrinae de re sacramentaria*, found in the 1582 edition of Beza's *Tractationum theologicarum* (3 vols. in 1, 2nd ed., Geneva, 1582, I, 206-210, does not substantiate the allegation.

the Sacramentarians on the one hand, and the Lutherans on the other. Lorraine, for his part, confessed that he believed in the defensibility of transubstantiation, but felt that theology could get along without the term—that is, it should not remain a stumbling block to reunion.[59]

The cardinal then made an oblique reference to the Lutheran interpretation, though professing that he had not had time to examine it at length. At this, Beza perhaps started, for the one thing that he dreaded was the introduction of anything that could advertise the Calvinist-Lutheran schism. He promptly confessed a want of agreement with some of the Lutherans, but stressed that they were of one mind in condemning transubstantiation and all that follows from it. They both acknowledged, moreover, a true reception in the sacrament. "Do you confess then," asked Lorraine, "that we communicate truly and substantially the body and blood of Jesus Christ?" Beza replied in the affirmative, though with the qualification, "spiritually and by faith."[60] The cardinal, who was apparently surprised to learn that the Calvinists held to the Real Presence,[61] did not pursue the finer distinctions, but closed with a positive note: "This also do I believe." He then expressed his great satisfaction with the interview to the Queen.[62] Beza, rehabilitated, now himself addressed the Queen: "Behold, Madam, these, then, are the Sacramentarians that you have so long vexed and oppressed with all kinds of calumnies." And she to Lorraine: "Do you hear, Lord Cardinal? He says that the Sacramentarians have no other opinion than this, with which you agree."[63] One source indicates that Lorraine reddened, but found no response.[64] Nevertheless, in taking leave, inquisitor-general embraced

59. *Ibid.*, 494-495.
60. La Place, *Commentaires*, p. 157.
61. *HE*, I, 495.
62. Beza, *Correspondance*, III, 136.
63. *Ibid.*
64. Jules Bonnet, "Laurent de Normandie," *BSHPF* XXXII (1883), 151.

heresiarch, professing: "I am very happy to have seen and heard you, and I adjure you in the name of God to confer with me, in order that I might understand your reasons and you mine," adding, "and you will find that I am not as black as they make me out to be."[65] Beza expressed his own gratitude, urging that should the cardinal pursue the colloquy in this spirit, it might bear good fruit.[66] Beza was somewhat more reserved in reporting to Calvin, repeating an ominous remark of one of the ladies at court about Lorraine and the meeting: "A good fellow for today, but tomorrow what?"[67]

This initial encounter caused a sensation and provoked a rash of contradictory rumors. Some held that Lorraine had convinced Beza; others, the reverse. While Lorraine recounted his success in the meeting,[68] an indignant Beza claimed the opposite.[69] There was wild speculation that Lorraine would dispose of his ecclesiastical dignities and become a Protestant.[70] There was even hope that the Duke of Guise would become an "earnest Protestant."[71] This was probably occasioned by the fact that he and Condé—at the behest of the Queen—had joined in the agape, and sealed a rather contrived reconciliation with an embrace. Few had illusions about this.[72] Catherine seems to have been swept away with the

65. *HE*, I, 497.

66. *Ibid.*

67. Aug. 25, 1561, Beza, *Correspondance*, III, 136. The remark was made by one of Catherine's maids of honor, Madame de Crussol, a zealous Protestant. She also said that one had better get pen and paper and make Lorraine subscribe to the things he had avowed, for in a few days he would say the contrary. *HE*, I, 497.

68. *Die Römische Kurie*, ed. Šusta, I, 241. Lorraine also pleaded to the nuncio that he was forced into the interview by the Queen and withdrew from it as soon as possible. *Ibid.*, 241-242. This is dubious: it looks as though his defense to Rome was a case of protecting his flank. See also *Suriano, Despatches*, p. 40.

69. Beza, *Correspondance* III, 136.

70. This was noted, but properly discounted by Michel de Castelnau, *Mémoires*, ed. J. le Laboureur (3 vols., Brussels, 1731), I, 72. See also *Throckmorton to the Queen, Aug. 8, 1561, CSP: Foreign*, No. 461(3).

71. Throckmorton to the Queen, Aug. 8, 1561, *CSP: Foreign*, No. 461(3).

72. There was some disapproval of this stagy reconciliation, notably from Beza, *Correspondance*, III, 135, and Jeanne d'Albret, who arrived at court on August 29. *Suriano, Despatches*, p. 39.

tide; she represented Beza himself as half converted and already foresaw some 100,000 other Huguenots converted by his example.[73] This was hardly the case: the next day Beza was preaching before the Bourbons, and with such success that it is said people were packed in the doorways and windows.[74] It is indeed conspicuous that no one seems to have drawn the logical deduction from the meeting of August 24: it offered some hope of an understanding. Beza and Lorraine were at least off to a good start. It is fatefully symptomatic of the sixteenth century that the talk was of conversion and not of convergence.

The court on the eve of the colloquy provides other insights into the psychology of the sixteenth century. It was soon enough patent that any optimism engendered by the meeting between Beza and Lorraine was premature. There was, for example, a confrontation over procedure. As has already been said, the bishops proscribed open discussion with the ministers and, in general, felt the heretics were there to be instructed and judged. The ministers had come primarily to defend the principles of the Reformation in the colloquy and to proclaim the Gospel outside it. Calvin apparently had little hope for the venture. Beza may have had more; he at least hoped to win a more equitable treatment for his coreligionists.[75] But none of the Protestants had come to be judged by the prelates. This was made explicit in a request that two of the ministers, Marlorat and Saint Paul, presented to the court on August 17. They set forth their conditions for a proper colloquy: the prelates were to be parties, rather than judges, in the conferences; the King was to preside, assisted by the Queen Mother and the princes of the blood, which implicitly underscored the first

73. As reported by Chantonnay, A.N., K 1494, No. 93.
74. Geisendorf, *Théodore de Bèze*, p. 140.
75. *Ibid.*, p. 143; Beza, *Correspondance*, III, 161-162; *CSP: Foreign*, No. 461(3), Aug. 30, 1561.

point; differences would be resolved by Holy Writ alone, with
Hebrew for the Old Testament and Greek for the New
Testament; and each party could choose its own secretaries
to record the discussions. The King agreed to submit the
request to his council.[76] But as no action was forthcoming, a
similar request was presented to the court on September 8.
This time the ministers made it clear that, short of compliance, they could not enter the colloquy in good conscience.
A written reponse was requested.[77]

Confronted by a threatened walkout on the part of the
Protestants and a potential lockout on the side of the
prelates, Catherine temporized. She, along with Navarre and
the Chancellor, personally favored the request. Because she
had to placate the prelates, the ministers had to be resigned
to a verbal promise accepting their requirements.[78] They
could realistically hope for little more, and the impasse was
avoided.

There is persuasive evidence that, despite the religious
truce, the anomalous presence of Protestants and Catholics at
court was exacerbating rather than easing emotions. The
Triumvirate were united in common indignation as never
before. The Duke of Guise, who had just arrived at court on
August 23, after escorting his niece, Mary Stuart, to Dieppe
and the ordeals of Scotland, reportedly spoke of the colloquy
as "humbug."[79] That the Constable was attacked by the gout
has already been recounted.[80] Saint-André, the last of the

76. *HE*, I, 491-492. Attached to the request was a copy of the Reformed
Confession of Faith as drawn up at the National Synod of 1559.

77. *Ibid.*, 498-499.

78. Beza, *Correspondance*, III, 143, 149, 151.

79. Romier, *C&H*, p. 188.

80. The strength of the Constable's feeling was revealed in an interview he had
with Catherine in June, when he presented a protest from the Parisians against the
Huguenots and their excesses of that time. He tendered the petition with these
words: "Madame, I am also one of those who would sacrifice their substance, and
their lives, and their children for God's honor, and if it be not sufficient for me to
subscribe (this declaration) with ink, I am ready to do so with my own blood."
Suriano, Despatches, p. 28.

trio, denounced Navarre before the court for confronting good churchmen with apostate monks. They almost came to blows, and a duel seemed imminent, but Catherine intervened and Saint-André took ill, retiring to his château.[81]

Interests beyond France were involved, especially a potential ally of the Triumvirate, Spain. The Spanish ambassador was incensed over developments at court and told Catherine he could no longer write to King Philip of the things he saw. She told him to write whatever he pleased.[82] Catherine became so vexed with his continued protests that she wrote her daughter, Elizabeth, wife of Philip, that Chantonnay mixed "in all our affairs" and found "all my actions bad," and went on to request his recall.[83] But Chantonnay's services were vital. Elizabeth assuaged her mother with assurances of the friendship of Philip and admitted that Chantonnay "always plays tricks," but withheld hope of his recall.[84] Moreover, by now the nuncio was weary of Lorraine's various promises[85] that the assembly would be kept within the bounds desired by the Pope. On September 8, the day before the colloquy opened, Viterbo sent a long message to Rome, reviling the dissimulation of Catherine, the procrastination over Trent, and the menacing presence of the Huguenots at court. Now was the time for action, and the impetuous Viterbo recommended that a league, headed by Spain but assisted by Savoy and the Duke of Guise, be formed to preserve Catholicism in France.[86] Without waiting, Viterbo then dispatched an appeal to arms to Philip.

81. Lucien Romier, *La carrière d'un favori: Jacques d'Albon de Saint-André* (Paris, 1909), pp. 339-340; Ruble, *Bourbon*, III, 155-156.

82. A.N., K 1495, Nos. 70, 97, 101, Sept. 1561; *Die Römische Kurie*, ed. Šusta, I, 228.

83. *Négociations,* ed. Paris, p. 873.

84. *Ibid.*, p. 876.

85. For example, on August 30, Lorraine assured Viterbo that the Assembly of Prelates would soon dissolve. *Die Römische Kurie,*ed., Šusta, I, 240; see also *ibid.*, 228, 236.

86. *Ibid.*, 250-254.

There was nothing explicit about the league, but this was enough to stimulate Philip's imagination. This was the opportune time: the enemy was without money, without counsel, and without German captains of reputation. Viterbo appealed to the interests of the prudent King; the loss of religion in France would lead to a similar loss in Flanders and, later, in Spain itself.[87] Philip himself had already assumed a threatening posture and would increasingly intensify the threat.

Furthermore, some doctors of Paris made an eleventh-hour attempt to dissuade Catherine from the colloquy. On September 8 Jean Peletier, acting as their spokesman, referred with alarm to the most recent exploits of the Protestants and strongly urged that they should not be heard in the assembly, and especially that the young King should not be exposed to their blasphemies. But Catherine held that the Huguenots, too, were her subjects, and the protest passed without effect.[88]

There is evidence that the suspicions were mutual. Merlin wrote Calvin on August 25 about talk of an "ambush" against the ministers. He personally discounted it because the adversary was not "so foolish as to think that the Gospel would be ruined in France by the death of ten or twelve people." He may well have had some fear of poisonings, for he added: "I think there is more danger from the minestrone than from open violence."[89] He acknowledged that some of his partisans wanted to resort to force, which he himself did not completely disavow. He simply felt that "it is not now necessary for us."[90] Beza himself, upon arrival in Paris,

87. *Ibid.*, 255-257.

88. *Journal*, p. 26. The Sorbonne and the Parlement of Paris had earlier protested against the religious policies of the crown. *Suriano, Despatches*, p. 26; Jean Crevier, *Histoire de Université de Paris, depuis son origine jusqu'en l'année 1600* (7 vols., Paris, 1761), VI, 104.

89. Calvin, *Opera*, XVIII, 645. This was surely not a comment on the French (or Italian) cuisine.

90. *Ibid.*

alluded to the danger of war. He stoically preferred "to fall in the civil war than in the colloquy."[91] And if the Protestants feared poison, the Catholics feared arson, suspecting that the Huguenots would fire the convent at Poissy. Every house was ordered to have a cask of water on hand for the emergency.[92] It would appear that the Huguenots were chary of food and the Catholics of sleep.

Finally, the two sides had decidedly ungenerous images of each other. To the Protestants, the prelates were ambitious, avaricious, and even ignorant of letters.[93] And, at the very opening of the colloquy, the Venetian ambassador, himself of patrician stock, reflected that the Huguenots were "all vile and low fellows, odious to look at, and strange and rude in manners, or in a word, rascals."[94] At the same time, the intractable Tournon rudely murmured: "Here are the dogs of Geneva!" Beza, having overheard, turned the unflattering metaphor to his advantage: "It is necessary that there be dogs in the flock of the Lord, in order to guard against the wolves." This was not an auspicious way to begin a dialogue.

Against this background, the colloquy, by its very existence, can be seen as an expression of the triumph of hope over experience. And so, mixed in its motives, sponsored by an alien woman and a child-king, no more than suffered by a majority of the Catholics, as often as not supported by the Huguenots for reasons other than reconciliation, challenged by Tournon and the Triumvirate, disavowed by Pope and council, harassed by Spain, haunted by the specter of Lutheranism, inhibited by the passions of the populace, and compromised by deep-seated animosities and suspicions, the Colloquy of Poissy, so darkly prejudiced, began.

91. Beza, *Correspondance*, III, 132.
92. *Collection*, ed. Duranthon, I, 24.
93. *HE*, I, 489.
94. *Suriano, Despatches*, p. 42.

IV / The Colloquy of Poissy Begins:
September 9 and 16, 1561

Mais quel malheur a fait que les prélats de France
N'ont voulu contre Beze à Poissy disputer.
Craignoient ils qu'à l'essay on leur veuille imputer
Que leur sçavoir caché passe nostre espérance.
Pensoient-ils, les couars, par leur feinte assurance
Faire encorres des feux, les bons persécuter.
                                    Anonymous[1]

Tu dis des prelats la troupe docte & sainte
Au Colloque à Poissy tremble toute de crainte,
Voyant les predicans contre elle s'assembler:
Ie la vy disputer, & ne la vy trembler
Ferme comme un rocher qui iamais pour orage
Soit de gresle ou de vent ne bouge du rivage.
                                    Ronsard[2]

It was a distinguished company that, on Tuesday, September 9, 1561, filed into the refectory of the old convent at Poissy. Besides the royal family, the princes of the blood, and the Council of State, there were six princes of the Church, over forty archbishops and bishops, twelve theologians of the Sorbonne, and as many canonists. For the Reformed, besides their party at court, there were twelve ministers, including Beza and François de Morel, president of the first French National Synod, assisted by some twenty laymen. This official company has already been enumerated. Beyond them, there was a large and mixed group of curious spectators, including the poet Ronsard and the philosopher Peter Ramus.

1. Ruble, *Journal*, p. 56.
2. Soeur Mary Hilarine Seiler, *Anne de Marquets: Poétesse religieuse du XVIe siècle* (Washington, D.C.: Catholic University of America, 1931), p. 42.

Charles IX opened the colloquy with a brief statement of
intent. The assembly was to resolve the troubles of the
kingdom and to reform its Church. The child-king proclaimed: "I have decided that you are not to move from this
place until you have given us such good order that my
subjects can henceforth live in peace and reunion with each
other."[3] Then the Chancellor, who had perhaps inspired
these remarks, arose to elaborate upon the theme. Addressing
the bishops, he issued a new call for peace and harmony. He
reviewed the perils of the realm and the failure of force,
stressing the need to root out the abuses that had crept into
the ancient constitution of the Church. And, as the diversity
of religious opinions was the principal cause of the present
troubles, he recounted how the King had accorded a safe-
conduct to the Protestants, hoping that they might all
profitably confer together. They were to be received kindly
and to be instructed with no force save persuasion. The
bishops had the King's promise that he would continue as a
"protector and defender of his Church."[4] Despite the in-
nocuousness of these remarks, the Chancellor again refused
Tournon a copy of his address.[5] Then Tournon himself, as

3. La Place, *Commentaires*, p. 158.
4. *Ibid.* I prefer to cite La Place here, rather than l'Hospital, *Oeuvres*, ed.
Dufcy, because of the textual difficulty previously mentioned. Evennett, *Lorraine*, p. 307, n. 3, felt that the address given in *Oeuvres*, ed. Dufey, I, 485-489,
for September 9 was actually that of July 31, and that that ascribed to September
1 may be that of September 9. *Collection des procès-verbaux des assemblées
générales du clergé de France*, ed. Antoine Duranthon, (8 vols., Paris, 1767-1768),
I, 26, n. 1, would offer some support to Evennett, *Lorraine*; the anonymous
source, *Recueilly par les Calvinistes*, A.N., G8*589ª, fols. 158-159, suggests that
Oeuvres, ed. Dufey, is correct with reference to September 9, as some passages
repeat Dufey verbatim. The other sources are too partial to be helpful, and studies
like Henri Amphoux, *Michel de l'Hospital et la liberté de conscience au XVIᵉ
siècle* (Paris, 1900), provide no light. The question is not of great importance, for
the Chancellor's speeches at this time were variations on a common theme.
5. La Place, *Commentaires*, pp. 158-159. The *Recueilly par les Calvinistes*,
A.N., G8* 589ª, fols. 160-161, records an altercation between the Chancellor and
Tournon.

president of the Assembly of Prelates, probably somewhat icily recited his pleasure at seeing the company and expressed his gratitude that the royal family had wished to be present. The incongruity of the scene was complete when the Duke of Guise, hammer of heretics, formally introduced the ministers. Colloquies made strange bedfellows.

If Tournon and Guise spoke without conviction, this was not the case with Beza. Beza, elected spokesman for the Reformed, arose to deliver the first full-length oration of the colloquy. The address was important not only for its intrinsic merits but also because it gave a certain direction to the later course of the colloquy. It warrants recounting at length. Beza gained permission from the King to speak and, falling to his knees, prefaced his address with a short prayer of thanksgiving for the assembly and of hope for the peace of the kingdom. Rising and addressing the King, he pledged the loyalty of his colleagues, so "destitute of help," "the lowest and most contemptible of the world." He appealed for an end of persecution and lavished a flurry of generous praise upon the young Charles, whose face represented "as it were a certain visible majesty of God." He expressed the hope that Charles would be "our defender and protector" and that the prelates "would strive with us to manifest the truth rather than to obscure it more."[6]

Beza then pledged himself to concord. He sounded a fine ecumenical keynote. It was his desire that "the ruins of

6. *HE*, I, 506. Beza's address is found *ibid.*, 503-521; La Place, *Commentaires*, pp. 159-168; and Calvin, *Opera*, XVIII, 687-702. It was first printed only a few days after its delivery. The reproductions of La Place and *HE* are faithful to the original, apart from minor variations. See *HE*, I, 502, n. 2, for details on the early printings, and Frédéric Gardy, *Bibliographie des oeuvres théologiques, littéraires, historiques et juridiques de Théodore de Bèze*, with the collab. of Alain Dufour (Geneva, 1960), pp. 85-92. I have chosen to cite the copy of *HE* because Beza himself supervised the work and was in a position to ensure its accuracy. Its veracity is confirmed by the editor of *Diario*, pp. 118-119. Beza's address seems to have been treated too sparingly by the historians. See Geisendorf, *Théodore de Bèze*, pp. 147-149; Romier, *C&H*, p. 213; and Evennett, *Lorraine*, pp. 307-309.

Jerusalem be repaired" and the "scattered and dispersed sheep ... might be brought together into the fold of our sovereign and single Shepherd." And, again, "I would to God that, without further ado, instead of disputations and arguments, we could all with one voice sing a canticle to our Lord, and take each others hands, as sometimes happened among even infidels, while their armies were already ranged against each other and the battle lines drawn." He concluded this refrain with the noble thought that God would bring this to pass "when it will please Him to cover our sins by His goodness and to drive away our darkness with His light."[7]

He then got to the heart of the matter, noting that there were two things to be avoided: the denial of any substantial differences between the two faiths and the assertion that there were no similarities. Neither was the way to concord.

In his polished and refined oratory, Beza went on to synopsize the Reformed beliefs by way of reviewing the Apostles' Creed. He first stressed the things that Rome and Reformed shared. These included belief in a single but Trinitarian God, in Jesus Christ, true God and true man, and in the perpetual virginity of his mother, the Blessed Virgin Mary. There was also a common belief in the "Holy Catholic Church," which he qualified as the Church Universal and defined "as the company and community of Saints, outside of which there was no salvation."[8]

Then he was obliged to consider the differences, of which there were two kinds: matters of interpretation; and unnecessary accretions. Should the necessity of the latter be demonstrated, he volunteered to acknowledge "our error." He first dealt with soteriology. There was no satisfaction for sins save Christ, whose sacrifice was not to be repeated, lest he be deprived of his priesthood. Moreover, to make new laws

7. See *HE*, I, 507, for both citations.
8. *Ibid.*, 509.

binding conscience degraded him from his position as "King of the Church." He observed disagreement on the effects of faith, but left some place for good works, which were characterized as inseparable from faith, as are heat and light from fire. But given the total depravity of nature, "the beginning, middle and end" of all good works are to be attributed to grace alone. They serve to glorify God and provide assurance that we are among the number of "the elect predestined to salvation."

Sola gratia was followed by the doctrine of *sola scriptura*. The Fathers and the general councils were accepted, however, if they were congruent with Scripture, "for the Holy Spirit never contradicts Himself." Beza supported this with the Fathers,[9] but it was clear where his first loyalty lay: there have been "Councils and Councils, Doctors and Doctors" even as there are now "false prophets" in the Church. And Beza backed up this unhappy allusion by a passage of Holy Writ frequently turned to polemical effect.[10]

He then treated the sacraments, which were defined as "Visible signs, by means of which the conjunction that we have with our Lord Jesus Christ, is not simply signified or figured, but also is truly offered to us from our Lord, and consequently ratified, sealed, and as it were, engraved by the power of the Holy Spirit on those who by a true faith apprehend what is thus signified and presented to them."[11] He seemed to underscore the word "signified," which was not to diminish the sacraments, but to distinguish the sign of the thing from the thing signified. They were to be distinguished, but not separated. This is best illustrated with reference to the sacrament that received emphasis, the

9. See esp. St. Augustine: If there is some difficulty in the interpretation of a passage, the Holy Spirit has so tempered the Holy Scriptures that that which is more obscure in one place is clarified elsewhere. *De doctrina Christiana*, PL 34:39.

10. 1 Tim.: 4; *HE*, I, 512.

11. *HE*, I, 514.

Eucharist. Though more than a commemoration, the bread and wine were transformed not into the very body and blood of Christ, but into the sacrament of the body and blood of Christ. There was no change in "the substance of the signs," but only in the use for which they were instituted. No doubt the prelates were a bit uneasy at this point, but Beza asked them to suspend judgment and to show a little patience. If convinced by the Scriptures of the contrary, he and his company would embrace it and retain it to the death. He rejected the doctrines of transubstantiation and *ex opere operato* as gently as possible. "It seems to us, according to the small measure of knowledge that we have received from God," Beza pleaded, "that this Transubstantiation is not related to the analogy and suitability of our faith, rather it is directly contrary to the nature of sacraments." He held that the signs are, as it were, the substance of the sacrament; if they are transformed, the sacrament is abolished.[12] This is the firm distinction between the sign and the thing signified. He also rejected consubstantiation as both unscriptural and unnecessary.

Beza continued with the sacrament, but at this point, for all his finesse, made what most writers consider an unfortunate error. He affirmed that the Reformed doctrine did not render Christ absent from the Eucharist, then added: "but if we regard the distance of things (as we must, when there is a question of His corporeal presence, and of His humanity

---

12. Beza follows Calvin in this doctrine. The latter adhered to it with characteristic awe before the divine majesty, in order to ensure against sacriligious receptions. The worthy receive the thing signified; the unworthy only the sign. Calvin wrote: "On this you are everywhere told that the sacrament is thus separated from its truth by the unworthiness of the recipient, so that nothing remains but a vain and useless figure." *Institutes*, IV, xiv, 15. He cited in support a curious passage of Augustine: "We all receive visible food this day, but the sacrament is one thing, the power of the sacrament another. Why is it that many receive from the altar and die, and die in receiving? For the Lord's morsel was poison to Judas, not because he received evil, but because an evil man evilly received a good thing."*John's Gospel*, PL 35: 1611.

considered separately): We say that His body is as far removed from the bread and wine as is heaven from earth."[13] Genuine Calvinism or not, Calvinism was scarcely ever so inopportunely expressed. The horrified prelates broke the hitherto polite silence with cries of "Blasphemavit!" The Venetian ambassador reported that "the faces of all those who were within the hall changed color, and it was remarked that even Coligny covered his eyes with his hands."[14] The refectory stirred with the murmuring and hissing of the prelates, some of whom began to walk out. Tournon, who had been seated in the front, interrupted the address and turned to Catherine, "trembling with wrath": "Will you, Madam, permit yourself to hear these horrible blasphemies, in the presence of the King and your other son, both of such tender age and so innocent?"[15] But the royal family was unmoved, and quiet was finally restored. Beza was understandably shaken by the disturbance, but entreated the audience to hear him out: "My Lords, I pray you to await my conclusion, which will satisfy you."[16]

Beza then proceeded to explain his remark, noting that the

13. *HE*, I, 516. For contemporary reactions, see n. 16 and 21, below.

14. *Suriano, Despatches*, p. 42; also, Hubert Languet, *Arcana seculi decimi sexti. Epistolae secretae ad principem suum sax. ducem & S.R.I. septemvirum* (3 vols. in 1, Halle, 1699), III, 139.

15. *Suriano, Despatches*, p. 43. The *Recueilly par les Calvinistes*, A.N., G⁸* 589ᵃ, fol. 165, relates that the prelates clapped their hands.

16. *HE*, I, 521. *Suriano, Despatches*, p. 43, whose account is hostile, said that after the interruption Beza "lost courage and was silent . . . He endeavored to continue his discourse, but became so confused that he did not know what he said, and finished it after uttering a few words." Pierre Bruslard, a canon of Notre Dame, reported that Beza "lost his original line of argument, without easily being able to return to it." See his journal, *Condé*, I, 51. This was perhaps to be expected, but is not really confirmed by Beza, *Correspondance*, III, 177. Reporting the incident to the Elector Palatine on October 3, he recorded that he was well heard by all, including the prelates, until his remarks on the Eucharist, when the prelates began to murmur, despite which he was allowed to finish. The *Journal*, p. 29, reports that Beza reddened at the incident and that his printed text did not entirely conform to the remainder of his address. Claude Haton, *Mémoires* (2 vols., Paris, 1857), I, 164, who apparently was not an observer, provides an unusual account in wihch Catherine urges Beza to "take courage."

glorified body of Christ can now be only in heaven, "and not elsewhere, and we are on earth, and not elsewhere." We participate in Christ's presence in a spiritual manner, and by faith. Finally, the principal function of the sacrament is our conjunction with Christ, not that the Eucharist be adored, preserved, carried in processions, or offered to God. He noted that he had now summed up the essence of his faith, but was not yet ready to conclude.

He briefly surveyed the other sacraments: he observed the agreement on baptism; he remarked on the parallel between confirmation and the preliminary instructions the Reformed gave the young before admitting them to the Eucharist; he mentioned penance, which could be satisfied either publicly or privately; he touched on the Reformed approval of matrimony, and of its perpetuity, their acceptance of the degrees of ecclesiastical charges, and their view of the visitation of the sick as a principal part of the ministry.[17]

He broached the subject of ecclesiastical polity in as sensitive a way as possible. Addressing the prelates, he solicited their concurrence that all was now so perverted, in such confusion and ruin, that the greatest architect of the world could scarcely recognize the vestiges and marks of the primitive Church. He sought to recall the Church to the "naïve purity and beauty" in which it had flourished in the days of the Apostles. As to adiaphora, he suggested as a rule that those things found superstitious or manifestly contrary to the Scriptures be abolished, that those superfluous be curtailed, and that things useful or proper to edification might be retained, though they should be weighed against the ancient canons and the authority of the Fathers.[18]

Then Beza concluded. While he affirmed that his primary obedience was to the "King of Kings," he diplomatically appealed to Rom. 13:1 as an expression of the Calvinist

17. *HE*, I, 517-518.
18. *Ibid.*, 518-519.

respect for the temporal order. He pledged the loyalty and affection of the Huguenots to the crown, exonerated them from any charge of treason, and conjured up the image of his hopes for the future glory of the King, whom he apostrophized as "little King Josias," while he skillfully compared Catherine "to the renowned Queen Clothilde." He ended, knee bent to the ground, and rose to present another confession of the Reformed faith to the King.[19] Romier states that he desired "above all to win over the royal family."[20]

This was understandable. If Beza did woo the royal galleries, apart from the exception noted, his was a model presentation of the doctrines of the Reformed Church. He accentuated, without exaggerating, the not inconsiderable common element of the two confessions. The address was conspicuously free of scurrilous attack on the Papacy, and he avoided more than an oblique reference to the labyrinthine doctrine of predestination. Presumably these questions could wait. It would seem prudent that the dialogue proceed from more agreeable to less agreeable subjects. Because of the stir over his remark on the Eucharist, one could readily overlook that he several times allowed that the Calvinists professed belief in the Real Presence, though the statement was qualified in the terms of Calvinist orthodoxy. Again, he several times confessed an openness toward any clearly warranted modification of his faith. In the main, then, the address was in an ecumenical spirit and provided a foundation for positive dialogue.[21]

19. *Ibid.*, 520.
20. Romier, *C&H*, p. 214.
21. Not to speak of its capacity to charm. Even the Venetian ambassador considered it "eloquent," despite other criticism. *Suriano, Despatches*, p. 42. Languet, *Arcana seculi*, II, 138, wrote that it was a "splendid oration." A Calvinist minister, Pierre Fornelet, boasted that Beza's speech "toppled down the Papacy and all false doctrines in order to restore the reign of Christ." "Le Protestantisme en Champagne, au XVIe siècle, Documents inédits et originaux,"

Beza's oration would not sway the royal family if Tournon could prevent it. As soon as Beza finished, the indignant prelate made a plea to Charles, beseeching him not to accept "the errors" of Beza, but to live in the faith his ancestors had professed since Clovis. This was said for the Queen and the entire company. Catherine assured Tournon that she and the King would live and die in the Catholic faith.[22] Tournon then encouraged the crown to refuse Beza's proffered confession, but the King, to the contrary, beckoned the Duke of Guise to accept it for him. Then, in apparent heat, Tournon asked that a day be fixed so that a proper response to Beza might be made. At first he expressed the hope that the King might be in attendance, but then suddenly corrected himself, finding better security in seeking only the King's support.[23]

Catherine herself viewed the eucharistic blunder as a setback to the colloquy. On September 14 she wrote her ambassador in Vienna that Beza had forgotten himself "in a comparison so absurd and offensive to the ears of the audience" that some even asked that she impose silence on him and dispatch the ministers forthwith.[24] Beza's own concern was revealed in a private message to Catherine the next day, attenuating the offensive expression and attempting to put it in better light. He now emphasized Christ's presence in the sacraments, though in a spiritual manner. What was most significant in his message was the request for a private meeting with the Queen. He suggested that such a

---

BSHPF, XII (1863), 365. On the other hand, Roland Bainton, in his general study, The Reformation of the Sixteenth Century (Boston: Beacon Press, 1960), p. 167, lamented that Beza "not only failed to conciliate the Catholics but succeeded also in alienating the Lutherans by stating in the baldest terms the Calvinist doctrine of spiritual communion." Incidentally, Beza's comment here was probably a variation on Isa. 54: 9, which may have inadvertently heightened the thought.

22. Journal, p. 29.
23. HE, I, 521.
24. Lettres de Catherine de Médicis, I, 608. Geisendorf, Théodore de Bèze, p. 150, insists, however, that she had to appear vexed, which is likely.

meeting, in the company of the learned men of her choice, might be conducive to the establishment of religious concord.[25] The interview did not come to pass, and Catherine's reaction is unknown. But the suggestion may have influenced future developments.

The morning after Beza's speech the prelates conferred on their course. Opinions varied. The bishop of Saint-Brieuc expressed the fairly general sentiment that inasmuch as Beza had directed his speech to the King, the Queen, and the princes of the blood, there should be no reply as such, because this would make it appear that the crown was the arbiter between the two parties and would be to "enter the lists" against the heretics. Rather, a remonstrance should be made that the matter could only be dealt with by the general council and that others ought to be neither audience nor judge. Montluc replied that the crown had no desire to act as judge in a religious suit.[26] But then Lorraine's thinking seemed to have dominated the conference. He was conspicuous in his denunciations of Beza's "errors and blasphemies" and even lamented: "Oh! That he had been mute or we had been deaf!"[27] This may have been his genuine sentiment, but it may also have been calculated to induce the prelates to accept the necessity of a rejoinder—and a declaration that he was possessed of just the unimpeachable convictions that this reply should represent. He pleaded that it was necessary to

25. For the letter, see *HE* , I, 522-525; Calvin *Opera*, XVIII, 703-705. Beza's concern about the possible ill effects of the point was communicated to Calvin on September 12. Beza, *Correspondance*, III, 152. Calvin, however, congratulated Beza. Beza, *Correspondance*, III, 159. He himself had written something of the same sort, though not out of season. *Institutes*, IV, xxiv, 24.

26. *Diario*, pp. 120-121. It is odd that this source alleges that Montluc nevertheless supported Saint-Brieuc's position. This does not square with the events before and after and is probably erroneous. It was apparently Coligny's hope that the crown would act as an impartial tribunal to decide which of the religions was best. This would follow the pattern of the Swiss Reformation. See Noël Valois, "Les essais de conciliation religieuse au début du règne de Charles IX," *Revue d'histoire de l'Église de France*, XXX-XXXI (1944-1945), 253.

27. *Journal*, p. 29.

elect someone to confute Beza's errors and, in what was perhaps a play at magnanimity, nominated the not illiberal Pierre du Val, bishop of Séez, for the assignment. But Lorraine himself was the unanimous choice of the prelates.[28]

The reply was to represent a consensus of the prelates' views, thus providing a governor for Lorraine and a spot test of orthodoxy. Lorraine was charged to treat four articles only: the Church and its authority; general councils; the authority of Holy Scripture; and the Real Presence. He invited the suggestions of the company, and it was agreed that the finished product would require the prior subscription of all the bishops. It was further affirmed that the King would be neither a judge nor a superior in the matter. The cardinal of Bourbon declared with spirit that the King should be informed that the prelates would shed their blood for the truth of the articles of the response. The company, now braced and resolute, agreed wholeheartedly.[29]

By the time news of the prelates' action reached the ministers, it had been considerably enriched by rumor. It was understood that the prelates had not only refused the Huguenots debate, which was true, but that they had also determined to pass judgment in the form of a confession of faith that would anathematize the Protestants, which was doubtful.[30] The alarmed Calvinists reacted with a strongly phrased statement to the King. It declared that if the prelates usurped the role of judges, this would "close the door" to further conversation. They required that their grievance be taken to heart and the action of the prelates reversed.[31]

28. *Ibid.*, p. 30. Evennett, *Lorraine*, p. 310, says: "It was the Cardinal of Lorraine who ensured the continuance of the Colloquy." It was an open secret at court that he burned to joust with the Calvinists. De Thou, *Histoire universelle*, III, 55, 64. The whole matter of his motivation will be considered later.

29. *Journal*, p. 30; *Diario*, pp. 120-121.

30. It is not revealed by the two sources privy to the meeting, *Journal* and *Diario*. Perhaps this opinion was expressed by some prelates and not recorded. Such a condemnation was, in fact, composed later.

31. *HE*, I, 526-527.

Calvinist exasperation was soon assuaged by the arrival of a reinforcement in the form of an able second to Beza: Peter Martyr Vermigli. Peter Martyr, as he is known, has been termed "an unlaureled hero of the Italian Reformation."[32] This is to confer a somewhat scanty wreath, for most of his reforming activities took place north of Italy; he was a genuinely cosmopolitan figure. Martyr was one of the most competent and least known of the Protestant Reformers, an incongruity that scholarship is now correcting.[33]

Martyr was born in Florence in 1500 of a distinguished family of that singularly distinguished city. At sixteen he became an Augustinian friar; by thirty he was abbot of Spoleto; ten years later he had risen to the rank of visitor-general of the order. He was not only a classical scholar, learned in Greek and Hebrew, but held the doctorate in theology from the University of Padua. Martyr's formation included membership in the circle of Catholic Evangelism in Italy, but he developed views of a more heterodox nature, and by 1542, the year of the Roman Inquisition, he was clearly a Protestant. He was then forced to leave Italy. Martyr went first to Zurich, then Basel, later Strasbourg, and was, in 1547, the first Regius Professor of Divinity at Oxford. He became a seminal figure in the English Reformation.[34] His writings included numerous commentaries on Scripture and a

32. Benjamin F. Paist, Jr., "Peter Martyr and the Colloquy of Poissy," *Princeton Theological Review*, XX (1922), 645.

33. For example, Joseph C. McLelland, *The Visible Words of God: An Exposition of the Sacramental Theology of Peter Martyr Vermigli, 1500-1562* (Grand Rapids, Mich., 1957); Philip McNair, *Peter Martyr in Italy* (Oxford: 1967).

34. McNair, *Peter Martyr*, p. xiii; John E. Booty, *John Jewel as Apologist of the Church of England* (London, 1963), p. 67; Alan Beesley, "An Unpublished Source of the Book of Common Prayer: Peter Martyr Vermigli's *Adhortatio ad Coenam Domini Mysticum,*" *Journal of Ecclesiastical History*, XIX (1968), 83-88. Pontien Polman, *L'élément historique dans la controverse religieuse du XVIe siècle* (Gembloux, 1932), p. 119, spoke of Martyr's *Defensio doctrinae veteris et apostolicae de sacrosancto eucharistiae sacramento* (1559) as "perhaps the most erudite that the Protestant polemic of the sixteenth century had produced on a special subject of the history of dogma."

Loci communes, or systematic theology. He was an exegete and dogmatic controversialist with a Scholastic turn and had engaged in eucharistic disputations in both England and Germany. In 1556 he returned to Zurich, where he became Reformed pastor to the Italian colony. Unfortunately, however, he was now advanced in years with fixed views and an intractable spirit. Though he would strengthen the ranks of the Calvinists, he would not enhance the prospects for conciliation.

And yet it was Catherine who sought Martyr's presence at the parley. No theologian herself, Catherine reportedly desired his participation "because he is of her nation."[35] Beza had acted as liaison and negotiated the conditions under which Zurich reluctantly allowed the revered pastor to leave.[36] By September 9 Martyr was courteously received in Paris, and shortly he was at court.

The colloquy was in French in deference to the royal family. Martyr could only understand, not speak, that language. Hence Beza was still the spokesman for the Reformed, and Martyr more a counselor. He participated indirectly, working behind the scenes. Perhaps above all, he essayed to be the confidant of the Queen, and on September 12 he enjoyed a warm interview with Catherine. He sensed, nevertheless, a basic conflict in their purposes. She desired the reform of the Church, but peacefully, and with the support of the prelates. This he considered impossible. Instead he praised the wisdom of Beza's oration and underscored the duty of the prince to reform the Church. She was animated by a sense of political realities; he, by a zeal for doctrinal integrity. Martyr would remain close to her counsels, and

35. Senate of Geneva to Senate of Bern, Calvin, *Opera*, XVIII, 568.
36. Beza, *Correspondance*, III, 124. For the rather involved particulars, see Calvin, *Opera*, XVIII, 567, n. 1, 599, 610, 612-613; see also Peter Martyr Vermigli, *The Common Places of the most Famous and Renowned Divine Doctor Peter Martyr*, tr. Anthonie Marten (London, 1583), p. 149, which contains, among many other things, translations of Martyr's letters from Poissy.

when the prelates tried to exclude him from the colloquy as an "alien," she overruled them.[37] It is conceivable that she came to regret this action.

It was Tuesday, September 16, one week after Beza's address, when the company convened for the second session. Nerves were still taut—there was apparently even a fear of assassination. The Duke of Guise, who kept the keys of the refectory, carefully searched the hall prior to the meeting to ascertain that no one had hidden himself there during the night.[38] The commuters from Saint-Germain took their place, the royal family acknowledged its readiness, and the spokesman for the prelates took the floor.

The cardinal of Lorraine bore the colors for the Catholic Church. He began with the customary amenities, pledging his loyalty and obedience to the crown. He went out of his way, however, to give the crown a polite lecture on the primacy of the spiritual. Though the King's power is of God, it is subject to him and his Church. The King was "within the Church, not above it," its son rather than its chief. He recited historical precedent from Ambrose and made only a dutiful reference to the superiority of the Holy See. He then acknowledged the ministers and, in a condescending tone, presumed that "they have shown a desire to learn and to be instructed." Should they decide to recognize the Church of their fathers, they would be "embraced as children." Lorraine felt compassion with "their infirmity" and sought "not to reject them, but recall them, not to separate them, but to reunite with them."[39] Perhaps after this righteous preamble

37. Martyr to Bullinger, Calvin, *Opera*, XVIII, 709-710; see also Martyr's own *Relatio, ibid.*, 760-763; McLelland, *Visible Words*, p. 61.

38. Throckmorton to Elizabeth, Sept. 20, 1561, *CSP: Foreign*, No. 516(7).

39. For the address, see La Place, *Commentaires*, pp. 170-177, which omits long passages, and the *HE*, I, 528-553. There is only a résumé in the *Diario*, pp. 122-124. Lorraine's speech was published later that year at both Reims and Paris. For a fine manuscript copy, see A.N., G[8]* 589[C], fols. 19-35; see also Evennett, *Lorraine*, pp. 313-324. It may be well to recall that his address was something of a joint effort. He acknowledged the help and cooperation of others. *Journal*, p. 31.

both Catherine and the Calvinists had some doubts, but this was an accepted method of initiating dialogue in the age of the Reformation.

Lorraine announced that he would first treat ecclesiastical authority—the Church, Holy Writ, and councils—and then the Eucharist. The Church was "the column and firmament" of the truth; the Eucharist, the "sacrament of unity." As regards the first, he made no distinction between a Church visible and invisible; it was thus bound to include both the elect and the nonelect, the "wheat and the chaff." He supported the point with abundant citations of Scripture. He made an effective response to Beza's unseemly comment about "false prophets," by speaking of the Church as the rock against which hell will not prevail, in spite of "false Christs, false prophets, false apostles, abuses, errors and heresies."[40]

He then sought to clarify "the rule of faith," a matter at the heart of Reformation controversy. The Gospel he understood, as did the Calvinists, as more than coextensive with Holy Writ. It was "the root of truth, not the leaves of pages." Though the Gospel was older than and prior to the Church, which preceded all "scriptures," it was proclaimed long before it was written. This reserved a place for tradition, and he invoked St. Paul's saying that we should hold fast to traditions whether received by word or epistle.[41] As regards councils, the provincial is subject to the general, and one general council can be corrected by another—but this only in matters of custom and discipline. In matters of faith the direction of the Holy Spirit precludes error. Single men can err, but the Church Universal never. In matters of controversy, it is incumbent upon us to turn to the ancient churches, among whom Rome's primacy stood out, so that its bishop was called "Primae sedis episcopum." This is as close as Lorraine the conciliarist came to the Papacy. He

40. *HE*, I, 534.
41. He cites 2 Thess. 2: 15 and also refers to Acts 15. *Ibid.*, 535.

concluded the section on authority with an oblique ascription of primacy to Holy Writ: "Above all . . . give way to the express Word of God, and to the witness of the Scripture." Apparently well satisfied with himself thus far, he patronizingly wondered how those who "have gone astray" could possibly prefer their novelties to the wisdom of the ancients.[42]

Lorraine now arrived at what he described as the last, but principal part, of his oration: the Eucharist. Beza's slip had made this kind of focus easy. The cardinal introduced the subject by regretting that what had been given as a "bond of union and peace" had, through a certain curiosity to search things higher than ourselves, become a bone of contention. The fruits of the sacrament were considered fourfold: the union and reconciliation that we ought to have with each other; the union obtained with Christ; the remission of sins; and the prize of eternal life.

He proceeded to argue for a literal exegesis of the words of institution: "This is my body." The case was supported with biblical texts and references to the early councils and to a long list of the Fathers. In case of doubt, he pleaded, who should judge the difference but the Church? His approach emphasized mystery: here "faith is necessary, reason superfluous." And the stress was upon the action of the Holy Spirit rather than the celebrant: "the ineffable operation of the grace of God, and power of his Holy Spirit, to be present in these holy mysteries." He specifically excluded Aristotelian terminology or any philosophy of the schools, though he observed that the Fathers did not shrink from adverbs like *substantialiter, naturaliter*, and *corporaliter*.[43] He did not require a local or circumscriptive presence and, leaning as far as he could, professed that the union with Christ is not itself "corporeal," but rather "supernatural,

42. *Ibid.*, 537-538.
43. *Ibid.*, 544-545. He drew on, for example, Hilary, *De trinitate*, PL 10: 249.

supersubstantial, spiritual, invisible, ineffable, special, and proper to the sacrament." "Take it on God's word," he beseeched the ministers, "for His word is infallible."[44] This was his first and only usage of that foreboding expression.

Lorraine then directed his argument toward the problem of a conflict between the Ascension and a corporeal presence. As far as he knew (but he did not know enough),[45] the ministers were the first to posit an opposition between the two. The Fathers were "not so subtle, ingenious or curious." They simply preached that when Christ ascended into heaven, he left us with this sacred mystery: "to be here, to be there." He supported the point with a prayer of St. John Chrysostom: "You who are seated with the Father, and here conversing invisibly with us, deign to give us from your omnipotent hand your immaculate body and precious blood."[46] Lorraine maintained that Calvin misinterpreted Augustine on this point and that the bishop of Hippo himself held that Christ's body could be conceived as other than visible,[47] thus making bodily ascension compatible with corporeal presence. But it was, to be sure, "inscrutable."

44. *HE*, I, 546.
45. The idea descends from Augustine and was not uncommon among the Swiss and the more radical Reformers. Among others, see the fine and ecumenical study of Kilian McDonnell, O.S.B., *John Calvin, the Church, and the Eucharist* (Princeton, N.J., 1967), esp. pp. 40-46.
46. *HE*, I, 547. The prayer is from *De sacerdotio*, lib. 3, and appears to be a free translation of the passage found in PG 48: 642, though Lorraine is faithful to the sense.
47. The question of misinterpretation turns on Letter 187 to Dardanus, PL 33: 832-848, cited as Letter 57 in *HE*, I, 549. Calvin had used the letter in his polemic of 1558 against the Lutheran Joachim Westphal, in *Ultima admonitio Ioannis Calvini ad Ioachimum Westphalum*, Calvin, *Opera*, IX, 137-252. See also Beza, *Correspondance*, III, 157, n. 2. As Lorraine did not adequately specify particulars, there is no need to analyze the lengthy letter in order to investigate the accusation. Augustine, who was not a systematic theologian, could be cited with equal ease in support of contrary doctrines. Sometimes he speaks of the Eucharist with great literalness. For example: "In doubt I turn to Christ and find how the earth can be adored without impurity. Flesh is from the earth and He received flesh from the flesh of Mary. He walked here in the very flesh and gave that flesh to us to eat for our salvation; but no one eats that flesh without first adoring it . . .

Lorraine joined the appeal to the Fathers with one to the "German Protestants"—obviously meaning Lutherans. Even they agreed to a corporeal presence, as against the "Sacramentarians." He referred to a man of great renown, presumably Melanchthon, who warned that discord over the Eucharist could menace and ruin the entire Church.[48] Attempting an *argumentum ad absurdum*, he repeated the now unwarranted assertion that the Calvinists held that Christ was no more "in the host then in a theater, nay, in mud."[49] He then played on Beza's remark: "We are as far from your opinion in this case, as is the highest heaven from the lowest earth."[50] He undoubtedly situated his own doctrine in the former. He chided the ministers: the "first heresy" was among those disciples who took Christ's words as "a hard saying" and no longer walked with him.[51] This assuredly delighted the prelates more than it convinced the Reformed, which Lorraine sensed. He paused: "It seems to me that I have wearied you more by my length than I wanted, but not persuaded you so much as I had desired." Perhaps the

---

Not only do we not sin by adoring, but we sin by not adoring." *Enarratio in Psalmum XCVIII*, PL 37: 1265. Hence, he speaks not only of a carnal presence, but also enjoins its adoration. Yet he says, on the same page: "You are not about to eat this Body that you see . . . I have entrusted a sacrament to you; spiritually understood, it will give you life." This would sound more like a Calvinist interpretation. See the well-organized effort of Eugene Portalie, S.J., *A Guide to the Thought of Saint Augustine*, tr. J. Bastian (Chicago: Henry Regnery, 1960), to reconcile the two faces of Augustine's eucharistic doctrine. Perhaps confessional peace consists in the simple acceptance of both sides of Augustine.

48. The editors of *HE*, I, 550, n. 1, conclude that this was Melanchthon to Johannes Oecolampadius, Apr. 8, 1529. Melanchthon, *Opera*, I, 1048-1050, however, does not contain exactly what Lorraine said. The admonition reads: "Teque rogo, ut considereres, quantam rem quamque periculosam susceperis." Lorraine probably exaggerated for effect.

49. *HE*, I, 549. In Latin rather than French, perhaps in concern for the sensitivities of the crown and its policy of conciliation, perhaps because of the fine rhetorical effect of the Latin: "In coeno, quam in sceno, imo."

50. *Ibid.*, 549. While Lorraine became more aggressive toward the end, a moment earlier he had even tendered a disparaging remark about the Scholastics: "We do not separate Christ from heaven . . . as even our Scholastics dogmatize the contrary." *Ibid.*, 548.

51. *Ibid.*, 550-551.

ministers, like students, appeared disconcertingly eager for
the bell that would terminate the lecture. His ultimate appeal
was to non-Roman churches. He pointed to the doctrine of
the Greek Church on the Eucharist and, then, undoubtedly
to Beza's increasing discomfort, referred to the Confession of
Augsburg. If the Reformed could not agree with each other,
there was no hope. He concluded with the ministers in a
partisan cry: "And if you like only your opinion, you should
become solitaries. And if you find our faith and our works so
distasteful, then remove yourselves far from us, and no longer
trouble our flocks, to whom you have not been charged."[52]

Lorraine closed with a plea to the King and the court. He
appealed to Charles to remain steadfast in the faith of his
fathers, held since Clovis, and matched Beza's allusion to
Catherine as Clothilde. He bid for the fidelity of Navarre and
the princes of the blood. He climaxed the oration in an
emotional appeal on his knees, pledging the blood of the
Gallican Church to the defense of Catholicism and the service
of the crown.[53]

No sooner had Lorraine finished than Beza was on his feet,
seeking the King's permission to reply "on the spot."[54] But,
apparently before the young monarch could react, Tournon,
who, with some of the other prelates, was already beginning
to leave the refectory, seized the moment. He proclaimed
that if the ministers were willing to subscribe to the declared
articles on the Church and the sacrament, "they would be
received as penitents with open arms." But should they
remain obstinate, the Catholics would not confer with them
any longer, for they would never have anything but "one
God, one faith, and one King."[55] Catherine, torn between

52. *Ibid.*
53. *Ibid.*, I, 551-553.
54. Beza to Elector Palatine, Oct. 3, 1561, Beza, *Correspondance*, III, 177; see
also his description to Calvin, Sept. 17, 1561, *ibid.*, 156; *HE*, I, 553.
55. *Diario*, p. 124. François, *Tournon*, p. 413.

her vision of peace and the thunder of Tournon, responded to Beza's request evasively.[56]

Before considering the future of her colloquy, it may be well at this point to evaluate the past. Lorraine's presentation, following Beza, had all the advantages. His ground was laid out; his targets fixed. The address was longer than Beza's—reportedly lasting an hour and a half[57]—and circumstances enables it to be perhaps more erudite. It was profuse with citations from Holy Writ and the Fathers. It was delivered in the grand manner, imperious and paternalistic in tone. And though Lorraine clearly saw the quarrel as one of venerable traditions versus ill-conceived novelties, it must be borne in mind that the oration required the approval of the intransigents.

There was another and irenical side to the address. It had biblical appeal, so that it met the Protestants on their own ground. And if the Reformed were treated cavalierly, so were the Scholastics. It was un-Scholastic and lacking in categorical definitions. Charged terms like the Mass, transubstantiation, and the *ex opere operato* formula were eschewed. The Papacy was merely touched on, and infallibility applied only to Holy Writ. The address might be characterized as magisterial in form and relatively accommodating in substance. And if it was calculated more to convince heretics than to win friends, given all circumstances, it was perhaps the most that could be expected. Whether they were the wisest words possible is debatable, but they were undoubtedly the best words the conservative prelates had for the

56. There are variations of detail in the sources here. In Beza's letter to the Elector Palatine he wrote that "it did not please the Queen to grant this in order to avoid a tumult." Beza, *Correspondance*, III, 177. In the earlier missive to Calvin, of September 17, he said that "it was replied that a day would be appointed us." *Ibid.*, 156-157. The *HE*, I, 553, follows this. The *Journal*, p. 32, reports that Catherine "responded that he would be advised."

57. As reported by Martyr, cited in Vermigli, *Common Places*, p. 152. This was one reason the ministers became restive.

Huguenots and, if they were to have their way, the last words. This evaluation seems generally borne out by the attitude of the audience. Catherine considered it a "very prudent and catholic [sic] response."[58] The Venetian ambassador was favorably impressed,[59] and Pierre Bruslart, the canon of Notre Dame, felt the address was "So fine . . . that even our enemies admired it."[60] This would perhaps include the nuncio, who seems to have found only a few passages of dubious orthodoxy.[61] The Protestants had mixed reactions. The Prince of Condé was reportedly "greatly pleased."[62] To Hubert Languet it was "more moderate than the Saxons,"[63] meaning the Lutherans, while Peter Martyr conceded to Bullinger that Lorraine "abstained from insult and acted placidly enough,"[64] an interesting commentary on the usual heat of sixteenth-century religious exchanges. There were some voices of dissent. Nicolas des Gallars, of the Huguenot Church of London, was obviously antagonized and felt Lorraine's speech was "so weak that a child would have laughed at it."[65] And, finally, Beza, Lorraine's opposite

58. *Lettres de Catherine de Médicis*, I, 239.
59. *Suriano, Despatches*, p. 43.
60. *Condé*, I, 52.
61. No details were provided. Evennett, *Lorraine*, p. 322; *Suriano, Despatches*, p. 45.
62. *Suriano, Despatches*, p. 43.
63. He even conceded, reluctantly, that "maior pars vincit meliorem." Languet, *Arcana seculi*, III, 139-140.
64. He also reported that the cardinal sounded like a Lutheran. Calvin, *Opera*, XVIII, 724; *Relatio, ibid.*, XVIII, 764. Geisendorf, *Théodore de Bèze*, p. 151, cited with apparent approval the opinion of Romier, *C&H*, p. 219, that almost all the audience considered Lorraine's discourse "brilliant, courteous, not devoid of a certain spirit of conciliation." The view of Ruth Rouse and Stephen Neill, *A History of the Ecumenical Movement, 1517-1948* (2nd ed., London, 1967), p. 40, that the speech was "uncompromising," does not seem clearly warranted by the text.
65. To the bishop of London, Sept. 17, 1561, *CSP: Foreign*, No. 507. And the speech allegedly made a Protestant out of philosopher Peter Ramus, or so he reported years later to Lorraine, his former patron. Paul Van Dyke, *Catherine de Médicis* (2 vols., New York, 1928), I, 217; Charles Waddington, *Ramus, sa vie, ses*

number, wrote scathingly of the discourse: "Never have I
heard such impudence, such ineptitude . . . the old arguments
a thousand times refuted . . . moved me to nausea."[66] This
view only reflects the more or less characteristic partisanship
of the period. A consensus would probably be that there was
more impudence than ineptitude.

When Beza put down his views on Lorraine's address, he
also assailed "the rubbish of Westphal" in the discourse,[67] an
allusion to its real or alleged Lutheran overtones. There was,
as a matter of fact, a demarche to enlarge the colloquy by
providing for Lutheran representation at Poissy.

At least three efforts can be discerned to establish some
sort of nexus between the colloquy and the supporters of the
Confession of Augsburg. The first attempt was largely made
on the initiative of the Lutherans. It will be recalled that
Navarre had long been in contact with the German princes
through his special emissary, Francis Hotman; they showed
an interest in a French national council. Christophe, duke of
Württemberg, invited Anthony to sponsor the Confession of
Augsburg in France.[68] And Christophe did this in conscious
opposition to "the false teachings" of the Swiss Reformers.[69] Calvin reacted sharply against such interloping; in
late August 1561 he implored Anthony to preserve his
fidelity to and protection of the Confession of the Reformed
Church, sealed by "the blood of the martyrs." He went on:
"Concerning the Confession of Augsburg, how does the Duke
of Württemberg make bold to ask you to receive it, seeing
that he and his likes condemn the author, who is Melanch-

écrits et ses opinions (Paris, 1855), pp. 134-135. This was apparently due to the
cardinal's vanity and Ramus's positive attraction to the Calvinist delegates.

66. Beza to Calvin, Sept. 17, 1561, Beza, *Correspondance*, III, 156. But Beza
did appreciate Lorraine's stylistic expertise. *Négociations*, ed. Paris, p. 799.

67. *Négociations*, ed. Paris, p. 799.

68. Bernhard Kugler, *Christoph, Herzog zu Wirtemberg* (2 vols. Stuttgart,
1872), II, 291-293, 303-304.

69. *Ibid.*, 292.

thon? . . . the fact is that those of renown of their party are like cats and dogs."[70]

A second attempt to establish rapport between Poissy and Lutheranism was made by Francis Baudouin, Navarre's emissary to Cassander. Baudouin seems to have encouraged Anthony to invite some German princes.[71] On his way to visit Cassander, he stopped over at Heidelberg and discussed his irenical projects with Frederick, the Elector Palatine. This was perhaps on his own initiative.[72] He also contacted the Duke of Württemberg through Pietro-Paolo Vergerio, once a papal nuncio, now a Protestant and pensioner at the court of Württemberg.[73] But it was in vain. Baudouin's moderation made him suspect to Württemberg, and Geneva alerted the Elector Palatine.[74] Baudouin could only pass on to the more congenial quarters of Cassander at Cologne.

But shortly after Lorraine's oration of September 16 Anthony himself decided that it would be advisable to have Lutheran representatives on hand. His motivation is somewhat unclear, but it is not unthinkable that the démarche was stimulated by the conciliatory side of Lorraine's address. Lorraine's notion of the Real Presence without transubstantiation may have suggested that a little Lutheranism might be instructive to both parties.[75] In any event, Anthony issued an official invitation, and the Duke of Württemberg and the Elector Palatine were responsive.[76] Hence, there was not

70. " . . . sont comme chiens et chats." Calvin, *Opera*, XVIII, 659.
71. Julius Heveling, *De Francisco Balduino* (Bonn, 1871), p. 27.
72. J. Duquesne, "François Baudouin et la Réforme," *Bulletin de l'Académie Delphinale* (1917), p. 65.
73. Calvin, *Opera*, XVIII, 627, 658-659. Calvin had a low opinion of Vergerio, who aspired to play an important role at Poissy. *Ibid.*, 466; Evennett, *Lorraine*, pp. 327-328.
74. Duquesne, "Baudouin," 65 ff.; Chandieu to Calvin, July 22, 1561, Calvin, *Opera*, XVIII, 569; August Kluckholn, *Briefe Friedrich des Frommen Kürfursten von der Pfalz, 1559-1566* (2 vols., Braunschweig, 1868-1870), I, 188-189.
75. As Evennett holds, *Lorraine*, pp. 330-331. The complexities of the matter will be explored in Chapter VIII.
76. Languet, *Arcana seculi*, II, 152.

only a danger to Calvinism from a Lutheran confession; there was the possibility of the imminent arrival of Lutherans themselves.

The diplomacy of irenicism was still further complicated. While Anthony was taking it upon himself to extend the hospitality of Poissy to new delegates, uninvited and unwelcome guests had arrived. The newcomers were not from Germany but from Rome, equally jealous of the proceedings in France. These were the emissaries of Pius IV—the cardinal of Ferrara and Diego Lainez—come, as it were, to administer extreme unction.

Ippolito d'Este, cardinal of Ferrara, was both a peculiar and a politic choice for a mission to save the eldest daughter of the Church for the faith. He was the son of Lucrezia Borgia and the grandson of Pope Alexander VI, of unhappy memory. Ferrara was hardly a fanatic. His was one of the few voices to be heard at Rome in opposition to the selection of Trent as the site for the council. But his was a case of mediocrity as much as moderation, a residue of the frivolous and decadent side of the Renaissance. Paul IV had driven him from the Papal States for his vices. With the ambivalent Pius IV he came upon better days and was now at court, having been accompanied by a grandiose entourage that contained six hundred knights for protection, a company of musicians for leisure, and some eight bishops and nine theologians for counsel.[77]

Ferrara's reception at court, on September 19, would remind him more of Paul than of Pius. He was received coldly by the King and the Queen Mother. The Chancellor affixed the royal seal to his faculties only under protest. It is even

77. Vincenzo Pacifici, *Ippolito II d'Este, Cardinale di Ferrara* (Tivoli: Società di storia e d'Arte in Villa d'este, 1920), p. 297; Romier, *C&H*, p. 223. On Ferrara, see also Heinrich Lutz, "Kardinal Ippolito II. d'Este (1509-1572). Biographische Skizze eines weltlichen Kirchenfürsten," *Reformata Reformanda: Festgabe für Hubert Jedin*, ed. Erwin Iserloh and Konrad Repken (2 vols., Münster, 1965).

reported that the valets at court hooted that he was a "fox" and threw stones at him.[78] But six bishops from the Assembly of Prelates were delegated formally to greet him and tender their obedience. It is noteworthy that there was now, with Tournon and Lorraine, a trio of papal legates in France. That they were so conspicuous at the court is a measure of the Pope's concern.

If Ferrara had personal shortcomings he possessed a redeeming virtue: he was a diplomat. Moreover, he knew the French intimately. He had a long association with them, having been something like minister of cultural affairs under Francis I—he had urged him to build the palace at Fontainebleau—and held numerous benefices in France. And he enjoyed excellent connections: he was related to the royal family through a daughter of Louis XII and to the Duke of Guise by the marriage of a brother. Given his background and experience, he was not the kind of man who was apt to act precipitously. His tactic was not to condemn the colloquy, which in view of his position might serve only to stimulate it further. Este seems to have felt that the dialogue would expire of itself. He is even credited with playing a role in the reconstitution of the conferences and seems to have offered the colloquy his patronage. To him, the schemes of Tournon, Chantonnay, and the Triumvirate were equally maladroit. He particularly exercised his talents in an effort to entice Catherine toward Trent and the vacillating King of Navarre toward Catholicism.[79] He preferred to woo an adversary gently.

If Ferrara represented the fading spirit of the Renaissance,

78. *Journal*, p. 33; *HE*, I, 555.
79. Pacifici, *Ippolito II d'Este*, p. 308; *Suriano, Despatches*, p. 45; *Condé*, II, 17. Geisendorf, *Théodore de Bèze*, p. 155; Romier, *C&H*, pp. 228-229. Vargas, the Spanish ambassador in Rome, said that "Ce personnage est passé maître en fait de cajoleries, prodigue de belles paroles." *Papiers d'état du Cardinal de Granvelle d'après les manuscrits de la bibliothèque de Besançon*, ed. Charles Weiss (9 vols., Paris, 1841-1852), VI, 415.

he had in his company someone who represented the rising spirit of the Counter-Reformation. This was the indomitable Diego Lainez, general of the fledgling Society of Jesus, recently held suspect by Paul IV and still denied legal status in France. Lainez was uncompromisingly committed to Rome and the Council of Trent. Now serving in France, he visited the small company of Jesuits on the Rue de la Harpe in Paris and then moved into the château at Saint-Germain—along with his counterpart, Beza. There he and his company[80] exercised an apostolate to counterbalance that of Beza and his companions. Lainez was resolute in his opposition to the colloquy and held poised over it his slight but mighty weight. Martyr was not far wrong when he wrote Calvin that Este had brought with him "most learned men, who have determined in this disputation to devour us like a morsel of bread."[81] Lainez, like Martyr himself, reinforced partisanship but inhibited Poissy.

The long and laborious trip of Ferrara and Lainez might have proved vain. It will be recalled that Beza was embittered at the conclusion of Lorraine's oration, and not without cause. He had been frustrated in his effort to reply while the speech was fresh in mind, and if Tournon's ultimatum meant anything, there might be no reply at all. Catholic spirits were buoyed high by Lorraine's address, which had vindicated their position, and the intransigents were determined to bring the whole affair to a hasty conclusion. Lacking in sympathy with the cause of the colloquy from the beginning, they now wanted to quit while they considered themselves ahead.[82]

80. His company included Jean Polanco, Annibal du Coudret and his brother Louis, and a Franciscan, Angelo Giustiniani. On Lainez's arrival and tour in France, see Henri Fouqueray, *Histoire de la Compagnie de Jésus en France des origines à la suppression, 1528-1762* (5 vols., Paris, 1910-1925), I, 257-268. It can be mentioned that Este seems to have suggested that some Jesuits accompany him; the Pope selected Lainez. *Ibid.*, 249.

81. Vermigli, *Common Places*, p. 154.

82. Beza, *Correspondance*, III, 157. And the Constable wanted the ministers whipped and sent out of the kingdom. *Suriano, Despatches*, p. 44.

Rumor had it that the prelates would treat with the ministers only with "condemnations and excommunications."[83]

The Calvinists did not themselves require much provocation. When several days had passed without word about a rejoinder to Lorraine, they dispatched a militant statement to the crown. It held that they had been brought from afar to remonstrate against "the errors and abuses" planted in the Church by the Pope and his underlings, yet also "to confer amiably and fraternally" with the prelates. They assailed the "ravishing wolves" and "ministers of Satan," who had crushed and despoiled the Church, conspiring to abolish the name of Jesus "by the ruses, counsels, and help of Satan." The Huguenots now appealed for direct action: "it was the office of a Christian King to take up his shield and arms . . . and, following the example of Ezechias and Jonas . . . reestablish the word of God." The request was so impassioned that it did not even ask for another hearing.[84] This was perhaps the more familiar language of the Reformation.

Meanwhile, in less heated quarters, there were forces working toward continuance. They seemed to be principally the civil authorities. Directly after Lorraine's speech, the admiral and Condé invited Beza and Martyr into private conference. The statesmen suggested that Lorraine's discourse was "moderate and calm" and sounded out the theologians. They hinted, above all, to Martyr that the Queen might ask his counsel the next day, and, if so, they would like him to try to mollify her and not compromise the colloquy.[85]

This was an effective rehearsal for what was to follow. The next day the entire quartet was called into private audience with the Queen. Catherine concentrated upon her country-

83. La Place, *Commentaires*, p. 178.

84. *Ibid.* The editors of Beza, *Correspondance*, III, 257, n. 3, mention that it had always been the desire of the Calvinists to be installed in France by the royal government. Cf. McLelland, *Visible Words*, p. 61, on Martyr.

85. Martyr to Bullinger, September 19, 1561, Calvin, *Opera*, XVIII, 725; *Relatio, ibid.*, XVIII, 764.

man and took him off to the side. Taking his lead from the meeting of the previous day, Martyr volunteered a more sanguine evaluation of the situation than he personally held. Questioned by Catherine, he felt that the speech of Lorraine was "eloquent enough," not sharp, and that he advanced many good and true things: for example, the inclusion of the chaff with the wheat in the Church[86] and the obedience due the magistrate.[87] While he could not approve Lorraine's exposition of the Eucharist, he suggested that in future conferences the cardinal might be found more tractable.[88] Martyr also intimated that, pending some later settlement, the article on the Eucharist might simply be left to conscience so long as the churches preached what seemed conformable to the Word of God and lived together in fraternity. Catherine warmed to the thought. He finally urged that, inasmuch as the prelates allegedly opposed the truth only because of their material interests, if they were allowed to maintain their property until death, they would be more theologically pliable in the interim.[89] Martyr had made his contribution to the colloquy—and to Calvinism. The colloquy, among other things, was a capital pulpit for the Reformed. And the proximity to the purple was making Calvinism "respectable."

There were other impulses at work. Naturally, l'Hospital urged that they persevere with the conferences. Two progressive bishops, Valence and Séez, maintained that it would be shameful to refuse to confer with ministers who had been invited by the King. And Lorraine wanted continuance in

---

86. It is dubious if this was Martyr's own opinion. See Evennett, *Lorraine*, p. 334. Beza himself castigated Lorraine for this notion. Beza, *Correspondance*, III, 156.

87. A cursory reading of Lorraine's discourse will reveal that the emphasis was upon the obedience *of* the magistrate.

88. He wrote to Calvin, September 17, 1561: "This I said, not that I so hoped, but that the purpose and hope of the conference might not be cut off." Vermigli, *Common Places*, p. 153.

89. *Ibid.*; Calvin, *Opera*, XVIII, 725.

order to win the Protestants over and to satisfy the Queen.[90] In sum, then, there was enough support among people of consequence to ensure continuation of the colloquy.

On September 22 the court finally resolved the dilemma, by way of a compromise. The colloquy would continue, but on a new basis. Twelve Calvinists would, henceforth, meet as many Catholics in private conference. To placate the prelates, the King would be absent, and, perhaps to encourage a more conciliatory atmosphere, the great majority of the prelates would be absent also[91] —no doubt to their relief. The sources do not elaborate upon the mechanics by which this resolution was reached. The notion appears implicit in Beza's letter to Catherine of September 14, when he suggested that a private meeting of theologians might be profitable. L'Hospital was among those who worked to effect the new arrangement.[92] Lorraine played some role, and the prelates generally none.[93] With the majority of the prelates and the King absent, it would seem that both playing to the galleries and interference from them could be eliminated. The theologians would have their day at court.

Thus passed the eventful month after Beza's arrival. The optimism engendered by his remarkable confrontation with Lorraine on August 24 was not so much dampened by the healthy clash of opinion on September 9 and 16 as it was by the general disaffection of the prelates, who were washing their hands of the whole affair. And the ministers, who had earlier burned so much for debate, realizing that they were *personae non gratae* to the prelates, appealed to Caesar for

90. As reported Bruslart, *Condé*, I, 52-53. But at Lorraine's peril. The intransigents reportedly said that those who further conferred with the heretics "would be excommunicated." *Ibid.*, 52. For the others, see Amphoux, *L'Hospital*, p. 223, and De Thou, *Histoire universelle*, III, 71.

91. *Lettres de Catherine de Médicis*, I, 239; *CSP; Foreign*, Sept. 19, 1561, No. 511; Beza, *Correspondance*, III, 177.

92. Amphoux, *L'Hospital*, p. 223, though faulty on some details.

93. *Négociations*, ed. Desjardins, I, 463. Evennett, *Lorraine*, pp. 334-335, maximizes the role of Lorraine.

justice and the restoration of the City of God. But Caesar was a realist: the meeting was to prevent civil war, and a loss of good feeling did not excuse a loss of good sense. The civil authorities were not theologians and decreed the reshaping and continuance of the parley, preferring present evils to unknown hazards, hoping against hope for a visitation of the Spirit and some magic formula that would usher in accord. Given the nature of the alternative, even this was not without a certain wisdom.

The colloquy had survived its first test. It soon had to face a new crisis, which proved even more critical, if not catastrophic.

V / Sacrament of Unity and Apple of Discord: September 24 and 26, 1561

I tell you most solemnly, if you do not eat the flesh of the Son of Man and drink his blood, you will not have life in you.

John 6:53

It is the spirit that gives life, the flesh has nothing to offer. The words I have spoken to you are spirit and they are life.

John 6:63

The critical feature of the second part of the colloquy was the focus upon the Lord's Supper. This was partially in the nature of things, partially by accident, and partially by design. It was in the nature of things because of the profound centrality of the sacrament in the traditional divine liturgy. Communion was not only the summation of the Christian life—union with Christ—it was a supreme bond and synthesis of the Christian community, the great mystical act before which all orders were leveled and all men made equal, kings humbled and commoners ennobled. And "the bread of life" was that foretaste of heaven and token of eternity through which mortal anticipated immortality, providing a kind of continuum between the sacred and the secular, heaven and earth. But its potential for division, paradoxically, was as striking as its power to unite, and since Marburg the Sacrament of the Altar had been the principal basis for two separate ecclesiastical traditions within Protestantism, the Evangelical and the Reformed. At the same time, it had already been central to a number of colloquies and, lamentably, even more polemics. Thomas Cranmer summed it up in a letter of 1552 to Melanchthon: "the sacrament of unity has become, through the devil's malice, food for disagreement and, as it were, the apple of discord."[1]

The significance of the sacrament for the assembly was partially accidental, and this accident must be attributed to Beza, with his infelicitous remark on the Eucharist and its all too graphic comparison of the distance between Christ and the host. The almost electric reaction of the prelates, with their cries of *blasphemavit*, meant that a fresh emotional charge was added to the theological contention, so that the Eucharist was seized upon as a symbol of everything that separated the two parties.

The third cause lay in design. The subject was deliberately introduced by the cardinal of Lorraine. Lorraine viewed the Eucharist as a way to eventual European reunion. This construction is particularly conspicuous in a noteworthy memorandum on reunion, which, though possibly inspired by Baudouin or d'Espence, was drafted by Lorraine earlier in the summer. The memorandum argued the case for the forthcoming national council and urged that the conference find some key to reunion, some formula so incontrovertibly true that it would compel the assent of conscience. He even mused, by way of example, over the *Henoticon* (482) of the Emperor Zeno, though conceding that it had caused a schism between Greek and Latin. Lorraine's key was the Eucharist. Upon this, he reasoned, turned the subsidiary questions of transubstantiation, adoration of the Host, eucharistic processions, private Masses, Masses for the dead, Communion under one or two species, and a Latin versus a vernacular liturgy. He sought a fresh and searching study of the Bible, the Church Fathers, and sacred history in order to find some eucharistic formula so demonstrably true as to command general acceptance. This, along with genuine moral renewal, would lay

1. Philip Melanchthon, *Opera quae supersunt omnia*, ed. Carolus Gottlieb Bretschneider, in *Corpus Reformatorum* (21 vols., Halle, 1834-1854), VII, 971.

the foundation for general religious concord.[2] Moreover, Lorraine entertained, whether for mediation or malice, a certain fascination for the Confession of Augsburg.[3] Given the cleavage between Lutheran and Calvinist, this fascination could be fatal.

The Confession of Augsburg was one of the new elements introduced into the colloquy. As early as August 30 Beza reported to Calvin that Lorraine "has the Confession of Augsburg on his tongue."[4] Calvin counseled him against any wiles of the cardinal and warned that the Lutheran confession would be "a torch to ignite a fire that would conflagrate all Gaul."[5] But the interest in a Lutheran confession was not restricted to Lorraine. Jean Bouteiller, a liberal Catholic theologian, sounded out Beza on the subject. Beza was noncommittal, but suggested that, given significant alterations, it might be acceptable to him.[6] And, as Martyr put it, a number of bishops "of the better judgment" asked him about consubstantiation, though they would keep the subject out of debate.[7]

The fact is that the court was humming with talk of the Confession of Augsburg. This was revealed in Martyr's first audience there. Catherine expressed the thought, seconded by Navarre and l'Hospital, that there would be better hope of conciliation if the Calvinists would accept some form of the Confession of Augsburg. All three of them allegedly had a

2. Though the memorandum was known to other historians, it was first fully discussed by Evennett, *Lorraine*, pp. 264-276, who published a Latin copy of it as his appendix VII, pp. 485-495. Copies of it can be found in S.A., Frankreich, A 115, Büschel 17, Nos. 92b, 105b, 105c.

3. S.A., Frankreich, A 115, Büschel 17, No. 79b; Throckmorton to Robert Jones, June 23, 1561, *CSP: Foreign*, No. 269(1).

4. Beza, *Correspondance*, III, 144.

5. Calvin also scented maneuvers by Baudouin and Cassander. Sept. 10, 1561, *ibid.*, 149.

6. He did not specify particulars. Beza to Calvin, Aug. 30, 1561, *ibid.*, 144.

7. Martyr to Calvin, Sept. 19, 1561, *The Common Places of the most Famous and Renowned Divine Doctor Peter Martyr*, tr. Anthonie Marten (London, 1583), p. 153. Martyr did not identify the bishops; they probably included Montluc.

penchant for this confession.[8] Martyr replied that Holy Writ was sufficient; besides, the prelates would not accept the Confession of Augsburg themselves.[9] This quieted the matter for the moment.

When the colloquy reconvened the situation was thus: there was talk of the Confession of Augsburg, and the likelihood that it might somehow be intruded into the fray; invitations were issued to the German princes, and the possibility existed that they could jeopardize the proceedings; the uncompromising Lainez and the astute cardinal of Ferrara were present at court. It was as though the winds were carrying a storm toward Poissy.

The colloquy resumed on September 24. The company no longer required the refectory, but now met in the more private but apparently commodious quarters of the prioress. Catherine arrived without the King early in the afternoon. Other lay dignitaries were the King and Queen of Navarre, l'Hospital, Condé, Coligny, the Duke of Guise, and the constable. There were five cardinals, Lorraine, Bourbon, Guise, Armagnac, and Châtillon—Tournon being conspicuously absent—and three liberal bishops, Valence, Troyes, and Orléans. The Catholic component was completed by three theologians, Claude d'Espence, Claude de Sainctes, and Angelo Giustiniani, a Franciscan recently come from Rome with Ferrara.[10] The theologians brought with them a number of weighty tomes of the Fathers, for Lorraine had said that he would substantiate his contentions on the Eucharist from

8. Romier, *C&H*, p. 205. De Thou, *Histoire universelle*, III, 77, said that they, as well as Montluc, desired to see the Huguenots accept the Confession of Augsburg.

9. Martyr to Calvin, Sept. 12, 1561, Martyr, *Common Places*, p. 151; Calvin, *Opera*, XVIII, 709-710; *Relatio*, Calvin, *Opera*, XVIII, 762. It should also be mentioned that the Confession of Augsburg was being "sold publicly" in France. *Die Römische Kurie*, ed. Šusta, I, 242.

10. *Discours*, p. 61; *Négociations*, ed. Desjardins, III, 464; and *HE*, I, 555-556.

the universal consensus of all the doctors of the first 500 years of the Church.[11]

The Reformed protagonists entered a little late, which perturbed the anxious Catherine. There were the same twelve as before, with the addition of Martyr. It was reported that Beza was vexed with Martyr,[12] which might help account for their tardiness. Subsequent events offer some confirmation that there were differences of opinion between Martyr and the rest of his company.

Lorraine, who still led the Catholic side, had recently assured the Assembly of Prelates that he would expound only upon the authority of the Church and the nature of the sacrament, specifically promising that he would not enter into debate with the heretics.[13] He now opened the conference by asking the ministers if they consented to his previous points. Should they have any difficulties, they might state them freely. His biographer sees this as a plain invitation to debate.[14]

Beza took up the invitation. He first addressed himself to Catherine, repeating his earlier hopes for an accord and expressing the politic wish that her grandeur might be advanced. He noted the difficulty of replying without a copy of Lorraine's oration, but proposed to treat of the Church and the Lord's Supper. As a matter of fact, he avoided the dangerous subject of the Eucharist. The Church was described as "the body of our Lord, bone of His bone, flesh of His flesh; indeed, one could attribute to it the very name of Christ."[15] It was impossible to be a member of Christ and

11. *Diario*, p. 133; *HE*, I, 556.
12. And that Beza was apparently so upset that he told one of his companions that he regretted having accepted the assignment at Poissy. *HE*, I, 556. No details are provided on this point.
13. *Diario*, p. 125.
14. Evennett, *Lorraine*, p. 345; *Diario*, p. 125.
15. The complete speech is in *HE*, I, 556-577, and is this time generally paralleled by La Place, *Commentaires*, pp. 179-189, who abridged the first two addresses. See also *Diario*, pp. 125-127; Evennett, *Lorraine*, pp. 345-346.

"the devil" at once; reprobates were, therefore, excluded. He then rehearsed the two senses in which the term Church was understood, the Invisible and the Visible. The former is constituted only of the elect; the latter includes all those who make exterior profession. The one is the Church as seen by God; the other, as seen by man. The marks of the Church were the pure preaching of the Gospel and the proper administration of the sacraments. In charity, those who hold to these criteria ought to be counted as among the faithful. He specifically excluded the Donatists of old and the contemporary Anabaptists. All this was important, for "outside the Church there is no salvation." While he cited with approval Paul's saying that the Church is "the pillar of truth," he shrank from attributing too much to this. The Word of God, which is the truth, supports the Church, rather than the reverse. But the Church is "the mother of believers."[16] Hence, if there was a certain compensating emphasis upon the Invisible Church in the Reformation in the face of the disrepair of the Visible Church of the time, the Reformed Church was scarcely a Platonic idea.

Beza then took up the problem of apostolic succession. Here he made another distinction, that between a succession of persons and a succession of doctrine. The former was avowed, but it must be conjoined and subordinated to the latter, the "infallible" mark of the true Church. And evangelical doctrine was upheld for its antiquity, fulfilling the essential requirement. He avoided the snares of Donatism: even if the scribes and Pharisees be seated on "the chair of Moses," one must do what they teach, not what they do, but this only insofar as they teach pure doctrine. For he noted that "false prophets could succeed to true, and wolves to

---

Geisendorf, *Théodore de Bèze*, p. 155, allows it but a few lines. For printed editions, see Frédéric Gardy, *Bibliographie des oeuvres théologiques, littéraires, historiques et juridiques de Théodore de Bèze* (Geneva, 1960), pp. 92-94.

16. *HE*, I, 557-559.

shepherds."[17] Perhaps some of the prelates were getting uneasy.

He then addressed himself to the matter of personal succession. If this were held a mark of infallibility of the Church, it is necessary to show some promise of God that he would guarantee his grace to "certain seats or regions" where this guarantee would be situated. This was an obvious allusion to Rome. Beza maintained that God might favor some places for a time, contingent upon their merit, and later withdraw his grace and chastise them, according to their deserts. He avowed that the apostolic succession of Rome had been shattered by the frequency of schisms and antipopes, the heresy of Pope Honorius[18] as well as that of John XXII,[19] and the sex of "Popess" Joan.[20] He finished the point with force: "those who do not preach at all, or who in place of the apostolic doctrine teach their own, although they allege themselves to have a thousand consecutive predecessors, ought not to be heard as pastors, but to be put to flight as wolves, by the express commandment of Jesus Christ and his apostles."[21] This implied another appeal for direct action, conciliation tempted to conquest.

Beza next treated the related question of ministerial orders, or what was termed "legitimate vocation." Here he made another distinction, one between "ordinary vocation" and "extraordinary vocation." Ordinary vocation was the estab-

17. *Ibid.*, 561-562.

18. Honorius (625-638), sometimes accused of teaching Monothelitism. See *Dictionnaire de théologie Catholique*, ed. A. Vacant *et al.* (15 vols., Paris: Letouzey et Ané, 1903-1950), VII, 92-132; *New Catholic Encyclopedia* (2nd ed., 15 vols., New York: McGraw-Hill, 1967), VII, 123-25.

19. John XXII (1316-1334), whose alleged heresy relates to a quarrel with the Spiritual Franciscans over evangelical poverty. See *Dictionnaire de théologie Catholique, Tables générales*, II, 2444-2445; *New Catholic Encyclopedia*, VII, 1014-1015.

20. Mythical Pope of the Middle Ages against whom Baronius, Bellarmine, Mabillon, and Döllinger brought their scholarship to bear. See *New Catholic Encyclopedia*, VII, 991-992.

21. *HE*, I, 564; La Place, *Commentaires*, p. 182.

lished form of the Church. It entailed examination of the
doctrine and life of the candidate, legitimate election, and
the imposition of hands.[22] Extraordinary vocation lacked
one or more elements of the above. He cited examples from
the Old Testament, especially Moses, Jonas, and David. The
latter type of vocation was allowed because those who had
held the ordinary succession abused and even perverted it. He
anticipated an objection: if it be held that extraordinary
vocation required some miraculous external evidence of a
call, this is not always so.[23] This was to prove a matter of
contention.

He then enlarged upon the rule of faith. Beza would
attribute infallibility neither to individuals nor to the Church
assembled in general council. As regards individuals, he
supported himself from the Old Testament with Jer. 14:14,
who speaks of the "lies" of false prophets, and from the New
Testament with Acts 20:29, where Paul speaks of the "savage
wolves" who will invade the flock after his departure. He
questioned even the first general council, Nicaea, inasmuch as
it ostensibly proclaimed the law of celibacy, which wrought
such havoc in the Church. He insisted, morever, that councils
contradicted each other, and, referring to Lorraine, maintained that this was true of doctrine as well as of external
matters.[24] He anticipated another objection: it might be
alleged that if Christ promised to be where "two or three are
gathered" in his name, he ought *a fortiori* to be found in a
general council. This is to be presumed, Beza said, but there

22. *HE*, I, 564. McLelland, *Visible Words*, p. 63, n. 162, says Beza was "much
confused" on the necessity of the imposition of hands. Beza himself later clarifies
the point.

23. *HE*, I, 564-565.

24. *Ibid.*, I, 569. He defended the point, which challenged Lorraine's conciliarist penchant, by citing Augustine, *De baptismo contra Donatistas, lib.* 2.
Augustine in fact put this in the form of a question, but in such a way as to imply
his concurrence. He refers to such reversals occurring when "a trial opens
something that was closed." He does not specify whether doctrine or matters of
discipline are in question. PL 43: 128-129.

is a difference between "a presumption and a necessary conclusion." He insisted that he did not want to render doctrine doubtful, but rather to assert that we know only "in part." The whole thrust of his argument was toward a recourse to Scripture as the "rock" by which doctrine was to be tested.[25] But he avoided the word "infallible."

He finally considered the relationship between his two principal terms, Church and Scripture. He allowed the priority of Church to Holy Writ, but insisted that priority is not the same as primacy. God desired that the Gospel be written to obviate the reveries of men who might pervert the Word of God. Holy Writ is sufficient for our salvation; unwritten tradition is acceptable, if not contrary to Writ and if conducive to edification. There was no question as to where he stood: to ask if the Church is above Scripture is like asking if "the child is above the father, wife above husband, man above God."[26]

Beza's final remarks were addressed to the Queen. He observed that his response was directed toward that part of Lorraine's oration that dealt with the authority of the Church. As regards the Eucharist, he suggested that it was best not to tax the company with further representations at this time. He was prepared to consider any reply based on the Word of God.[27]

The second oration was more academic but less ecumenical than Beza's first. It was abundantly documented from the Bible and the Fathers, especially Augustine. His three uses of the word "wolves," and in a way unlikely to ingratiate him with the Catholics, was probably an implied acknowledgement that he had few friends among them anyway and a result of the recent heat over the ministers' protest against the intransigent prelates. Just as Lorraine's oration climaxed

25. *HE*, I, 569-570.
26. *Ibid.*, 574.
27. *Ibid.*, 577.

with the Eucharist, Beza's built up to the Bible. They both apparently wanted to shift the conversation to terrain on which they felt most comfortable. But Beza's reluctance to address himself to the main point of Lorraine's oration—with however much good reason—might facilitate Lorraine's taking a more aggressive stance and perhaps peremptory measures.

Lorraine, who was prepared to speak only on the Eucharist, waived the opportunity to respond. He signaled instead for his theologian and former tutor, d'Espence, to reply.

D'Espence was not an inappropriate choice. Schooled at the humanistic College of Navarre and presently affiliated with the Sorbonne, he was not only among the most learned of the Catholic protagonists, but he was an Erasmian moderate.[28] Evennett epitomizes him as having "more practical sense than Cassander, more religious knowledge than Michel de l'Hospital, more modesty than Erasmus."[29] Despite his "practical sense," d'Espence suffered the fate of many a proponent of the middle party. He himself lamented that the times were so contentious that if one remained a Catholic one was charged with approving abuses, while if one deserted the old Church one was accused of approving schism. In 1543 he was hailed before the tribunal of the Sorbonne and compelled to retract several unorthodox remarks; in 1546 and 1553 he saw several of his works proscribed or censured.[30] In his own Parisian days, Beza had known d'Espence both as a renowned preacher and as a friend. Beza wrote d'Espence a letter in 1550, mentioning that he had heard him

28. For his estimation of Erasmus, see d'Espence's *Apologie contenant ample discours, exposition, response, & deffense de deux conférences avec les ministres de la religion prétendue réformées en ce royaume* (Paris, 1569), pp. 9, 475-476.

29. As editor of his *Discours*, p. 40. As has been said, d'Espence was probably the author of the *Journal*, notwithstanding the doubts of Evennett. See Chapter III, n. 20, above.

30. Pierre Feret, *La faculté de théologie de Paris: Époque moderne* (4 vols., Paris, 1900-1907), II, 103-105, 101-117, for a sketch of d'Espence. He is even included in Haag, 2nd ed., VI, 97-102.

preach justification by faith and entreating him to abandon
the middle way for "the true way."[31] D'Espence preferred
truth to partisan orthodoxy. In 1546 he had theological
conversations with Peter Martyr and Martin Bucer at Strasbourg; in 1548, on the way home from Trent, he ventured
into Geneva to converse with Calvin.[32] D'Espence was
radically opposed to coercion. His maxim that we may "hate
errors, not men"[33] is refreshing for his time. He was
probably the most irenical figure in the room.

D'Espence prefaced his remarks by noting his own pacific
attitude and expressing his abhorrence of force. Addressing
Beza, he professed that he was unprepared to consider all of
his points, for he had apparently primed himself in the
theology of the Eucharist. He took up, nevertheless, several
key questions. He first considered the matter of ministerial
orders. He noted that Beza, by implication, included himself
among the extraordinary vocations, but questioned the validity of this. The Old Testament cases of an extraordinary
vocation—Moses, Isaiah, Daniel—were supported by compelling and miraculous evidence. As regards the New Testament, Christ himself expressly sanctioned the ministry of
John the Baptist. He questioned Beza: "Show us, I pray you,
which of you have performed miracles, or disclose to us
which passages of Scripture have prophesied or adverted to
your extraordinary vocation, and then we shall believe you
and gladly receive your new doctrine."[34] Lacking this, as
well as imposition of hands, d'Espence would have to
conclude that Beza could claim neither an extraordinary nor

31. Beza, *Correspondance*, I, 63-64. The editors properly note, I, 65, n. 1, the
want of a good monograph on d'Espence. The *Omnia Opera* (Paris, 1619),
includes only his Latin works. De Thou, its editor and something of a child of the
middle party, himself esteemed d'Espence highly.

32. D'Espence, *Apologie*, 141-144, 585-586.

33. *Ibid.*, pp. 4-5.

34. *Diario*, p. 128. D'Espence discusses the whole matter of orders at length in
his *Apologie*, pp. 133-327.

an ordinary vocation. He challenged the Reformed at their vital center.

Then d'Espence turned to the matter of Church authority. He professed that he himself shrank from saying that the Church is above Scripture—or the reverse. Rather they were equivalent authorities, that is, part of a common fund animated by the same Holy Spirit.[35] But in opposition to Beza, d'Espence held that the Church and general councils could not err in matters of faith, regardless of whether their decrees conformed to the express word of Scripture. He avowed that the Reformed belied their principle by their own practice. They confessed such doctrines as the consubstantiality of the Son with the Father, infant baptism, and the perpetual virginity of Mary, notwithstanding that Holy Writ does not expressly authorize these doctrines. Moreover, both orthodox and Arian defended their varying positions from the same Scripture at the Council of Nicaea. As for Beza's point, on the authority of Augustine, that general councils had had their decisions reversed by subsequent councils, there had been only three by his time, Nicaea, Constantinople, and Ephesus, and the second approved the faith of

35. *Diario*, p. 129. In his *Apologie*, p. 365, d'Espence holds that the Church judges the Scriptures only as a witness, and not as an author or superior. This would seem to confirm the *Diario*. But the *HE*, I, 577, reports that d'Espence confessed substantial agreement on this point with Beza, holding as blasphemous the opinion that placed the Church above Scripture. La Place, *Commentaires*, p. 189, holds that d'Espence concurred with "all which had been said of the Church, including succession," by Beza. D'Espence challenges the accuracy of La Place's account on this point as on some others. *Apologie*, pp. 74, 134. Yet d'Espence also notes the difficulties of his obligation to reply "on the spot." *Apologie*, pp. 136-137. This could suggest an attempt to excuse a slip of the tongue. But the following matter clearly contradicts La Place. The notion of a coinherence of Church and Writ was becoming lost at the time. See George Tavard, *Holy Writ or Holy Church* (New York: Harper and Brothers, 1959). Heiko Augustinus Oberman, *The Harvest of Medieval Theology: Gabriel Biel and Late Medieval Nominalism* (Cambridge, Mass.: Harvard University Press, 1963), p. 368, criticized Tavard's view. Yves M.-J. Congar, *Tradition and Traditions*, tr. Michael Naseby and Thomas Rainborough (New York: Macmillan, 1969), pp. 44-45, supports Tavard.

the first, and the third that of the first two. D'Espence suggested that Augustine was undoubtedly referring to matters of custom, not faith.[36]

D'Espence concluded by gingerly shifting to the sensitive subject of the Eucharist. As evidence of his good faith, he sought concord here on the most congenial terms he could devise: Calvinist subscription to the word of Calvin himself. D'Espence had explored Calvin's writings for passages in which the master spoke clearly and unequivocally of a real and substantial presence. Calvinists generally avoided the term "substantial presence," preferring "sacramental presence." But d'Espence was successful in his researches. He proceeded to read aloud to the ministers three passages from the *Dilucida*, a work of Calvin of that same year, wherein a substantial presence was taught.[37] D'Espence implored the ministers: "Since he says the body and blood of Jesus Christ to be in the Eucharist, to be substantially exhibited, given and received there, which he puts in a substantial, but not local, presence, may we not agree here on the true presence?"[38]

Before Beza could rise to respond, an impetuous and dogmatic Sorbonnist, Claude de Sainctes, seized the moment. De Sainctes spent virtually a whole lifetime in contention with Beza, to which Poissy was no exception.[39] De Sainctes

36. *Diario*, pp. 131-132; d'Espence, *Apologie*, pp. 449-450, n. 1.

37. *Discours*, pp. 61-62; Beza, *Correspondance*, III, 162. The tract is the *Dilucida explicatio...ad discutiendas Heshusii nebulas*, Calvin, *Opera*, IX, 457-524, a bitter polemic against the militant Lutheran, Teleman Heshusius. The pertinent passages, given by d'Espence in the *Apologie*, p. 478, and reprinted by Evennett, *Lorraine*, p. 498, and in Beza, *Correspondance*, III, 168, n. 17, are: "Ubique admitto substantialiter nos pasci Christi carne et sanguine, modo facessat crassum de locali permixtione [d'Espence and Evennett render this *commixtione*; see Beza, *Correspondance*, III, 168, n. 17] commentum." Calvin, *Opera*, IX, 467. "Substantialiter Christi carnem et sanguinem nobis offerri et exhiberi in Coena... " Calvin, *Opera*, IX, 470. "Omnino isthaec piis tenenda est regula, ut quoties symbola vident a Domino instituta, illic rei signatae vertitatem adesse certo cogitent, ac sibi persuadeant." Calvin, *Opera*, IX, 472.

38. D'Espence, *Apologie*, p. 479; Beza, *Correspondance*, III, 162.

39. Some ten years earlier, de Sainctes advanced grave personal charges against

did not say much that was novel; he reiterated much that
d'Espence had already sought to establish. But he employed
just that harsh, if not abusive, tone that d'Espence had so
studiously avoided. He compared Beza and his company to
the Anabaptists, who also claimed the Holy Spirit as their
own, in spite of good ecclesiastical order. He charged that
Beza had misused the Fathers and recommended that he read
the ancients three or four times before he invoked them
again. And he alleged that Chrysostom had written that God
never intended that the Gospel be reduced to Scripture.[40] He
emphasized that it was necessary to follow not only Scripture, but also nature—presumably meaning reason—and tradition.[41] De Sainctes's foray was so sharp that even Lorraine,
his patron, was annoyed.[42] His would be a diminishing role
in the colloquy.

Beza finally got his chance to respond. He first protested
against the pugnaciousness of de Sainctes and appealed to
Catherine to establish better order at the conferences. She
seems to have remained mute, and so Beza proceeded to take

Beza, apparently based on the *Juvenilia*. See the article by Natalie Zemon Davis,
"Peletier and Beza Part Company," *Studies in the Renaissance*, XI (1964), 204, n.
64; and Geisendorf, *Théodore de Bèze*, pp. 19, 23-24, 30. After the colloquy de
Sainctes launched the attack with the *Examen doctrinae Calvinianae et Bezanae
de Coena Domini* (Paris, 1566). Beza immediately issued a rejoinder, *Apologia ad
libellum Sorbonnici theologastri F. Claudii de Xainctes cui titulum fecit: Examen
doctrinae Calvinianae et Bezanae de Coena Domini ex scriptis authorum ejusdem
collectum* (Geneva, 1567), found in his *Tractationum theologicarum* (3 vols., in 1,
2nd ed., Geneva, 1582), II, 288-363. De Sainctes came back with the *Responsio
F. Claudii de Sainctes Parisien, theologi ad apologiam Theodori Bezae, editam
contra examen doctrinae Calvinianae & Bezanae de Coena Domini* (Paris, 1567).
The quarrel was still being waged in 1577. Geisendorf, *Théodore de Bèze*, pp.
274-276. The latter work of de Sainctes, the *Responsio*, is valuable for the
conferences. Pontien Polman, *L'Elément historique dans la controverse religieuse
du XVIe siècle* (Gembloux, 1932), p. 133, wrote that their polemic produced
nothing really original. On de Sainctes see Feret, *La faculté*, II, 123-30.

    40. *HE*, I, 579. The reference is somewhat obscure.
    41. La Place, *Commentaires*, pp. 189-190; *Discours*, p. 62.
    42. As relates Beza, *Correspondance*, III, 162; see also La Place, *Commentaires*,
p. 192. De Sainctes, *Responsio*, p. 65, denies this. The subsequent reduction in his
role suggests that Beza's account may have been correct.

up his case for the defense. He first considered the objections of d'Espence, touching on the question of the imposition of hands. This, he clarified, was more a formality than a necessity. He likened the preaching of the Word of God to the administration of sacraments, and, just as Catholics allowed women to baptize in case of necessity, so the Reformed proclaimed the Gospel without the traditional formalities. This undercut a Catholic argument put forward: "Nemo dat quod non habet." Beza, responding to a query of Lorraine, located the Reformed basis for orders in proper examination and election by the college of elders, approval by the magistrates[43] and people, and solemn institution into the ministry. He noted, no doubt with some complacence, that the Reformed had renounced the Roman Church and were not tempted to seek orders where a horrible disorder reigned. In the beginning, then, they had to claim an extraordinary vocation. He reverted to the Old Testament, citing the cases of Samuel and Elias, who were outside the regular priesthood. Miraculous proof was not necessary, but if it should be reduced to this, Beza proffered the paradox of the success of his party in spreading the Gospel, despite the persecution of powers and principalities. He then took the offensive, challenging the orders of the prelates who, he maintained, possessed external ceremonies instead of the Word of God. In the main, he vindicated Reformed orders by the purity of Reformed doctrine, and he justified withdrawal from Roman orders by the contrary.[44] As to the taunt of de Sainctes, who had admonished him to read the Fathers, Beza assured him that he had read the tract of Chrysostom more

43. *HE*, I, 579-580. The *Journal*, p. 37, which is only a summary account, records that after Beza said "the civil magistrate," Martyr, sitting behind him, prompted, whispering in his ear "the ecclesiastical magistrate." In any event, Beza did not alter his response. The Catholic argument on "Nemo dat" was advanced by either Lorraine or d'Espence. Evennett, *Lorraine*, pp. 366-367; *Diario*, p. 132.
44. *HE*, I, 581-582.

than eighteen times and had yet to see the blasphemy that it
was not God's intent that the Gospel be written.[45]

This was enough to provoke a spirited exchange between
the two. De Sainctes took the initiative and repeated the
query about the inconsonance of *sola scriptura* with the
Huguenots' acceptance of the doctrines of the perpetual
virginity and infant baptism. For the first, Beza replied that it
was not an article of faith, but could be held with probabil-
ity; as to the second, he cited the precedent of circumcision,
to which baptism succeeded. De Sainctes rejoined that by
such reasoning it was only necessary to baptize males, and
that on the eighth day. Beza retorted that the point was to be
taken analogously rather than literally and noted New Testament illustrations where entire families were baptized. De
Sainctes followed up another line of attack. He reverted to an
earlier position that there were three foundations of faith:
nature, Scripture, and tradition. He sought to make a case for
nonscriptural sources by citing 1 Cor. 11:6, that women must
be covered in church, thus indicating that Holy Writ implies a
sanction of tradition and custom. Beza replied with a
smirk[46] that it was badly argued. In the first place, Paul was
not concerned here with an article of faith, but only a point
of discipline. The passage, then, did not have the force
alleged by de Sainctes; moreover, the fundamental articles of
our faith were contrary to the order of nature. Beza concluded the exchange: "Scrap, if you please, this nature" of
your schools when there are questions of such pertinence.[47]
The clash emphasizes the difference between a Scholastic and
a classical Protestant frame of mind. Philosophical assump-
tions appear superfluous in dialogue.

D'Espence relieved de Sainctes and pressed his own previ-

---

45. *Ibid.*, 583.
46. Given the context, it would seem appropriate thus to translate *en se
sousriant. Ibid.*, 585.
47. *Ibid.*

ous line of questioning. He returned to the matter of ecclesiastical orders and marveled that the ministers could not cite a single case of vocation without imposition of hands in 1,500 years of history. Beza replied that all that has happened has not been recorded in history; moreover, God was not bound to historical precedents. He argued that the question had now been adequately discussed,[48] but betrayed some embarrassment on the subject.[49] D'Espence then darkly referred to 2 Tim. 3:16, which, he said, apparently in an effort to broaden the base of authority, should read *omnis doctrina* is inspired by God, rather than *omnis scriptura*. Beza held the contrary and was immediately sustained by one of the doctors in attendance.[50] They tilted awhile at the secrets of the *filioque* clause and the enigma of the Trinity. But the Eucharist was not forgotten, and d'Espence finally reverted to the quotations from Calvin's *Dilucida*. Beza, however, did not feel that the passages referring to a substantial presence were extraordinary. Calvin simply used the term *substantialiter* in contradistinction to an "imaginary" presence. Beza repeated: "the symbols are on earth, the things in heaven."[51] D'Espence's researches had been in vain.

General debate if not mayhem followed. De Sainctes interjected again comments about infant baptism and the perpetual virginity, and it seems the whole company joined in the fray. Lorraine attempted to restore order. He endorsed

48. La Place, *Commentaires*, p. 190; *HE*, I, 586. The question of an extraordinary ministry is elucidated in an article by the irenical Dutch Jesuit, Frans Josef van Beeck, "Towards an Ecumenical Understanding of the Sacraments," *Journal of Ecumenical Studies*, III (1966), 57-112.Van Beeck allows that "necessity knows no law" and roots an extraordinary ministry in the priesthood of believers. It is interesting that Ignatius Loyola made his confession to a comrade-in-arms at the Battle of Pamplona in 1521.

49. According to the irascible de Sainctes, *Responsio*, p. 64, who also said the milder d'Espence became, the fiercer Beza. *Ibid.*, p. 63.

50. *HE*, I, 586. See also *ibid.*, 583, n. 1, for proof that someone other than Beza edited at least parts of this section. There is a considerable divergence between the *HE* and La Place, *Commentaires*, pp. 190-191, at this point.

51. D'Espence, *Apologie*, p. 480.

the views of d'Espence, then narrowed the field of discussion
to the fateful subject of the Eucharist. The Lord's Supper
was poison to the colloquy.

The crisis began with Lorraine announcing, hyperbolically,
that the Eucharist was the cause of all the divisions in
Christendom. There had been enough discussion of the
subject; the time had come to seek a formula for agreement.
Failing this, he added, the conference could not continue.
Beza protested to the Queen about the impropriety of such a
maneuver and pleaded that there were other things to discuss
that might render easier a later resolution.[52] Though Catherine took Lorraine's move "in ill part,"[53] he was able to argue
that Beza's oration of September 9 had already been printed
and that his provocative remark on the Lord's Supper had to
be clarified, lest the faithful be scandalized.[54] Lorraine, then,
without elaborating upon his own preoccupation, shifted the
responsibility back to Beza. He could diminish his own
responsibility for any consequences by pointing out that the
prelates had agreed not to permit further discussion unless
the ministers accept "the existence of the flesh of our Lord
in the Sacrament of the Altar."[55] Lorraine might well have
felt obliged to protect himself against charges of being "soft"
on Calvinism.

Lorraine forthwith presented the ministers with what must
be considered an ultimatum. He produced first one, and then,

52. Beza added, in what appears a different sense, that he and his companions
had come to defend their Confession of Faith and had no other mandate from
their churches. La Place, *Commentaires*, p. 192; Beza, *Correspondance,* III, 163.
This is a significant idea and reinforces the notion that the Reformed viewed the
colloquy as a disputation along Swiss lines.

53. Martyr to Calvin, Oct. 2, 1561, Vermigli, *Common Places*, p. 154; *Relatio,*
Calvin, *Opera*, XVIII, 767.

54. La Place, *Commentaires*, 192; *HE*, I, 587.

55. De Sainctes, *Responsio*, p. 63; La Place, *Commentaires*, p. 192. Lorraine
also referred to the opened but unused tomes of the Fathers. *Diario*, p. 132.

either here or later, a second *Lutheran* formula,[56] for the Huguenots to sign as a condition of continuance. Needless to say, as a follow up to Calvin's articles proferred by d'Espence, this was unacceptable. This was the act H. Outram Evennett called "the dreaded blow" and Paul Geisendorf "la bombe."[57] It is ironic that on that very day Calvin wrote Coligny: "Above all, I pray you, my Lord, to see that the Confession of Augsburg does not come into play, which would be only a torch to light the fires of discord."[58] Their worst fear—a complete Calvinist-Lutheran schism—seemed about to be realized. Calvinist historians have traditionally seen this as a wedge employed by Lorraine to split the Protestant ranks, to play one confession off against the other.[59] A more recent Catholic reaction has been to view Lorraine's action as both sincere and conciliatory: it would save the ministers from having to submit to completely Roman Catholic terms.[60]

In fact it had neither effect. Beza, pressed into a corner, responded by asking Lorraine if he would volunteer to subscribe first. Lorraine replied evasively, but loosened his grasp. This bought precious time for the ministers to confer,

56. The precise nature of these formulas is far too technical a question to be unraveled here. It is my contention that Lorraine used both the Confession of Augsburg and a Confession of Württemberg of 1559, although this view has been challenged. Chapter VIII, below, reviews this matter. For the texts, see Appendixes A and B below.

57. Evennett, *Lorraine*, p. 351; Geisendorf, *Théodore de Bèze*, p. 156.

58. Calvin, *Opera*, XVIII, 732-734.

59. La Place, *Commentaires*, p. 189; Émile Doumergue, *Jean Calvin: Les hommes et les choses de son temps* (7 vols., Neilly-sur-Seine, 1927), VII, 263. Moreover, La Place, *Commentaires*, p. 189, perhaps following Beza, *Correspondance*, III, 162, who viewed d'Espence as Lorraine's tool, also saw d'Espence as acting in collusion with the cardinal. D'Espence later took issue with La Place on this point, maintaining that he personally disapproved and had even attempted to prevent the use of "this expedient." *Apologie*, pp. 597-598, 726 ff. The editors of Beza, *Correspondance*, III, 168, no. 17, are inclined to absolve d'Espence of the old charge.

60. Romier, *C&H*, p. 230: Evennett, *Lorraine*, p. 365.

while the whole company implored them to consider the terms for the sake of peace. Wary lest they incur the blame for the collapse of the colloquy, the pastors announced that they would take counsel and submit their response the next day. The reckoning was later deferred until the second day, that is, September 26.[61] Thus, the impasse was temporarily averted, and the session hastily concluded.

As the company slowly filed out of the room, Catherine made a last-minute effort to secure more favorable terms for the ministers. Taking Lorraine aside, she pleaded that he devise some alternative formula. The resourceful Lorraine obliged. After a moment's discussion with some of the theologians, he produced the following: "We confess with a firm faith in the most holy sacrament of the Eucharist the true body and blood of Christ really and substantially to be and to exist, to be exhibited and eaten by the communicants."[62] This seemed, apart from the absence of the term transubstantiation, designed more for a clarification of Catholic doctrine than for conciliation of the Calvinists. When it was given Beza, he privately asked de Sainctes if it would be acceptable to the Catholics without the important verbs *esse et existere.* This would put the emphasis upon reception, giving it a vehicular turn. De Sainctes replied that he could not speak for the rest, but to remove these terms would make the formula sound Calvinist or at least excessively ambiguous.[63]

If the formula did not go far to placate the ministers, it went too far for some of the Catholics. They disapproved its silence on transubstantiation, the inclusion of which they had urged on Lorraine. And many wanted the Calvinists ejected at once, instead of by what was described as a "step-by-step"

61. Beza, *Correspondance*, III, 163; La Place, *Commentaires*, p. 192, *HE*, I, 588-589.
62. For Latin text, see Appendix C, below.
63. De Sainctes, *Responsio*, pp. 64-65.

refutation.[64] The day engendered the usual mixed emotions. While some of the Catholic triumphalists boasted victory, some of the ministers did the same, caricaturing the Mass and the Catholic understanding of the Eucharist.[65] Sixteenth-century dialogue was just a shade short of war.

But Catherine was as determined as ever to be a peace-maker. The next day, September 25, she sent two of the most conciliatory Catholics, Montluc and d'Espence, to the "neutral place"[66] of Saint-Germain to confer with Beza and des Gallars. None of the four had binding authority. Lorraine's formula of the previous day was used to initiate the discussions, but as it availed nothing, it was soon modified beyond recognition. The new formula not only stressed the usage of the sacrament, adding that it was eaten by the "faithful" communicants, but made it explicit that the modality of the presence was "spiritual."[67] The finished product was essentially a Protestant document. It was agreed, nevertheless, that it would be referred to both parties. It is curious that the article was rejected even by the ministers. This appears to have happened because it did not adequately preclude Christ being "here below."[68] Most important was the opposition of the uncompromising Peter Martyr, whose prestige was such that he seems to have been able to turn the

64. *Ibid.*, p. 65.
65. *HE*, I, 589.
66. The *Discours*, p. 62, says "en lieu neutre." One is tempted to say, under a flag of truce. De Sainctes tells us he was to be sent on the mission with d'Espence, but he was apparently rejected. De Sainctes, *Responsio*, p. 64. The reasons should be obvious.
67. Montluc and d'Espence resisted the changes, but unsuccessfully. *HE*, I, 604-605. For the text, see Appendix D, below. The *HE*, I, 603, also gives another formula, implying that it was presented by the two Catholic emissaries. Evennett, *Lorraine*, p. 357, n. 3, properly regards it as coming from staunch Catholics, because it allows *ex opere operato:* "Credimus & confitemur in augustissimo Eucharistiae sacramento esse & existere verum Christi corpus natum ex Maria virgine, et de manibus sacerdotum eorum ore consecratum exhiberi & sumi a communicantibus." This can hardly be considered a formula of concord and was probably not used in the conference.
68. *HE*, I, 605.

pastors against it.[69] To d'Espence, Martyr was "a pure Zwinglian."[70] In any event, if the Reformed could not agree upon a formula largely of their own making, their reaction to a Lutheran confession imposed upon them by an outsider was a foregone conclusion. But the rejection of the one ensured the immediate reappearance of the other.

The day of reckoning was September 26. One would like to think there was an unspoken bond of affection between Beza and d'Espence, and as they took what seemed a last walk into the chambers, Beza had to inform d'Espence of his inability to secure assent to the previous day's formula. He commented darkly that it was now "all or nothing."[71] Inside there was a capacity crowd to witness the climax to Lorraine's ultimatum. It included the Queen and the civil dignitaries, twenty-five bishops, and as many theologians.

Lorraine still held an uneasy and elusive initiative. He had hoped to cover himself with glory at Poissy, but he was clearly a man in trouble. His position was almost as vulnerable as that of the Huguenots. If they rejected his terms, the crown could blame him for the failure of his tactics. At the same time, the prelates were disturbed by his handling of the colloquy. They had just let him know that, in allowing debate with the ministers, he had exceeded their instructions at the previous session. And henceforth, as they informed

69. Benjamin F. Paist, "Peter Martyr and the Colloquy of Poissy," *Princeton Theological Review*, XX (1922), 442, notes with approval that Johann Baum, *Theodor Beza nach handschriftlichen Quellen dargestellt* (2 vols., Leipzig, 1843-1851), II, 344-345, long the standard biography of Beza, blamed Martyr for the rejection of this article, which he considered prevailingly Protestant, and in general for his unwillingness to take a conciliatory attitude on the Eucharist. Geisendorf, *Théodore de Bèze*, p. 158, accepts Baum's opinion, and says that Martyr "raised himself violently" against the formula. The *HE*, I, 604-605, here and throughout, avoids the dissension within the Reformed delegation. See also Evennett, *Lorraine*, p. 359.

70. D'Espence, *Apologie*, 469. Needless to say, the prelates would never have accepted the formula.

71. *HE*, I, 605.

him, "what transpired in these conferences concerning doc-trine was without their consent."[72] It would be impolitic, to say the least, to defy the prelates and menace the Huguenots at once. This would make him a man without a party. But Lorraine had well-developed political instincts. The day before he had assured the prelates that if the ministers rejected his terms they would no longer be heard.[73] This time he opened the meeting by abruptly asking Beza point blank if he was ready to sign.[74] There was no alternative offered, and no invitation to debate was given.

Beza and his companions were not ignorant of the resolution of the prelates. They knew that if they refused to subscribe, they would kill the colloquy[75] and risk incurring the wrath of Lutheranism; on the other hand, should they accept, they reasoned that not only would the prelates triumph, but that the Huguenots might then be thrown out of their pulpits as traitors, leaving French Calvinism divided and paralyzed.[76] It was to extricate themselves from these perils that Beza and his company prepared a long and adroit statement of their case, which Beza now read.[77]

It was a reply to Lorraine and an appeal to the Queen. Beyond the particular issue, Beza lamented Lorraine's whole conduct of the colloquy. He proceeded to argue that the success of the conference had been prevented by two ma-neuvers: the irrelevant questioning of ministerial orders; and the inordinate emphasis upon the Eucharist and the introduc-

72. *Diario*, p. 133: "che passava in queste conferentie circa la doctrina era senza consenso loro."
73. *Journal*, p. 38.
74. *Diario*, p. 133.
75. This was one thing Calvin wanted avoided. Beza, *Correspondance*, III, 189, 192.
76. *Ibid.*, 163, 178; *HE*, 590-591.
77. La Place, *Commentaires*, p. 193. Geisendorf, *Théodore de Bèze*, p. 159, suggests that Beza's reading from a prepared text is itself illustrative of the divergence between Martyr and Beza, who was "perhaps a little too indulgent." If so, this would be relative only to Martyr.

tion of a Lutheran confession. It was an effort to toss responsibility for any impending collapse back to the Catholic side and to Lorraine.

Beza countered the attack on Reformed orders by imagining a bishop inquiring into the propriety of the procedure by which the prelates were raised to their dignities. While acknowledging that he lacked imposition of hands, he pointed out that this was a lesser evil than simony, a subject that it might be inconvenient to explore. As regards the Eucharist, Beza, no doubt with tongue in cheek, expressed regret that some in the audience were scandalized to hear something expressed that seemed novel; he himself would prefer the language of the ancient doctors, by which Lorraine had promised to convince all. But instead Lorraine had said: "Sign here; otherwise we cannot pass beyond."[78] Such a procedure was unworthy both of the dignity of the prelates and the importance of the subject. Appealing to Catherine's political sense, Beza intimated that such intimidation would not go down well with the enormous ranks of the Reformed. Their principals in Geneva would know if they had succumbed to constraint and not been convinced by sound arguments and Holy Scripture.

Having carefully laid the groundwork, Beza addressed himself to the ultimatum. He managed to strike a fine compromise. He announced that his company approved "all that had been read by Monsieur d'Espence from the book of Monsieur Calvin that had been given us, without otherwise conferring upon it."[79] Thus he accepted the pleadings of d'Espence in order to avoid the perils of Lorraine. Regarding "the tenth part of an article," patently a reference to the Confession of Augsburg, Beza took the offensive. He held

78. La Place, *Commentaires*, p. 194; *Journal*, p. 39; and Beza, *Correspondance*, III, 170, n. 30.
79. *HE*, I, 595.

that it was necessary to consider the entirety of the confession, not just one single line from a solitary article. It was also essential to know if the cardinal proposed "the Confession of Augsburg"[80] on his own account or that of the prelates. If the latter, Beza thanked God that the Gallican Church had condemned transubstantiation. This accounts for Beza's insistence upon the entirety of the text, for the Confession of Augsburg implies such a rejection. He also urged that in fairness Lorraine should be first to accept the article that he had required of others, in other words, that the host should sip from the suspect cup he had set before his guest. He hoped this would unceremoniously dispose of the ultimatum.

Beza suggested to Catherine, as an alternative, the following article on the Eucharist: "We say that our Lord Jesus Christ is in the usage of the Holy Eucharist, in which he presents, gives and truly exhibits His body and blood for us by the operation of the Holy Spirit, and that we receive, eat and drink spiritually and by faith this very body which has been delivered to the death for us, and this very blood which has been shed for us, in order to become bone of His bone and flesh of His flesh, and to be quickened and to receive all that which is required for our salvation."[81] On the surface this sounded Catholic. It involved not only a real but a carnal presence; there was joined, nevertheless, the important qualification that this was "spiritually and by faith." Moreover, the entire thing was predicated on the usage of the sacrament and therefore was not really indulgent toward Catholicism. He ended by asking Lorraine to produce his promised texts from the Fathers and imploring Catherine to establish a

---

80. Both La Place, *Commentaires*, p. 195, and the *HE*, I, 594-595, speak of "the tenth part of an article." This confirms that Lorraine used the Confession of Augsburg, for its tenth article treats the Eucharist.

81. For the text, see Appendix E, below.

proper procedure so that the colloquy might yet bear good fruit.[82]

Beza had taken his stand. The riposte, rendered in desperation, appealed over Lorraine's head, but struck a discerning mean between maximum persuasion and minimum offense. As to the latter, the scarcely oblique challenge implicit in Beza's dialogue with the imaginary bishop was not dismissed as fantasy by the prelates. Beza himself said that Lorraine was "boiling"[83] as he rose to respond. Nevertheless, Lorraine mustered his composure and spoke as moderately as possible.[84] Ignoring Beza's approval of the articles offered by d'Espence, which apparently had not impressed the prelates, particularly as it specifically precluded further clarification, Lorraine launched a counterattack. Beza, he asserted, had not only degraded the sacerdotal authority, but the royal as well. For in challenging the procedure by which bishops were instituted, he had impugned the concordat[85] between the late Francis I and the Pope that regulated these matters. Thus, Beza, who had "little experience" in the ways of France, had tampered with the royal authority, and if he wanted to impeach the vocation of the bishops, he had better take the matter up with the King.[86] In this Lorraine cleverly parried Beza's thrust and matched his zeal for crown and country.

Though Lorraine's remarks seem to have occasioned some astonishment, Beza answered with change of "neither voice nor visage."[87] Eager to dissociate himself from criticism of

82. La Place, *Commentaires*, pp. 195-196; *HE*, I, 596. According to de Sainctes, the texts had already been opened, but were not utilized. *Responsio*, p. 63.

83. Beza, *Correspondance*, III, 164.

84. *HE*, I, 596-597.

85. The Concordant of Bologna, 1516, a basic document for the Gallican Church, which recognized the transfer to the monarch of the dormant right of the people in the election of bishops.

86. La Place, *Commentaires*, p. 196; *Diario*, pp. 134-135.

87. *HE*, I, 597.

the monarchy, he protested that the crown had been con-
strained to alter the ecclesiastical order because of the
"horrible confusion" to which it had been reduced by "the
ambition, avarice and intrigues" of the clergy. And, as to the
solemn form of episcopal consecration to which Lorraine had
alluded, this was a mere "farce." Beza concluded with force:
"in the midst of the extreme dissipation and confusion of the
Church," our ministry is legitimate, "however vilified and
mocked without cause."[88] The tone was no longer strictly
academic.

Lorraine retorted by alleging that the ministers had begun
the inquiry into orders by attacking "our kings." Having
posed again as defender of the purple, Lorraine thereupon
reverted to the "Confession of Augsburg." He asked the
ministers why they did not want to subscribe.[89] They
responded that this was an unreasonable request since Lorraine and the prelates did not themselves approve it in its
entirety. The pastors conceded that if the prelates would
subscribe to it first, this would be a means of facilitating
accord. It was again pleaded, moreover, that the ministers did
not know if Lorraine's request was his own or whether he
represented the whole body of prelates.

Lorraine responded that he would not be compelled to
subscribe either by the authors of the Confession of Augsburg or by the ministers, but he was prepared to subscribe,
"if you say that which is the truth." In effect, then, he made
his signature contingent upon that of the ministers. Rather
than indicate that he was acting in behalf of the prelates, he
simply noted that he had done nothing contrary to their
common purpose. Beza retorted: "since you yourself do not

88. *Ibid.*, 597-598; La Place, *Commentaires*, p. 196; Beza, *Correspondance*, III, 164.
89. La Place, *Commentaires*, p. 196, and *HE*, I, 598, here, as almost every-where, say the Confession of Augsburg.
90. *HE*, I, 598.

want to subscribe to the confession, it is not reasonable to
ask that we subscribe to it."[90]

General debate followed. D'Espence entreated the ministers
to accept the corporeal presence of Christ in the Host,
expostulating that if he was not in the bread, he could not
otherwise be eaten.[91] He blamed the ministers for con-
trariety to the teachings of Calvin, again displaying the tract
against Heshusius. He exhorted them to accept the very
important verb *adesse* (to be present) as well as *exhiberi* and
sumi, which concerned usage, arguing that the latter imply
the first.[92] They reiterated that they were prepared to
subscribe to the articles from Calvin's tract. The whole
matter turned on the word "substance." To the ministers, it
was employed to distinguish a real from an "imaginary
reception."[93] To d'Espence, it distinguished the presence of
Christ and the appearance of the bread. Calvin's tract could
not bridge the gap.

At this juncture, an individual whom d'Espence characterized as "the man who under heaven had written the most on
this matter"[94]—Peter Martyr—intervened to elaborate. Not
knowing French, he obtained permission from Catherine to

91. La Place, *Commentaires*, p. 197. But in the *Apologie*, p. 470, d'Espence
protests that he had not spoken so rudely of such a great mystery.

92. D'Espence, *Apologie*, pp. 464-465, the point being that for the ministers
Christ was "really" offered, but "spiritually" present.

93. La Place, *Commentaires*, p. 197; *HE*, I, 598-599. For Calvin and "sub-
stance," see McDonnell, pp. 232-248; François Wendel, *Calvin: The Origins and
Development of His Religious Thought*, tr. Philip Mairet (New York and
Evanston: Harper and Row, 1963), p. 342; and G.S.M. Walker, "The Lord's
Supper in the Theology and Practice of Calvin," in *John Calvin*, ed. G.E. Duffield
(Grand Rapids, Mich., 1966), p. 134, who propounds the view that Calvin
generally understood the term in a dynamic rather than a metaphysical sense. A
recent trend is to observe some ambiguity and apparent contradiction in this area.
For example, Walker, "The Lord's Supper," p. 141; Wendel, *Calvin*, pp. 342,
350-354. McDonnell, *Calvin*, pp. 210-211, stresses Calvin's personalism, his fear
that Christ as bread destroyed his humanity. McDonnell's study notes some
failings as a whole, but sees Calvin's emphasis upon union with Christ as
unassailable. See his appendix, pp. 367-381.

94. *Discours*, p. 64. Later, when obviously himself under fire, he would feel
compelled to explain away this compliment. D'Espence, *Apologie*, pp. 591-594.

speak in his native Tuscan, which she no doubt was pleased to grant.[95] He referred the word "substance" to "the true and natural body of Christ," not to a "fiction or phantom," on the one hand, nor to the sacred species, as did d'Espence, on the other. He categorically rejected both transubstantiation and consubstantiation. Communion is a heavenly matter, and Christ's body is found in heaven. When we communicate, Christ does not descend to us; rather, "we are carried up into heaven" by our faith and the power of the Holy Spirit. This is the controversial *sursum corda*.[96] Given this, Martyr could logically hold that one truly receives Christ, yet the bread and wine are mere "corruptible creatures which serve only as signs." The relationship between the signs and the thing signified, the species and Christ, is one of "simple analogy."[97] This weighty philosophical construct, derived from Martyr's Aristotelian background, was fundamental to his understanding of the sacrament.[98]

Lorraine, though he understood Italian, grumbled that he did not want the business at hand to be treated in other than French. Perhaps this was to prevent any future "foreign intervention" by Martyr. Nevertheless, Catherine overruled the cardinal, asking d'Espence to reply. He first pleaded that he knew no Italian and that to converse with Martyr would be like a "dialogue of the deaf," which would only provide

95. *Relatio*, Calvin, *Opera*, XVIII, 768. For his speech see *ibid.*, 769-771; *Diario*, pp. 136-137. McLelland, *Visible Words*, pp. 287-288, provides translations of the key passages; and my quotations are taken from him.

96. McLelland, *Visible Words*, p. 205, who notes that Martyr supported the concept in his *Tractatio*, with St. John Chrysostom: "We must ascend into heaven when we communicate, if we would enjoy the body of Christ." *Homily 24*, PG 61:202-203. For Calvin and this construct, see McDonnell, *Calvin*, pp. 191-193 *et passim*, and for its background history from Augustine onward, Chapter II. Perhaps any difference between Beza and Martyr here would be the difference between Calvin and Martyr: "Many of the Christological factors found in Calvin's Eucharistic doctrine are found in a more explicit and developed form in Peter Martyr. His theology is much more philosophically structured." McDonnell, *Calvin*, p. 225, n. 59.

97. McLelland, *Visible Words*, p. 288.

98. See *ibid.*, pp. 79-85.

the company with a "laugh."[99] But he did his best to oblige.
There followed an exchange between the two over tropes, or
figures of speech, and their employment in eucharistic theology. Martyr urged, as a particular, that the Bible refers to
Christ as "the rock." D'Espence rejoined that this was an
obvious figure.[100] And, in a friendly spirit, he argued for a
literal acceptance of the words of institution, opposing the
est to Martyr's *significat*.[101] Martyr concluded in a pronounced Zwinglian vein: "Christ . . . in the Last Supper
wanted the external symbols of bread and wine to seal a
perpetual memory of the thing."[102] There was no middle
way between *est* and *significat*.

We can doubt whether the dialogue between Martyr and
d'Espence furnished the company with a "laugh"; we can be
sure that the next speaker did not. This was the heir of
Loyola as general of the Jesuits, Diego Lainez. Opposed to
the colloquy in general and to the intervention of Martyr in
particular, he finally broke his silence. He gained permission
from Catherine and, like Martyr, spoke in Italian. This time it
was the language of Rome.
But he began his celebrated and much-criticized speech
with an international theme: "Madam, although a stranger

99. *Discours*, p. 64; *Apologie*, pp. 583-584.
100. *Relatio*, Calvin, *Opera*, XVIII, 722.
101. D'Espence, *Apologie*, p. 584. But, as he wrote later, d'Espence felt that
Martyr's position was logically sounder than that of Beza. Martyr did not use
exhiberi and *sumi* without *esse* and *adesse*, that is, postulate a real reception
without requiring a Real Presence. *Ibid.*, pp. 469-470. Wendel, *Calvin*, p. 350,
would agree.
102. *Relatio*, Calvin, *Opera*, XVIII, 772. Martyr's eucharistic theology would
seem to stand somewhere between that of Zwingli and Calvin. McLelland, *Visible
Words*, pp. 227-228, perhaps overstresses his proximity to the latter. The
difference may illuminate the tensions in the Reformed ranks. De Sainctes,
Responsio, p. 67, recounts that Martyr's speech interrupted Beza, whom he would
not allow to finish; d'Espence, *Apologie*, pp. 468-469, reports that when Martyr
spoke, Beza himself grumbled. There was, of course, no unanimity in the Catholic
ranks either.

ought not to pry into affairs of the republic of others, nevertheless because the faith is not of particular nations, but universal and Catholic, it would not seem inappropriate to propose some comments to your Majesty, speaking in general of things treated herein, as also in particulars, responding to some objections made by fra Pietro Martire . . . "[103] The "fra," repeatedly used, was undoubtedly a taunt to the former Augustinian. Perhaps taking a tip from Beza's use of the word "wolves" in the previous conference, Lainez observed that the Scriptures speak of those who have left the Church as "serpents, wolves in sheep's clothing, and foxes."[104] Citing the Pelagians as an example, he warned that one must beware of their "falsehoods." All claim to be Catholic, but in "particular ways."

He posited that there were two remedies for the present dangers. One was the Council of Trent, the proper forum for such discussions. He attacked the legality of a national council when a general council had been called, maintained that the Huguenots—with safe-conduct—should be packed off to Trent, and berated the secular authorities for assuming direction of spiritual affairs. As he put it none too flatteringly: "It is generally agreed that the blacksmith should stick with his craft." Again, the ministers wanted to teach, rather than be taught, and to "spread their venom" and preach their sermons which endure as long as "an hour and a half"![105] A second solution, but far less preferable, would be to restrict the disputes to the presence of "learned men" alone, who would be in no danger of "infection" and who might, with "charity," win the dissidents over. These would be private meetings that would exclude the magnates about court, including the Queen.

103. The speech is in the *Monumenta historica Societatis Jesu* (93 vols. to date; Madrid, 1894-1965), VII, 759-768 [hereafter cited as *MHSJ*].
104. *Ibid.*, 760.
105. *Ibid.*, 761.

Lainez went on to offer a few substantive comments. He acknowledged the evils of simony, but insisted that this did not invalidate orders, and he held that experience had shown that the popular election of ministers ultimately led to simony. He countered the *sursum corda* of Martyr by arguing that, though Christ was present in heaven naturally he was present in the host supernaturally. Christ was omnipresent. He finished the argument with an allegory of a prince who periodically reappears in a festival that reenacts his great victories.[106] Lainez improved upon Martyr's exhortation to the audience to confess his faith by professing his preparedness to die for his own. He finally insinuated that Catherine might lose her crown as well as her soul if she departed from the faith of her fathers. Thus spoke "the impetuous Lainez."[107]

This was an effort to destroy the conference, and the forces of moderation were stunned. Catherine, seeing her policy publicly attacked and her hopes waning, broke down in tears.[108] Martyr said even "the Papists" were offended.[109] Chantonnay, of course, eulogized the speech,[110] and the intransigents undoubtedly glowed. Lainez had well acquitted the suspect Society of Jesus, "to whom moderation was error"[111] and of which the prelates were now induced to take a new view.[112] It is difficult, in fact, to evaluate the

106. *Ibid.*, 766.
107. As put by a modern Jesuit historian, James Brodrick, *The Origin of the Jesuits* (New York: Doubleday Image Books, 1960), p. 184.
108. *Journal*, p. 39. The author, presumably d'Espence, was resentful. Martyr described it rather differently. He said that Catherine would have taught Lainez a lesson in modesty had not Este intervened to make a diverting speech. *Common Places*, p. 155. It seems doubtful that Catherine could have mustered the courage at that moment.
109. *Relatio*, Calvin, *Opera*, XVIII, 774.
110. To Philip II, Sept. 30, 1561, A.N., 1495, No. 73.
111. As Constant, *Concession*, I, 166, put it.
112. The Assembly of Prelates formally accepted the Society of Jesus on September 15. *Procès-verbaux des assemblées générales du clergé*, A.N. G^8*589^a, fols. 147-52.

effect of Lainez' intervention. For Geisendorf, it "spoiled all."[113] Even the Jesuit historian, Joseph Lecler, concedes that it gave a "new and grave check to the politics of conciliation."[114] Any appraisal must consider the prospects for success prior to the intemperate speech. They would scarcely warrant optimism. And Lorraine, the only prelate with perhaps the will and certainly the weight to secure and enforce a solution, was quickly losing ground. When the forces of moderation fail, those of intractable orthodoxy will take the initiative.

An exasperated Beza immediately protested Lainez' abuse. He seemed especially disturbed by Lainez' assumption that the Calvinists were convicted heretics, on charges that still awaited proof. He heaped ridicule upon the allegory of the Eucharist, which was rather a "comedy," in which Christ was "the principal buffoon." Perhaps Beza took inspiration from Lorraine's recent strategem, in treating the Jesuit's reprimand to the civil authorities and his assertion that the Calvinists should be packed off to Trent. Beza, who had already addressed his remarks to Catherine, responded triumphantly that the princes knew what they were doing. This was Beza's opportunity to rally them to the colors, in their defense against the disruptive ultramontanism of that alien "Spaniard."[115]

Beza finished with the Spaniard only to turn to the Sorbonnist, d'Espence. He took issue with d'Espence's remarks on tropes. If the Bible rehearses the words "This is my body," it also says "This is my blood of the New Testament," or similarly, "the chalice is the New Testament in my

113. Geisendorf, *Théodore de Bèze*, p. 161; François, 414, felt it hastened the end of the colloquy.
114. Joseph Lecler, *Histoire de la tolérance au siècle de la réforme* (2 vols., Paris, 1954), II, 55. This to Fouqueray, another Jesuit, was more an occasion for congratulation (*ibid.*, I, 259).
115. La Place, *Commentaires*, p. 197; *HE*, I, 600; *Diario*, p. 139; Beza, *Correspondance*, III, 164.

blood." This can only be understood as a figure, or put another way, Christ speaks of His presence only "sacramentally." He concluded that the bread is spoken of as Christ only because it is similar to Christ. There cannot be a sacrament without a figure.[116]

D'Espence forthwith objected that if this was the case, there was no difference between the sacraments of the Old Testament and those of the New, whereas the former are held to be figures of the latter. Otherwise we would have to say that the old were "figures of the figure," which would be an absurdity. The ministers promptly attacked his contention. They urged that the word "figure" is broader than "sacrament" and, as applied to the Old Testament, is used in a different sense from that of the New. In the former, it is largely a matter of prefiguring; in the latter, more a case of distinguishing "common things from those which have become sacraments." Beza elaborated, employing such tropes as "the peeling" and "the veil" to describe the bread and wine.[117] The great fear of the Calvinists was that the sign might be confused with the reality.

This exchange was not as esoteric as that which followed. Jacques du Pré, doctor of the Sorbonne and theologian of the new University of Reims,[118] advanced and asked Beza and Martyr what they understood grammatically in the words "This is my body." His concern was to what the pronoun *hoc* referred. They replied that it referred to the bread, which is the sign of his body. Du Pré insisted that, to the contrary, it was grammatically impossible for *hoc* to refer to the bread. It had to refer to his body, to which the bread had been transformed by the utterance of the words. Du Pré said in his school this usage of *hoc* would be called an "individu

116. La Place, *Commentaires*, p. 198; *HE*, I, 600-601.
117. *HE*, I, 601-602.
118. *Discours*, p. 65, n. 1; Beza, *Correspondance*, III, 164; Feret, *La faculté*, II, 191-193, for biographical sketch.

vague."[119] Beza professed that the whole thing was vague to him and the argument alien to the necessity of a sacramental sign. Du Pré, magisterially shaking his finger, retorted sarcastically that Beza should go to school in order to learn his terms. Du Pré and Martyr continued the argument, but without effect.[120] By this time the debate must have become general, with the ministers affirming that all the ancient Fathers were in agreement with them. Lorraine took to the tomes that he had brought into the chambers and marked again certain passages of Augustine and other Fathers who contradicted this assertion. The Reformed, for whatever reason, refused to look into the books. Some felt that Lorraine wanted to reduce the dispute to writing and feared that the princes and lords would be unable to follow such proceedings.[121] This was perhaps another direct appeal to the purple.

The hour was growing late for appeals. This long and troubled session, so full of event but so feeble in effect, was quietly concluded, as evening slowly descended on Poissy, and on the colloquy. This memorable session, which lasted five hours, closed with increasing acidity.[122] The eloquent

119. *HE*, I, 602. The *Diario*, p. 140, speaks of this as "un pronome vago et non signato," which seems untranslatable. It is refreshing to observe that d'Espence deprecates "jargon" somewhere in the *Apologie*. The argument, only implicit in the sources, is that *hoc*, modifying *corpus*, is neuter gender, whereas *panis*, being masculine, would take *hic*. It is, of course, an argument for transubstantiation. See also Beza, *Correspondance*, III, 171, n. 41. See George Hunston Williams, *The Radical Reformation* (Philadelphia: Westminster Press, 1962), pp. 43, 101, for Carlstadt and this question.

120. *Diario*, pp. 140-141.

121. La Place, *Commentaires*, pp. 198-199. Lorraine's use of the tomes is corroborated in the *Recueilly par les Calvinistes*, AN, G^8*589^a, fol. 184. This was, of course, just what Beza had asked for in his opening protest. There may have been some basis, however, for the Calvinist presentiment that Lorraine, at this point, preferred to continue the debate in writing. Evennett, *Lorraine*, p. 371. He gave a list of patristic texts of more than twenty Fathers for de Sainctes to send the ministers. These citations were to support his position on the Eucharist, but the ministers reported them "lost." De Sainctes, *Responsio*, pp. 79-80.

122. *MHSJ*, VIII, 759; *Discours*, p. 65; and Calvin, *Opera*, XIX, 7.

speeches, the subtle formulas, the wasted texts had been tried and found wanting. Both means and participants were exhausted.

The colloquy can be seen as a study in diminishing alternatives. From the mixed content of the initial exchanges of September 9 and 16, there came an ominous focus upon the Eucharist on September 24. The rejection by the Reformed of the largely Protestant formula of September 25 ensured the revival of Lorraine's ultimatum on September 26. Lorraine's "bomb" did not explode the colloquy, which had begun to disintegrate earlier but endured some time longer. Lorraine's ultimatum did destroy the last chances of maintaining a dialogue on the principle of persuasion. The consequence of the crisis was that Beza and Lorraine desperately tossed the formula back and forth in an effort to pin the blame for the impasse on the opposing side. This provoked the unequivocal and restrictive intervention of Martyr and then the uncompromising Romanism of Lainez.

The conversations somehow survived, but they were no longer held at Poissy, and they were now exclusively on the Eucharist. This was a reduction to the sublime, perhaps the impossible.

VI / The *Petit Colloque* and Closure of the Assembly: The Decay of Dialogue

Messiurs de Valence et de Sees
Ont mis les papistes aux ceps;
Salignac, Boutillier, Despance,
Pour servir Dieu quittent la pance.

Marlorat, de Besze, Martyr,
Font mourir le Pape martyr:
Saule, Merlin, Sainct Paul, Spina,
Sont marris qu'encore pis n'ha.
                    Anonymous *huitain*[1]

Les apôtres, jadis, preschoyant, tous d'un accord,
Entre vous aujour'huy ne règne que discord.
                    Ronsard[2]

There are reasons for considering Catherine de' Medici the heir of Charles V as the foremost royal irenicist of that day. Though Lorraine, now disenchanted by failure and fallen farther from the grace of the Queen Mother than perhaps ever before, had advised her to compel national adherence to the Real Presence under pain of heavy penalties, she would hear nothing of this.[3] Catherine thought along other lines. The ministers were still at court, and glad to be, and all the old threats were no less menacing. One of these threats came from Lainez, who had spoken so proficiently, if rudely, for the view of things south of the Alps and the Pyrenees. But Catherine was more determined than intimidated. She had to find some way to avoid the stern eye of Lainez, or at least to

1. *Recueilly par les Calvinistes*, cited in Beza, *Correspondance*, III, 185.
2. Pierre Perdrizet, *Ronsard et la Réforme* (Paris, 1902), p. 79.
3. Evennett, *Lorraine*, p. 372; *Diario*, pp. 134-35.

assuage his passion. In this dilemma the adviser to whom she turned once more was none other than the cardinal of Lorraine, and this time she received more agreeable counsel.

Lorraine, backed by l'Hospital, advised that the conversations be continued, but on an entirely private basis. This meant, in effect, accepting the second solution and lesser evil put forward by Lainez in his controversial address at the colloquy. Lorraine suggested that five theologians from each side might confer, but the discussions were to be restricted to his favorite doctrine, the Eucharist. The ministers themselves were eager for dialogue, but not on that particular issue. Coligny and the Protestant princes of the blood were able, however, to prevail upon their coreligionists. The Eucharist was, so to speak, half a loaf. Though the choice of this only too familiar subject boded ill, Catherine required no encouragement. Before going to bed on Sunday, September 29, she dispatched a note to d'Espence summoning him and two other theologians, Bouteiller and Salignac, to court the following morning. The Catholic contingent was completed by Montluc, bishop of Valence, and du Val, bishop of Séez.[4] They were to be matched with a Huguenot quintet: Beza, Martyr, Nicholas de Gallars, Augustin Marlorat, and Jean de l'Espine.[5] The next morning the group promptly met at court.

This was more than a second reconstitution of the colloquy. (Strictly speaking, the last sitting of the Colloquy of Poissy was that of September 26.) For one thing, this group met in the more protected surroundings of the court, at Saint Germain-en-Laye. For another, the Catholic contingent was not authorized to represent the Assembly of Prelates, which

4. *Discours*, pp. 65-66; *Journal*, p. 40. The text implies that Lorraine suggested the Catholic personnel. For his role, see also Evennett, *Lorraine*, p. 373.

5. Beza, *Correspondance*, III, 181; *HE*, I, 606. The *Discours*, p. 66, speaks of François de Saint Paul instead of des Gallars. The latter was apparently substituted for the former on September 30. On the role of Coligny and the Protestant princes, see *CSP: Foreign*, Oct. 9, 1561, No. 595(1).

was still convened at Poissy, drawing up the canons for the reform of the Gallican Church. They neither represented nor were representative of the prelates. They were liberals—even radicals. D'Espence and Séez were liberal, but orthodox. The other three had been among the rebels in the Utraquist service of August 3 that had filled the prelates with such consternation. Salignac and Bouteiller had delivered radical speeches before the prelates in August. Bouteiller, who was vicar-general to Châtillon (which did not augur well for his orthodoxy), had advanced positively heretical ideas before the Assembly of Prelates, such as questioning the superiority of bishops to priests, and would later be taken for a Protestant.[6] Salignac, a theologian of the College of Marmoutier, had long held Calvinist sympathies and would some years later pass over to the Reformed ranks.[7] And Montluc was already being characterized by an irate Pius IV as "Pseudo-Episcopus."[8] As one of the traditional Protestant sources put it, they were "all men of knowledge and reason."[9] But the biographer of Lorraine complained that the colloquy was "reduced at last to the level of a court intrigue and stripped of the last vestige of properly constituted" authority.[10] The outcome was almost predictable.

Catherine, pressed by circumstances and impatient for results, fed the theologians and put them to work. The first meeting of the *petit colloque*, as Romier termed it,[11] was

6. August Kluckholn, *Briefe Friedrich des Frommen Kürfursten von der Pfalz, 1559-1566* (2 vols., Braunschweig, 1868-1870), I, 228.

7. In 1565. Haag, 1st ed., IX, 113-114; Beza, *Correspondance*, III, 217, n. 2. And for Séez, Feret, *La faculté*, II, 191-93.

8. *Annales ecclesiastici ab anno MCXCVIII.; ubi desinit cardinalis Baronius, auctore Odorico Raynaldo . . . accedunt in hac editione notae chronologicae, criticae, historicae . . . auctore Joanne Dominico Mansi* (15 vols., Luca, 1747-1756), (1561), No. 83.

9. *HE*, I, 606. While the Florentine ambassador was vexed by these "strange choices" of the Roman Church. *Négociations*, ed. Desjardins, III, 464.

10. Evennett, *Lorraine*, p. 374.

11. Romier, *C&H*, p. 235. The sources for the conferences are the *HE*, I, 605-615; La Place, *Commentaires*, pp. 199-200; *Discours*, pp. 65-77; *Journal*, pp.

after dinner on September 29, the day of their summons to court. They gathered in the congenial quarters of the King of Navarre. The objective of the Catholics was fundamentally unchanged: to persuade the ministers to agree to a corporeal or substantial presence in "good terms."[12] To this end they initiated conversations by again referring to the articles composed in connection with the private meeting of September 25. These were the *Firma fide* and the *Credimus in usu coenae.*[13] Both were still unacceptable to Martyr. His position was inflexible, stressing not only a spiritual presence but a spiritual reception, while emphasizing the faith of the communicant. As he told the Catholic protagonists, "for my part" Christ is to be found substantially only in heaven. Though d'Espence's account laconically adds merely: "and so they departed,"[14] the *Histoire ecclésiastique* notes that he and several of his companions were struck by the qualification, "for my part." In the *Histoire ecclésiastique* d'Espence is again said to have scented dissension among the ministers, and although there is evidence in the same source that seems to contradict this, Martyr himself does not do so. In a letter to Heinrich Bullinger he confessed that "we have adversaries meek enough and who do not disagree much with us"; he affirmed, nevertheless: "My colleagues seem to me to yield too much." He went on to acknowledge that "they say" he was more rigorous than his own companions and to recognize that he was not ingratiating himself with the Queen.[15]

40-44; and a letter of d'Espence to Eustache du Bellay, bishop of Paris, which is largely a posterior elaboration of the theology discussed, *Annales ecclesiastici* (1561), No. 91. See also an anonymous report in S.A., Frankreich, A 115, Büschel 20, No. 2; *CSP: Foreign*, Sept. Oct., 1561, Nos. 559, 569, 583, 595, and 611, together, of course, with Beza's letters.

12. *HE*, I, 606.

13. See Appendixes C and D.

14. "Et ainsy se departirent," both in *Discours*, p. 66, and in the *Journal*, p. 40. The two accounts are virtually identical here. Such passages constitute the strongest case against Evennett's view that d'Espence was not the author of the *Journal. HE*, I, 606.

15. Oct. 2, 1561, Calvin, *Opera*, XIX, 8-9; Martyr, *Common Places*, p. 156.

D'Espence epitomized him as a respectable but intractable "old soldier."[16] Yet Martyr's bearing would seem to have the blessing of Calvin. On October 15 Calvin wrote Beza a noteworthy letter cautioning against concessions, lest "the course of truth be arrested."[17]

The next meeting was on September 30, *cinq à cinq*, at the lodgings of Séez. Salignac was still Catholic enough to present an argument for transubstantiation. Dusting off an old Greek manuscript volume of sermons attributed to Cyril, bishop of Jerusalem, he noted that, according to the author, after the invocation of the Holy Spirit the bread of the Eucharist is "no longer common bread, but the body of Christ." The main thrust of his argument was against a spiritual presence and the *sursum corda*. Martyr, the specialist on the sacrament, countered with an argument based on the nuances of Cyril's terms. Had Cyril intended transubstantiation, he would not have said that the bread is "no longer common bread, but simply that it was no longer bread."[18] The subtlety here is that his usage of the expression "common bread" implies that the species becomes an uncommon bread after consecration. A solution was not forthcoming from the ancient doctors, any more than from Calvin's tract, the *Augustana*, or the Scholastics.

They turned instead to a new formula. The ministers had one ready, for they presented what was virtually the same confession as the one that Beza had suggested to Catherine in his protest which opened the session of September 26. It confessed that:

Inasmuch as faith renders present the things promised, and that this faith takes very truly, the body and blood of our Lord Jesus Christ, by virtue of the Holy Spirit, in this regard we confess the presence of His body and blood in the Holy Eucharist, in which he truly presents, gives

16. D'Espence, *Apologie*, pp. 591, 469.
17. Beza, *Correspondance*, III, 189.
18. The discussion is in *HE*, I, 606-607.

and exhibits for us the substance of His body and blood by the operation of the Holy Spirit, and we receive and eat spiritually and by faith this very body which died for us, to become bone of His bones and flesh of His flesh, in order to be quickened and to receive all which is necessary for our salvation.[19]

D'Espence realized that the prelates would never accept the formula and frankly expressed his dissatisfaction with it. His principal objection was the subjective element, the concept that faith "renders present the things promised." He preferred to attribute the Real Presence "to the power of God, working by faith." The ministers responded positively. They said that the two things went well together, inasmuch as faith is like the eye that sees what God presents to it by his power; without this faith, which God also offers, he is no more present to the understanding than is a visible thing present to a blind man.[20] This conceded that while the communicant's awareness of the Real Presence is contingent upon faith, the actual presence itself is independent of that faith. Such an accommodation was a significant approach toward a Catholic interpretation. Though the ministers would make these attenuations no more than verbal, it was agreed that they should try submitting the formula to the prelates. As d'Espence tells us, "nothing else could be obtained."[21]

This was not quite the same as an accord. Nevertheless, a rumor started that accord had been reached, perhaps engendered by Montluc, perhaps by Beza.[22] Catherine was prematurely elated with the prospect of agreement on this crucial issue, received Beza warmly, jubilantly accepted the

19. *Ibid.*, 607. Des Gallars sent a Latin version of this to London. Johann Baum, *Theodor Beza nach handschriftlichen Quellen dargestellt* (2 vols., Leipzig, 1843-1851), appendix, II, 83.
20. *HE*, I, 607-608; *Discours*, p. 67.
21. *Discours*, p. 67. Again the *Journal*, p. 41, employs exactly the same language.
22. Evennett, *Lorraine*, p. 378; A.N., K 1495, No. 85; Beza, *Correspondance*, III, 181. The last is not substantiated by the other accounts.

formula from Montluc, and delicately tendered it to the prelates at Poissy.[23] The expected occurred: on the same day that the assembly received the formula (October 1) it found it to be "very pernicious," even "damnable."[24] Though the rejoicing of the court had been short lived, Catherine was undaunted. Before the day was over she had the collocutors at the conference table for a herculean and, as it turned out, final effort.

This time d'Espence wanted to make explicit what the ministers had maintained was implicit in the previous meeting. That is to say, he sought to rephrase the formula in such a way as to comprehend both the subjective and the objective element. After consulting with his companions, he presented the following formula to the ministers:

We confess that Jesus Christ in the Holy Eucharist presents, gives and truly exhibits to us the substance of His body and His blood by the operation of the Holy Spirit, and that we receive and eat sacramentally, spiritually, and by faith this very body which has died for us, so that we become bone of His bones, and flesh of His flesh . . . and therein receive all which is required for our salvation. And *because the word and promise of God, on which our faith is based*, makes and renders present the things promised, and that by this faith, we take truly and really the true and natural body and blood of our Lord by virtue of the Holy Spirit.[25]

There were things to commend in the formula. It avoided transubstantiation and the *ex opere operato* doctrine. It embodied both a substantial and spiritual presence, but it must be pointed out that the use of the word "natural" involves a literalism that would seem to preclude the latter

23. *Journal*, p. 41; *HE*, I, 608, which, however, refers these events to October 4 and another formula. This is disproved by Beza's letter to Calvin of October 4, 1561. Beza, *Correspondance*, III, 181; *Journal*, pp. 41-42.

24. The *Diario*, p. 145, holds that some counseled acceptance, arguing that from a "bad debtor one had to accept what he could get." No particulars were provided.

25. D'Espence's own emphasis. *Discours*, p. 67.

and sound foreign to the Calvinist ear. It made a valiant effort to balance the objective and subjective, for while the Real Presence is operative by "the word and promise of God," the communicant partakes of it "by faith." The fact is d'Espence tried to do too much and did too little. The formula failed.

It took only a moment's examination for Beza to realize the essential modification that d'Espence had made. This was to attribute the Real Presence to the "word" in lieu of "faith." And this, notwithstanding the verbal glosses of September 30, was unacceptable. Beza properly saw and pointed out the well-intentioned contradiction implicit in an objective presence and a subjective communication. Martyr followed this with some finer points. D'Espence defended his formula against their arguments, but to no effect.[26] After consultation, the ministers presented the Catholics with a substitute formula identical with that of d'Espence with one important exception: "faith based on the word of God" replaced "the word and promise of God, on which our faith is based" as that which "makes and renders present the things promised."[27] It was a slight but significant difference. It was, nevertheless, far from a low doctrine of the Lord's Supper. It was not exclusively subjective. The Real Presence was still present, "by the operation of the Holy Spirit," but the stronger and more emphatic "makes present" was reserved to

26. For the discussion, see Beza, *Correspondance*, III, 181; *Discours*, p. 72.
27. This formula reads: "Nous confessons que Jésus Christ en sa saincte Cène nous presente, donne & exhibe véritablement la substance de son corps & de son sang par l'operation de son S. Esprit, & que nous recevons & mangeons sacramentellement, spirituellement & par foy, ce propre corps qui est mort pour nous, pour estre os de ses os & chair de son chair, à fin d'en estre vivifiés & en percevoir tout ce qui est requis à nostre salut. Et pource que la foy appuyée sur la parole de Dieu nous fait & rend presentes les choses promises, & que par ceste foy nous prenons vrayement & de faict le vray & naturel corps & sang de nostre Seigneur par la vertu du S. Esprit, en cest esgard nous confessons la presence du corps & du sang d'iceluy nostre Sauveur en la saincte Cene." *HE*, I, 608; *Discours*, pp. 67-68. A slightly modified version of this, with the Latin expression *seu realiter et re ipsa* added, is given in the *Journal*, pp. 41-42.

faith. Moreover, the document also contained the expression "natural body and blood of our Lord." It represented the maximum concession of the Calvinists, and d'Espence noted its approximation to his own formula.[28]

Despite this, it appears clear that no agreement was reached. But as before, the anxious launched rumors of an accord. Although there is some evidence to suggest that there had been some accord,[29] a careful study of the sources does not bear out the view. D'Espence noted the rumor that both parties signed the article, but denied it emphatically.[30] In the absence of any affirmations to the contrary from the two leading Calvinists, Beza and Martyr,[31] one may reasonably conclude that the meeting ended short of agreement.

D'Espence had some cause to be emphatic in denying that

28. *Discours*, p. 67. Evennett, *Lorraine*, p. 378, attributes these events to a fourth séance, held on October 3, rather than to the meeting on the first of the month. This is not borne out by the sources, though the peculiar organization of the description in the *Journal*, p. 41, can probably account for it. Evennett himself earlier put the date as October 1. *Discours*, p. 68, n. 2.

29. La Place, *Commentaires*, p. 199, affirms this, while the *HE*, I, 608, is so darkly phrased as to imply vaguely that the article was submitted to d'Espence himself. Des Gallars says that the deputies had no difficulty with the formula, but endeavored to make it ambiguous so that the bishops might accept it. Des Gallars to Throckmorton, Oct. 5, 1561, *CSP: Foreign*, No. 583. *Collection des procès-verbaux des assemblées générales du clergé de France*, ed. Antoine Duranthon (8 vols., Paris, 1767-1768), I, 31, holds that the Reformed started the rumor. The anonymous Catholic summary of the sessions published in Christian Friedrich Sattler, *Geschichte des Herzogthums Würtemberg unter der Regierung Graven* (4 vols., Tübingen, 1767-1768), IV, 186, maintains that the Reformed engendered the rumor out of pride in their own formula. Given the circumstances, it is easy to envisage the enthusiast misinterpreting a willingness to see the best in another's point of view.

30. The *Journal*, p. 42, recounts a story of positive refusal. See also *Discours*, p. 68. De Sainctes, *Responsio*, p. 81, and De Thou, *Histoire universelle*, III, 76, support d'Espence. See also Baum, *Beza*, appendix, II, 83-84.

31. Beza, *Correspondance*, III, 182, speaks of "proximum conventum," while Martyr wrote Bullinger on October 17, 1561, that the Catholics "seemed to consent with us somewhat in the matter of the sacrament." Calvin, *Opera*, XIX, 57. "Near agreement" undeniably means disagreement. Nevertheless, Geisendorf, *Théodore de Bèze*, p. 163, follows the *HE* in accepting that an accord was reached.

he had agreed with the Huguenots. A part of the current
rumor was that the Catholic members of the conference were
boasting that they had been deputed to attend Saint-Germain
by the congregation of bishops. An indignant assembly at
Poissy not only disavowed this, but on October 2 proclaimed
that the Catholic collocutors should be expelled from their
company and numbered among the ranks of the "heretics"
themselves.[32]   The next day the Catholic protagonists
pleaded the awkwardness of their position before Catherine,
Navarre, and l'Hospital. They complained that they had no
mandate from the prelates, had labored with the Huguenots
in vain, and that their continued presence smacked of schism.
There seemed no other recourse than to abandon the effort.
But Catherine was willing to take another chance with the
prelates—there was hardly an alternative now—and had Lorraine communicate the formula to their assembly at Poissy.

It has already been suggested that the assembly was
seething by this time. There were not only the galling
presence of the conferences at Saint-Germain and the disturb-
ing rumors associated with them; there had also been unseemly strife among the leaders of the prelates. On October 1
Lorraine returned from a few days at Meudon to find things
gone awry. He had allowed Tournon and some of the other
bishops to draw up the canons of the Assembly of Prelates in
his absence, but was not displeased by certain liberties they
had taken with his intentions. He complained sharply before
the whole congregation, directing his remarks specifically to
Tournon. The crusty Tournon retorted that Lorraine
"wanted to be above the congregation" and walked out.[33]
The bishops made a mild protest to Lorraine about his
domineering attitude and pointed out to him the satisfaction
the Calvinists would reap from any revelation of Catholic

32. *Diario*, pp. 144.
33. *Ibid.*, pp. 143-144; Calvin, *Opera*, XIX, 15.

disunity. Tournon was reasonable, and the quarrel was mended.

The new formula was duly conveyed to this assembly, excited and unsettled but conscious of the need for solidarity and unity. Lorraine may himself have liked the formula,[34] but, if so, the situation called for discretion. The formula was relayed to Montluc, who presented it to the assembly with one final politic hint that Catherine desired to see it accepted. Thereupon, on October 4, a commission was created to examine it and to draw up recommendations on behalf of the prelates. That this committee included such conservatives as de Sainctes and du Pré, who both played constraining roles in the colloquy, and Jean Pelletier,[35] dean of the College of Navarre, and that it spent a full five days scrutinizing the formula were not good omens.

The indictment was returned to the bishops on October 9. Not only was the confession "captious and heretical," but a vast bill of particulars was attached. The formula was found riddled with heresy, most of which centered on the "faith, based on the word of God" clause, plus such features as the *ex opere operato*, communication by faith, and the *sursum corda*. It was affirmed, as against the subjective interpretation, that Christ had said "This is my body," and not "this will be my body when you eat it," and that Paul had said that the unworthy receive, but to their own judgment. The formula was returned, but in a form altered beyond recognition.[36] The only positive aspect of the report was a Catholic confession: "We believe and confess that in the holy sacrament of the altar the true body and blood of Jesus Christ are really and substantially under the species of bread and wine,

34. *HE*, I, 608; Languet, *Arcana seculi*, II, 144; Evennett, *Lorraine*, p. 381.
35. Other theologians deputed were Vigor, Brochet, and de Mouchy. The bishops were Lavaur, Lisieux, and Chalons. *Journal*, p. 42; *Discours*, p. 68; *Diario*, p. 146. There are some minor variations between the *Journal* and the *Discours*.
36. For the report, see *Discours*, pp. 68-70; *HE*, I, 609-612.

by the virtue and power of the divine word pronounced by the priest, the only minister ordained to this effect, according to the institution and commandment of our Lord."[37]

The report of the committee upheld the convictions of the great majority of the assembly. Tournon did seem a bit puzzled that there could be so much heresy in a single formula, but characteristically concluded that this only showed one could not judge such things lightly.[38] The Catholic confession was circulated and read aloud by the prelates, who thus signified their approval. The bandwagon psychology prevailed. The cardinal of Bourbon offered to subscribe with his own blood. Lorraine not only sided with the majority; he added an anathema for all who held a contrary view.[39] The bishops followed this up with a statement on the colloquy—a kind of white paper—lamenting the "errors and blasphemies" of the Huguenots and requiring subscription to the Catholic formula as the price of any future hearing.[40] This was a means of ensuring that the ministers, with all their works and ceremonies, would soon be expelled from the private preserves of the Gallican Church.

There were a few voices of dissent. Seven of the bishops—including Châtillon, Valence, Uzès, Chartres, and Vence—dared oppose the rising tide. Being prudent, they seem to have absented themselves while the confession was being circulated. When they were asked about this, Uzès, Chartres, and Vence said they wanted time for deliberation, pleading that only a council or pope could constrain one to sign a confession of faith. Châtillon did not sign, alleging that the

37. *Discours*, p. 70.
38. *Ibid.*, pp. 71-72.
39. *Diario*, p. 147; *Journal*, p. 43. Consequently, if Lorraine did approve the formula the week before he was condemning himself. But, of course, now he was acting upon theological opinion.
40. *HE*, I, 612-614. To which the Calvinists could only respond with a decidedly Protestant statement. La Place, *Commentaires*, pp. 199-200; *HE*, I, 614-615.

confession was simply a device to effect his suspension. One avowed that had the condemned confession been found in the writings of Augustine or some Scholastic, it would not have been deemed heretical. Another anonymous voice observed that the ministers had not been treated graciously. Valence defended the censured article, but took issue with one of its particulars, which had stressed that Christ had said: "This is my body," and not "this will be my body when you eat it." He noted that Christ had prefaced these words with "Take, eat," thus arguing that the taking and eating, in faith, is primary and the cause of the Real Presence. Tournon suffered the mavericks, several of whom were already suspect, without pejorative comment.[41] Seven could not hold back the élan of seventy.

The assembly was about to conclude its day's anathemas, when Lorraine commented on the rumors that the Catholic five had accepted the Calvinist-sponsored confession. Inasmuch as he was patron of one (d'Espence), he felt that that person should have the opportunity to vindicate himself before the congregation.

D'Espence was a bit startled at being called upon to make an impromptu defense before a bellicose assembly. Though one source, no doubt with some exaggeration, comments that he was "judged to be beside himself,"[42] he immediately regained his composure, rose to the occasion, and delivered what was, perhaps more than any other single speech, the valedictory of sixteenth-century irenicism. He reduced his vindication to three main points.

First, d'Espence denied categorically that he had ever approved the Calvinist statement on the Eucharist. He narrated his role in the crucial conferences and his hapless arguments against the formula of the Huguenots. As a "lesser

41. For the seven and their dissent, see *Diario*, pp. 147-148; *Discours*, p. 71.
42. *Diario*, p. 148. For the defense, see also *Discours*, pp. 72-78; *Journal*, pp. 44-45.

evil," he had urged its acceptance, but this was not the same
as accepting it. He wanted rather to get beyond it: to treat
the adoration of the sacrament—as had been the instructions
of Lorraine—and other germane particulars. These points
would have clarified the Calvinist position and prevented the
conference signing an agreement based on a specious accord.
Nevertheless, he had never seen a Calvinist document on the
Eucharist so close to Catholic doctrine.[43]

This, said d'Espence, advancing to the second point, was
why he was so offended by the censures. He prayed that God
might "illuminate his eyes," for he failed to find the article
so full of heresy. He went on to put the whole matter into a
much broader perspective, using an eschatological frame of
reference that transcended the quarrel about whether "the
word or faith" renders Christ present.[44] Moreover, the
Scriptures allowed a role to the subjective. Holy Writ teaches
that if anyone eats this bread he will live forever. He argued
that it was unwarrantable to condemn the ministers for
holding that the unworthy do not receive, for he himself felt
the ministers did not adhere to this. The formula was not a
comprehensive statement, and it was unjust to condemn it,
a priori, for its deficiencies. He urged the bishops not to
publish their censures, for this might reveal that there are
"more censurers than writers" in this world and drive future
colloquies underground.[45]

The final point concerned the Catholic confession. D'Espence's conscience was not inordinately disturbed by the
confession, but he made it clear he would have used different
language. His complaint was against the anathemas of those
who professed otherwise. The ancients might have employed
such condemnations, but times had changed. Anathemas
could only be declared by a council, and the prelates had

43. *Diario*, p. 149; *Discours*, p. 73.
44. *Supra*, Chapter VI.
45. *Discours*, p. 74: " in umbra."

expressly abrogated that status. The prelates should be aware, moreover, that the Greek Church does not attribute the Real Presence to the words of consecration, but to certain "mystic prayers," the *Epiclesis*, which can be found in the canon of the Mass. He cited several of the Fathers in support.[46] This legitimate variation suggested the possibility of conciliation with the Reformed on this point, given a fresh and broader perspective. But the speech was a noble effort delivered out of season.

D'Espence did not make any friends that day. As he said, some of the prelates were offended by this remonstrance "more than he by their anathemas."[47] Pelletier, one of the committee of theologians, replied that the censures were only "simple advice" submitted to the prelates—a point easier asserted than defended. D'Espence got into an altercation with Guillaume d'Avançon, bishop of Embrun, and we are

46. *Ibid.*, pp. 75-76.
47. *Ibid.*, p. 76. *Collection des procès-verbaux*, ed. Duranthon, I, 36. And even a year later the new nuncio, Prospero di Santa Croce, wrote Borromeo that d'Espence was "molto sospetto." *Die Römische Kurie*, ed. Šusta, III, 369. As a moderate he was fated to be suspected by both Catholic and Calvinist. But it was the latter who gave him the most trouble. This was due to the charge that d'Espence and his companions had accepted the Calvinist-sponsored formula of October 1. Historiographically, this accusation seems to have begun with the anonymous *Recueilly par les Calvinistes*, G8*589ª fols. 186-187, incorporated into the *Ample discours des actes de Poissy*, a very abbreviated account published only weeks after the colloquy and written in a polemical spirit. It was incorporated into La Place, which lent the charge authority. D'Espence defended himself against La Place in his own small tract, *Traicté en forme du conférence avec les ministres de la religion prétendue réformée, touchant l'efficace & vertu de la parole de Dieu aux ministère & usage des saincts sacrements de l'église* (Paris, 1566). But d'Espence's arguments were without effect, and he introduces his formidable *Apologie* (1569) by telling us that he was treated with indignity by both friend and foe. This is a good source for miscellaneous information on the colloquy. The next year, d'Espence reinforced the *Apologie* with the *Continuation de la tierce conférence avec les ministres extraordinaries de la religion prétendue réformée en ce royaume* (Paris, 1570). Here he says the whole question of the formula was based on a simple misunderstanding, while he dismisses the author of the *Ample discours* as a "bird of night" who hides behind the cloak of anonymity; see esp. pp. 144-150. It would seem that after 400 years the evidence warrants dismissing the old charge. See also the discussion Evennett prefaces to the *Discours*, pp. 51-59.

told that the most temperate thing he could say was that Embrun "ought to go to school." Bouteiller, another of the collucutors, joined in, making it a free for all and exchanging insults with Embrun. When Pelletier impugned Montluc's opinion as heretical, the latter simply rejoined that "that monk seemed to be out for his blood."[48] It is well to remember that for good measure d'Espence had stepped on the toes of his patron, Lorraine, who had inspired the very anathemas that he had questioned.

The confrontation was finally concluded and peace restored. Lorraine himself bore no grudge against his theologian and used his good offices to reconcile d'Espence and Embrun. D'Espence seemed appropriately embarrassed when it was emphasized to him that Lorraine had started the anathema and remarked that in religious disputes we are not "like magpies in a cage," but often speak out of turn and without premeditation. The proper apologies were tendered, and all was forgiven between the two.

The Assembly of Prelates, having now completed its work without solving its problems, proceeded to dissolve itself. The final session was held on October 13. Lorraine, speaking in behalf of the aged Tournon, addressed the congregation. He thanked the prelates and theologians and asked for their continued assistance. He exhorted them to preach against heresy judiciously, that is, to avoid stirring up sedition and rebellion. They were, at last, free to leave. That day their canons, the decrees on reform, and the agreement on the subvention were tendered to the crown. The prelates dissolved without consulting Catherine, for fear she would not grant them permission.[49] And so her *fait accompli* was requited. As the prelates filed out of the assembly, some of them grumbled that they had never been told why they had

48. For the fracas, *Discours*, p. 77; *Diario*, p. 149.
49. *Suriano, Despatches*, p. 46.

really been summoned, and even d'Espence was discomforted at being made to speak without warning before his "elders."[50] This is how he pitifully ends his account. Religious experimentation was at an end, having given way to renewed conformity. Unity had failed; only uniformity was left.

As if in comic contrast, a few days before the dissolution the ubiquitous and quixotic Francis Baudouin rushed upon the scene. He brought a new irenic, if not now ironic, tract by George Cassander, which bore the splendid title *De officio pii ac publicae tranquillitatis vere amantis viri in hoc religionis dissidio.*[51] The tract was now inappropriate, but Cassander's name was introduced appositely. And on October 26 the small mission of German theologians summoned by Navarre straggled into Paris from Württemberg and the Palatinate. The danger of a confrontation between Lutheran and Reformed was now past, and Beza wrote in relief: "All is well because so very late."[52] The real danger no longer lay in the tilting of the theologians, but in the thunder of arms.

50. *Discours*, p. 78. Incidentally, some sources, for example the *Journal*, pp. 45-46, put the concluding session at October 14, but most favor October 13. *HE* I, 616; *Collection des procès-verbaux*, ed. Duranthon, I, 36.

51. George Cassander (Cassandri), *Opera quae reperiri potuerunt omnia* (Paris, 1616), pp. 781-791.

52. Beza, *Correspondance*, III, 196.

VII / The Eleventh Hour: Concessions and the Conferences on Icons

You shall not make yourself a carved image or any likeness of anything in heaven or on earth beneath or in the waters under the earth; you shall not bow down to them or serve them. For I Yahweh your God, am a jealous God . . .
Exod. 20:4-5

True art is made noble and religious by the mind producing it. For those who feel it, nothing makes the soul so religious and pure as the endeavor to create something perfect, for God is perfection, and whoever strives after perfection is striving for something divine.
Michelangelo[1]

Poissy satisfied no one. Catherine was offended that so little courtesy had been shown to her guests, the prelates were vexed by the crown's furtive invitations and less muted pretensions, and if the Huguenots were disappointed with the timidity of the one, they were repelled by the inhospitality of the other. Reformed and Roman Catholic refused mediation; Trent and the Pope's remedy were as remote as ever; faction at court was unchecked; and Philip of Spain was increasingly bellicose. Civil and religious war lurked on the dark horizon.

Against this background, Catherine surveyed the results of the assembly. Though she was hurt at the collapse of her plans, the convention had not been without a positive note. If the prelates had been unbending in matters of dogma, they had been rather more flexible as regards their purses. The subvention, agreed to on September 26 and signed on October 21, effected the redemption of the royal domains.

---

1. *Vasari's Lives of the Artists*, ed. Betty Burroughes (New York: Simon and Schuster, 1946), p. 301.

The clergy agreed to advance the crown 600,000 livres per year for a period of six years, on condition that they retain their privileges, properties, and benefices unmolested.[2] Though Catherine first felt that the subsidy "seemed small," Condé and Navarre urged its acceptance,[3] probably with the hope that the prelates might thereby be rendered more tractable. The action of the prelates on the subvention was coupled with their canons for the reform of the Gallican Church. They were of a fairly comprehensive nature, dealing with bishops, cathedral chapters, monasteries, and the clergy in general.[4] Though they would be texts for the French Counter-Reformation, the old structure was left fundamentally intact.

This was especially the view of things from the court. On October 3 Catherine sent a copy of the canons to her ambassador in Vienna, revealing her disappointment with the efforts of the prelates. She gently noted that they had "touched" many things dealing with reform. But as regards what concerned their own grandeur, not to mention benefices, they had "passed lightly." And none of their proposals provided for the troubles that beset the realm, which "is well to my great regret."[5] Her ideas do not seem to have been clearly formulated, but the day after this plaintive note Martyr reported somewhat quizzically that she was considering toleration and even toying with the idea of an "Inter-

2. *Collection des procès-verbaux*, ed. Duranthon, I, 21-23; *Diario*, pp. 150-151. For the significance of "the contract of Poissy," see J. Laferrière, *Le contrat de Poissy (1561)* (Paris, 1905), pp. 138-148. This became a valuable precedent, and the clergy were convoked thirteen more times before the end of the century. Conversely, as the Estates General had refused the requests of the crown, they were disregarded. Major, *Estates General*, pp. 113-114.

3. *Journal*, pp. 35-36, 39.

4. For the decrees, see *Procès-verbaux des assemblées générales du clergé*, A.N., G8*589a, fols. 45-80; see also Claude de Sainctes, *Confession de la foy catholique, contenant en brief la réformation de celle que les ministres de Calvin, présentèrent au roy, en l'assemblée de Poissy* (Paris, 1561).

5. *Lettres de Catherine de Médicis*, I, 239; see also *ibid.*, 243.

im.""[6] In any case, it appeared that Catherine herself would now seek to implement her policy of conciliation.

Catherine.had not yet depleted all her resources. Though the Guises left court on October 19, and Martyr followed suit at the end of the month, Beza and a number of the protagonists of both parties were still at court and accessible. Calvin hoped that Beza and his cohorts might obtain a "tolerable liberty"[7] for the Reformed Church, which would be little more, at this point, than reconciling law and fact. Beza was enjoying a splendid apostolate at court and at the end of September officiated at the marriage of Jean de Rohan, Lord Fontenay, and Diane de Barbençon-Cary, members of two of the greatest families in France. Martyr helped score a coup in the conversion of Antonio Caracciolo, bishop of Troyes, to the Reformed faith.[8] And throughout the realm the Huguenots, emboldened by the colloquy and their strong position at court, were preaching at will. Zeal was soon replaced by more aggressive crusading instincts: churches were seized, and pitched battles ensued. Both sides began mustering arms, and the Venetian ambassador reported in alarm that a "great fear" was sweeping the kingdom.[9]

Before pursuing developments in France, it may be well to review some international reactions to Poissy and the events in their train. First, there was the Pope himself. Pius found the Chancellor's opening address suspect and went into a tirade over Beza's discourse, with its indiscretion on the Eucharist. As far as he was concerned, all in France was in "extreme license and abandon." When Pius remarked ironi-

6. Calvin, *Opera*, XIX, 14. It is interesting to note that Henri Klipffel, *Le Colloque de Poissy* (Paris, 1867), pp. 204-205, writing from the vantage point of a politique, scolded Catherine, who was "not a Henry IV," for not forcing the prelates to come to terms with the Huguenots.

7. Beza, *Correspondance*, III, 192.

8. *Ibid.*, IV, 212; Joseph Roserot de Melin, *Antonio Caracciolo, Évêque de Troyes, 1515-1570* (Paris, 1923). Martyr died in December 1562.

9. *Suriano, Despatches*, p. 46; Beza, *Correspondance*, IV, 66, n. 15.

cally that the general council "is in being," the French ambassador used as delaying tactics the matter of precedence, noting that there might be quarrels between the French and imperial bishops over the niceties of protocol.[10] But the resolute Pius wrote the legates on November 19 that "we are *resuming* the Council of Trent," from which "we desire the union of all good *Catholics*," as well as perpetual peace in Christendom.[11] This was a more explicit statement that the council was to be a continuation of Trent and confirms that the mediatory possibilities of the assembly were exhausted.

It also provides another hint of the increasing part that Spain was playing in Pius' calculations. In a remarkable missive of October 18 Pius offered literally to crown the papal-Spanish rapprochement. He proposed to deprive the sovereigns of both France and England of their crowns and give their titles to Philip, if they did not send delegations to the council and accept the authority of the Holy See. And as though this were not enough, Pius even held forth a hope of the imperial dignity to Philip.[12] He took a similarly hard line on the whole problem of heresy. The next month he told the Spanish ambassador that "the time for gentleness has passed"; now was the time for "rigor" and "severity." Pius put all his hope in Philip as "protector" of the council and, indeed, of "religion itself."[13] Philip had been appointed, as it were, watchdog of the Council of Trent, and the Pope was about to unleash him.

From appearances, the King of Spain did not require much coaxing. Even before he knew of the regal prizes held forth by the Pope, Philip was threatening Catherine. Regarding her

10. Lisle to the King, Sept. 11, 1561, *Instructions*, ed. Dupuy, pp. 97-98; Noël Valois, "Les essais de conciliation religieuse au début du règne de Charles IX," *Revue d'histoire de l'église de France*, XXXI (1945), p. 255, n. 1.

11. *Die Römische Kurie*, ed. Šusta, I, 113-114 [italics mine].

12. For details, see "Instructions of the Pope . . . for Philip II," *ibid.*, 279-280.

13. Vargas to Philip II, Nov. 7, 1561, *Papiers d'estat du Cardinal de Granvelle*, ed. Charles Weiss (9 vols., Paris, 1841-1852), VI, 398-408.

dalliance with the Calvinists, he told Chantonnay on October 1 to "Let the Queen know that by such a course her son will lose his kingdom." A more sinister reproach followed later in the month.[14] But these were probably idle threats. Philip had just repudiated his government's debts in 1557, and his finances did not even allow him to travel to the Netherlands.[15] It would be a long time before Spain would engage itself in France. Nevertheless, although there were more designs than deeds, all Europe believed that Spain and other Catholic potentates would soon intervene.[16]

Catherine reacted to the menaces of Philip in characteristic fashion. As a counterweight to the pressure of Spain, she drew closer to the Reformed. Her son, the Duke of Orléans, actually joined the Calvinists; Beza hoped to convert the entire royal family.[17] Romier relates that she governed with the credit of Beza.[18] But Catherine was still making the effort to juggle contradictory policies. While this was going on, she managed to present the appearance of a dutiful Catholic and in October had twenty-six bishops chosen for the Council of Trent. This allayed the threat of Philip,[19] protector of the council, and seems to have been done to little other purpose. She humanely suffered the bishops "a little rest" after the hot summer at Poissy, for they were not ordered to be at the council until March of the next year.[20]

14. A.N., K 1495, No. 80, for the quotation; see also *ibid.*, Nos. 84 and 86; *Lettres de Catherine de Médicis*, I, 240, n. 1.

15. Philip to Granvelle, Oct. 6, 1561, *Granvelle*, ed. Weiss, VI, 375. Granvelle, Philip's representative in the Netherlands, was apparently for intervention: "the French are not people to leave us without likely pretext." *Ibid.*, 462. Romier, *C&H*, pp. 245, 248, considers that intervention was unlikely.

16. Romier, *C&H*, p. 275; *Lettres de Catherine de Médicis*, I, 253, 610-612; *Granvelle*, Ed. Weiss, VI, 460-461.

17. Beza to Calvin, Nov. 25, Dec. 16, 1561, Beza, *Correspondance*, III, 226.

18. Romier, *C&H*, p. 271. Beza, *Correspondance*, IV, 17, wrote Calvin on January 6, 1562, that Catherine "inclines openly to our party."

19. *Die Römische Kurie*, ed. Šusta, I, 297.

20. Ferrara to the Council-Legates, Nov. 3, 1561, *ibid.*, 292.

This provided time for Catherine to pursue what was still her primary goal: conciliation. For while Catherine oscillated between Geneva and Trent, she did not deviate from her more basic search for religious concord. But it was now the eleventh hour, and Frenchmen were mustering arms. It would require a heroic effort.

Catherine now sought to reconcile the religious parties by means of various disciplinary concessions. The notion was scarcely original. It will be recalled that this was one of the expedients of the irenicists in the German Reformation and had been attempted by the Emperor in the Augsburg Interim of 1548. The "third party" in France now embraced the idea. We can presume that, besides the Queen, this party included the Chancellor, and we know that other members were Montluc, Uzès, and the cardinal of Châtillon, all radical prelates.[21]

There had been some talk of various disciplinary concessions early in August. And it is curious that even the prelates at Poissy contemplated some restrictions upon images and the matter of Communion under both species, but resolved that any who so desired could make individual petitions to Rome in the matter.[22] Catherine took up this text and on October 24 submitted to Rome a request for Communion *sub utraque*. It was done in the best form. She was astonished that the Pope could be ill disposed toward her, for she had in mind some twenty-five able and carefully selected bishops for the council. As regards Poissy, she noted one thing that "all" the bishops and doctors had agreed upon: Communion under both species, as in the primitive Church. This could be authorized by the Pope independently of the council and would lead back many who were long separated. She stressed

21. *Ibid.*, II, 373-374.
22. *Diario*, p. 150.

that the request was "unanimous, necessary and urgent."[23]

Pius seems to have received the request amenably (his earlier attitude toward concessions will be recalled). But circumstances went against the petition. For one thing, Pius had little reason personally to be accommodating to a delinquent Queen. This attitude was reinforced when Rome discovered through independent sources that Catherine had misrepresented the unanimity of the request.[24] Finally, Spain interposed again, in the person of Vargas, the Spanish ambassador in Rome. Just as Lainez had intervened at Poissy, Vargas intervened at Rome. He declared that the request was "impudent and scandalous" and went on to warn that the French had in mind, beyond this, "a thousand other heresies."[25] Pius should "close the door on their nose."[26] The petition was submitted to a consistory for consideration, though Vargas attempted to dissuade the Pope from such a course.

Even before the adverse decision on the cup had been announced, the French court started to envisage more sweeping concessions. Sometime in earlier November the heterodox cardinal of Châtillon opened the matter with a new nuncio,

23. *Instructions*, ed. Dupuy, pp. 101-103. This seems to be her first such request. Various authors drawing on De Thou, *Histoire universelle*, III, 60-63, consider Catherine to have sent a far bolder request on August 4, 1561, calling for, among other things, complete abolition of images and frequent colloquies between the religious parties. The letter is published by de Thou. It seems, however, that this letter is not authentic or, at least, was never dispatched. *Die Römische Kurie*, ed. Šusta, I, 239. It cannot be found in the *Lettres de Catherine de Médicis*, I, or the supplementary volume, X. Ruble, in his commentary on the *Journal*, p. 15, held that Catherine used the colloquy to force the hand of the Pope on the concessions. This is contradicted by the fact that the request was subsequent to the colloquy.

24. The informant is not named. Lisle to the King, Dec. 9, 1561, *Instructions*, ed. Dupuy, pp. 116-117.

25. Vargas to Granvelle, Nov. 15, 1561, *Granvelle*, ed. Weiss, VI, 416-417.

26. " . . . leur fermera la porte au nez." *Ibid.*, 430. Fra Paolo Sarpi in his classic and antipapal *The Historie of the Councel of Trent*, tr. Nathaniel Brent (1st ed. 1619; London, 1676), p. 430, adds that the Spanish prelates called "the Prelates of France heretics, some schismatics, and some unlearned, alleging no reason but that Christ is in both the kinds."

Prospero di Santa Croce, who had just replaced the daunted Viterbo.[27] In the course of a two-hour interview, Châtillon proclaimed his goodwill and, perhaps to ingratiate himself with the nuncio, informed him that Lorraine himself had declared at Poissy that the popes really did not want a general council—they just paid lip service to the idea. Châtillon then broached the subject of the concessions. As the way to reunion, he sought—beyond the reformation of the clergy—the use of the vernacular in the liturgy, reduction of the number of Masses, the curtailment of Masses in private homes, and "some other things." He blamed the intransigent prelates for the fiasco of Poissy: had they heeded the good that the ministers had to say, made them understand their errors, and submitted the doubtful matters to the Pope, all would have gone better. Santa Croce temporized by replying that the council would accept all his suggestions that were found good. Châtillon seemed more or less agreeable about Trent, but sought this "provisional reformation" pending the council.[28] The nuncio maintained firmly, despite the various blandishments of the court, that Trent was "open," that there were learned men there, and that they would be willing to consider the desired concessions. And he still held out, as an enticement,[29] that the site could be changed after arrival.

If the third party made little headway with Santa Croce, they fared better with the more congenial Este, cardinal of Ferrara. Este's reputation had not been prejudiced by any

27. Santa Croce, bishop of Albano, had just arrived in Paris October 15. *Archives curieuses de l'histoire de France depuis Louis XI jusqu'à Louis XVIII*, ed. M.L. Cimber and F. Danjou (1st Series, 15 vols.; 2nd Series, 8 vols., Paris, 1834-1839), VI, 4. Pastor, *History of the Pope*, XVI, 176, n. 1, indicates that Cimber and Danjou published the nuncio's letters only partially and not without error. They must be supplemented by Šusta. Again, it has already been indicated that Châtillon professed adherence to the Reformed Church in April, but his religious orientation at this time appears equivocal.

28. *Archives curieuses*, ed. Cimber and Danjou, VI, 7-10.

29. Santa Croce to Borromeo, Dec. 28, 1561, *Die Römische Kurie*, ed. Šusta, I, 320-321.

unseemly hunt for heresy or any obtuse effort to break off
the colloquy. Nor had he compromised himself by the fact
that he had played a key role in a recent reconciliation of the
irresolute King of Navarre to the old Church.[30] This helped
improve Este's image in Rome, which had looked askance at
his rather casual attitude at court.[31] Este was now a most
promising intermediary.

Throughout December, Este had been conferring with
Montluc, Uzès, and Châtillon in order to regularize properly
their position vis-à-vis Rome.[32] This provided a fine entrée
for the same trio to take up their concessions directly with
him. These concessions were of a comprehensive nature and
included removal of icons to the exterior of churches,
suppression of Corpus Christi processions, simplification of
baptism, Communion under both species, the restriction of
the sacraments to the first Sunday of the month, the
elimination of the superfluity of Masses, some vernacular in
the Mass, and psalms in the vulgar tongue. They were even
emboldened to call for a reduction of dogma to that
contained in the Apostles' Creed and the canons of the first
six ecumenical councils. They pleaded that these concessions
were essential to save a kingdom that was already one-fourth
separated from Rome. Though the whole tone of the requirements indicated that they were intended to placate the
Calvinists, they were sweetened with a universal flavor by the

30. And as might be expected it was largely a political reconciliation. The King
of Spain was induced to offer him Sardinia as a settlement for Spanish Navarre.
For details, see Ruble, *Bourbon*, III, 251-314, IV, *passim*. It is ironical that before
the year was over he fell in battle at Rouen and reportedly died with a Huguenot
psalm on his lips. Pacifici, *Ippolito II d'Este*, p. 319. Ruble says he probably died
a Lutheran. *Bourbon*, IV, 373-374. The conversion to Catholicism resulted in his
estrangement from Jeanne d'Albret.
31. For details, see *Granvelle*, ed. Weiss, VI, 405; *Die Römische Kurie*, ed.
Šusta, II, 383.
32. François, *Tournon*, p. 418. Proceedings against the three dragged out
interminably, though Châtillon was deprived of his dignities and benefices by a
consistory in 1563. Their best protection was the fear in Rome of further
alienating France. Pastor, *History of the Popes*, XVI, 190-192.

hint that they would be a means to effect the reunion of the Greek and Latin Churches.[33] While Lainez offered his characteristic opposition,[34] the accommodating Este gave the program considerable endorsement and, on December 31, sent the requests to Rome.[35]

They arrived inopportunely. On January 18, 1562, the Council of Trent had finally reopened, with 113 prelates in attendance.[36] None of them were French. The Pope was scarcely in a humor to consider the concessions, which he assailed as "impious and wicked." His answer to Este was pointed and abrupt: if the French wanted a reply, "they could come to the Council now open and well attended, which would respond to them suitably."[37] It is ironical that the fear of Trent was a key motive in Catherine's whole independent policy of conciliation, while the failure of the French to make their scheduled appearance there provided a convenient excuse for the Pope to reject their petition.

The French reacted with a last desperate effort to counter the Council of Trent. In November Catherine had complained about the continuation of the former council, so hateful to Protestants, and longed for a new beginning. Using strong language, she accused the Pope of favoring "the conservation of his grandeur and authority more than the cause of God."[38] Now, and perhaps partially in a spirit of reaction, she sent the Sieur de Rambouillet to Germany on a secret mission to revive the French version of a general council. He visited the Duke of Württemberg, the Elector Palatine, the

33. Their memorandum, given under the title, "Remonstrance of the King to the Pope," is found in the *HE*, I, 651-665. See also *Die Römische Kurie*, ed. Šusta, II, 373-374. The *HE*, I, 651, and Valois, "Conciliation," pp. 263-264, note the hand of Montluc in the document.

34. *Die Römische Kurie*, ed. Šusta, II, 374.

35. *Ibid.*, I, 322-326; Pacifici, *Ippolito II d'Este*, p. 305, n. 1.

36. Jedin, *EC*, 173.

37. Borromeo to Ferrara, Jan. 28, 1562, *Die Römische Kurie*, ed. Šusta, II, 387.

38. *Instructions*, ed. Dupuy, p. 106.

Elector of Brandenburg, and Philip of Hesse, but their reactions were negative[39]—much as they had been at Naumburg. He was also to sound out the Germans on what aid they would provide should the King of France become a Protestant with the result that the French found themselves at war. They replied they would furnish as many men as the French could afford.[40] The Rambouillet mission was followed by the dispatch of the Sieur d'Auzance to Spain to solicit Philip's favor for "a universal and safe Council" in Germany, which would be attended by the Pope himself.[41] Philip, needless to say, could scarcely lend an ear to a project that would reopen the burning question of justification.

Meanwhile, someone else at court who had recently, as it were, turned irenicist, was laboring in behalf of the council. This was the indefatigable Lainez, who now scurried about court, urging upon all, including Beza, that the "free and General Council" already convened at Trent was the "instant remedy"[42] for the divisions of Christendom. Like Ferrara's, Lainez's tour at court was not fruitless. The Society of Jesus was finally admitted to France. Long suspect because of its Ultramontanism and for the presumption of its very title, the society was formally approved by the Assembly of Prelates on September 15.[43] It has been held that the bishops did this in retaliation for Catherine's indulgence to Beza.[44] It is not

39. Heidenhain, *Die Unionspolitik Landgraf Philipps von Hessen*, pp. 373-375; Beza, *Correspondance*, IV, 40, n. 22.

40. Santa Croce to Borromeo, "Mémoire sècret," Mar. 13, 1562, *Archives curieuses*, ed. Cimber and Danjou, VI, 50.

41. Crivello to Borromeo, Jan. 17, 1562, *Die Römische Kurie*, ed. Šusta, II, 369-370. Crivillo was nuncio at the court of Philip.

42. See his tract written at court: *Remedia instantium ecclesiae malorum*, *MHSJ*, , VIII, 785-788.

43. Henri Fouqueray, *Histoire de la Compagnie de Jésus en France des origines à la suppression, 1528-1762* (5 vols., Paris, 1910-1925), I, 256; A.N., G8*589ᵃ, fols. 147-152. It can be noted that this preceded Lainez's attack of September 26.

44. James Brodrick, *The Progress of the Jesuits 1556-79* (New York: Longmans, Green and Co., 1947), p. 60. This may well be, but Brodrick's particular assertion that they resented being forced to listen to a sermon from Beza at a

without irony that while Poissy approved the Jesuits, a Jesuit did what he could to subvert Poissy. In any event, the Jesuits, a major force in the Counter-Reformation, were now received into the kingdom of the "eldest daughter of the Church."

This occasions a moment's digression. The action of the French would later prompt the fathers at Trent to offer special praise and recognition to the Society of Jesus.[45] This appreciation was shared by the Pope, who increased the privileges of the order and annulled a rule of his hostile predecessor, Paul IV, restricting the general of the order to a tenure of three years. Pius was grateful for services rendered and treated Lainez, as well as his successor, Francis Borgia, with great distinction. The Pope summed it all up in a letter to Philip II of November 24, 1561, just several months after Poissy, when he wrote: "Among all the religious orders . . . the Society of Jesus deserves to be embraced with special love by the Holy See."[46] The Jesuits had come of age.

Catherine was not yet prepared to recognize this coming of age. Through the last months Catherine's thoughts on toleration seemed to have crystallized. She preferred reconciliation to toleration, but toleration to war. To this end she called to Saint-Germain deputies of the various parlements of the realm, carefully selected from among those favorable to moderation. The consequence was a new edict on toleration, the notable Edict of January (1562), which authorized the Reformed to hold their assemblies throughout the country-

---

reception on August 22 is wrong or at least inaccurate. Beza did not reach court until August 23. Opposition to the Jesuits came from the Parlement of Paris, doctors of the University of Paris, and the bishop of Paris, Eustache du Bellay, who later changed his position; friends of the Jesuits included Tournon, the cardinals of Bourbon, Armagnac, and Lorraine, and even Catherine herself. Fouqueray, *Histoire de la Compagnie de Jésus*, I, 244-53. The approval was not registered by the Parlement of Paris until February 1562, and acceptance was under the title of "The Society of the College of Clermont." *MHSJ*, VIII, 805-807.

45. Pastor, *History of the Popes*, XVI, 92.
46. *Ibid.*, 93-94.

side, but forbade them within the walled cities and towns. But Catherine's vision of peace served only to enrage the militant Catholics, and the parlements balked at registering the edict.[47] Widespread street fighting in Paris was narrowly averted. Lainez had warned Catherine against toleration in solemn language: "A kingdom divided against itself will be destroyed."[48]

Against this background, the court seems suddenly to have reconsidered the complexities of toleration. Catherine somehow seized upon the idea of another colloquy. Her intentions, as so often, are a bit obscure. Beza first wrote Calvin of a second colloquy on January 18, indicating that it purposed some accommodation on the religious terrain and was possibly an alternative to toleration.[49] For Chantonnay, it was simply another device to delay the French prelates' attendance at Trent.[50]

The various reasons are all part of the same problem. Catherine was desperate and beginning to grasp at straws. The Catholics would not accept the way of toleration; the Calvinists would not accept the way of Trent, and neither would accept each other. A colloquy, it would appear, had simply become the thing to do when in doubt. The new colloquy was really an anticlimax.

For this reason the Colloquy of Saint-Germain need not be treated with the same concern as Poissy. The conferences took place between January 27 and February 11, under the anxious royal eye at the château at Saint-Germain, in the Queen's own room. Catherine still had an adequate supply of partisans from the two confessions, and on January 27, 1562,

47. For some particulars, see *Condé*, II, 606-612; *HE*, I, 692; Beza, *Correspondance*, IV, 65, n. 2.
48. *MHSJ*, VIII, 782.
49. Beza, *Correspondance*, IV, 25.
50. *Condé*, II, 22.

they convened for the initial meeting. There was a considerable company. Present were the Queen Mother and the King, the King and Queen of Navarre,[51] the cardinals of Ferrara, Bourbon, Châtillon, and Tournon, Coligny, the bishops of Valence and Séez, the Privy Council, and the twelve presidents of the parlements who had recently assisted with the Edict of January. Among the Reformed theologians were Beza, Marlorat, François Pérussel (or La Rivière), a former Franciscan now attached to Condé, and Arnaud-Guillaume Barbaste, described by Beza as a "good and whole man," a chaplain of Jeanne d'Albret.[52] Among the Catholics were Jean Maillard, dean of the faculty of the Sorbonne, and a host of names from Poissy: d'Espence, Salignac, Bouteiller, Antoine de Mouchy,[53] Vigor, Pelletier, Lainez, and Angelo Giustiniani, and in addition, Jean de Hans, a monk and stormy preacher, and Pierre Picherel, a scholar whose theological works had been censured by the Sorbonne.[54] The large proportion of liberals and heterodox in the Catholic party favored a profitable dialogue.

After a few faint words from the King, l'Hospital delivered the opening oration. He observed that pending "a free and legitimate General Council" it had seemed proper to the government and the deputies of the parlements to organize such a conference. After a fresh call for a conciliatory spirit, he itemized the agenda. They were to consider images, the administration of baptism, the Eucharist, the Mass, the imposition of hands and ministerial vocations, and, if there

---

51. The estrangement was apparently not yet complete, though Anthony was now out of sympathy with such arrangements about court. He now felt such discussions should be held at Trent. *Archives curieuses*, ed. Cimber and Danjou, VI, 34.

52. Beza, *Correspondance*, IV, 30, III, 204, n. 15.

53. Antoine de Mouchy, or Demochares, the Latinized form of his name. See Feret, *La faculté*, I, 239, II, 51-55.

54. *HE*, I, 692, n. 13. Languet, *Arcana seculi*, II, 197, speaks of the first three and Picherel as "brilliant and learned men."

seemed hope of accord, doctrine. These were obviously more than disciplinary matters. L'Hospital wanted them to discover why the ministers remained separated from the Church and, above all, to see what the usages of the primitive Church were, in order to find some means to effect a good union, "with the approval of the Holy Father."[55] As it turned out, the collocutors did not get beyond the first item of this ambitious program: images.

Reformation attitudes on this subject may not be as familiar as the theological questions that formed the basis of the earlier discussions. The catacombs were "the cradle of Christian art," which was born in cemeteries, as an expression of hope. Nevertheless, the early Church inherited the Jewish exegesis of the Second Commandment and was generally hostile to religious art. This was no doubt reinforced by the real dangers of idolatry in an age when the pagan cults were practiced side by side with the Christian. By the time of Constantine the situation was changing, and the differences in opinion finally led to the iconoclasm controversy of the eighth and ninth centuries. Iconoclasm was generally foreign to the West, where the example of Gregory the Great and Bernard of Clairvaux reinforced the general acceptance of Christian art. As we approach the Reformation, doctrine and piety become increasingly mediated through sense experi-

55. B.N., MS. Moreau 740, fol. 46r°; B.N., Fonds Dupuy 309, fol. 25. As regards the acquiescence toward Rome, Este's reluctance to be present was overcome by Catherine's assurances that the record would be submitted to the Pope. See Hyppolite Este, *Négociations, ou lettres d'affaires ecclésiastiques, et politiques. Escrittes au Pie IV, et au cardinal depuis saint Borromée, par Hyppolite d'Est, cardinal de Ferrare, légat en France au commencement de guerres civiles*, tr. J. Baudoin (Paris, 1650), p. 17. Among the major sources for the Colloquy of Saint Germain are the summary in Este, *Négociations*, pp. 48-58; the *HE*, I, 692-717 (though this account is somewhat disjointed); Theodore Beza, *Tractationum theologicarum* (3 vols. in 1, 2nd ed., Geneva, 1582), II, 356-363; résumé of d'Espence (another "Discours") in *Procès-verbaux*, A.N., G[8]* 589[a], G[8]* 589[b]; and B.N., Fonds Français 5812; and an anonymous Catholic "Relation" in B.N., MS Moreau 740, fols. 46-56. There is a short but scholarly study, with citations to the sources, in Valois, "Conciliation," pp. 264-275.

ence—at best, instructive and inspiring, at worst, a banal overfamiliarization with the holy. And Protestants, especially the Reformed variety, were inclined to see the worst in religious art. Andreas Carlstadt anticipated the liturgical radicalism of Ulrich Zwingli, who developed a systematic attack upon it. So successful was Zwingli that not a single pre-Reformation statue survived in Zurich, and hardly a tenth of its painting has been preserved.[56] Zwingli's strictures found their echo in Calvin, and Calvin now found his echo in Beza, at Saint-Germain-en-Laye, on January 28, 1562.

Beza opened the debate with an address of two hours. He informed the company that the whole matter of images, with the consequent idolatry, was a key reason why he and many others had left the Roman Catholic communion. To images and the related incensing, prostrating, and other originally pagan rites, he opposed the absolute proscription of the Decalogue. It was "absurd" to render an invisible being visible. He maintained that images were unknown in the first five centuries of Christianity. Beza rejected the authority of the Empress Irene's Second Council of Nicaea (787), which upheld images and condemned iconoclasm, preferring Charlemagne's Synod of Frankfurt (794), which impugned the authority of the former. Beza also rejected any distinction between adoration of God and veneration of images, observing that any supernatural power attributed to icons by the faithful prevented their raising themselves up toward the real seat of the supernatural. He supported his case particularly with the Old Testament, the unanimous condemnation of icons at the Synod of Elvira, the example of St. Epiphanius, several passages from Augustine, and, less appropriately,

56. For some of these thoughts, see Walter Lowrie, *Art in the Early Church* (New York: Pantheon, 1947), esp. p. 39, for the reference to the catacombs; Charles Garside, Jr., *Zwingli and the Arts* (New Haven, Conn.: Yale University Press, 1966), pp. 90-91, 93, 80, n. 14, though I think the author exaggerates Erasmus' antinomy between the external and the internal, e.g., pp. 36-37, 94; and Calvin's *Institutes*, I, xi.

Gregory the Great.[57] Beza's lengthy address seems to have been enough to constitute the day's work.

The Catholic rejoinder was not delivered until January 31, in order to allow a few days to verify Beza's citations. The principal speakers were Pelletier, of the College of Navarre, and Lainez. A distinction was made between the representation and the thing represented, and the paintings found in the catacombs were cited for proof of images in the early Church. They sought to reestablish the authority of the Second Council of Nicaea and to clarify the disputed text of Gregory the Great.[58] Their arguments were basically traditional.

But the Catholics presented far from a united front. The unorthodox theologian Salignac spoke and came closer to seconding Beza than supporting his own colleagues.[59] Tournon was so disturbed that he left during Salignac's discourse, under pretext of the heat.[60] Beza seems to have got in the last word for the day, denouncing images as a violation of the Decalogue and supplicating Catherine not to tolerate such idolatry. In the sixteenth century this would not be con-

57. *HE*, I, 696-714; Beza, *Correspondance*, IV, 30-31; Este, *Négociations*, pp. 49-50; Geisendorf, *Théodore de Bèze*, p. 187. For Calvin and Empress Irene, see *Institutes*, I, xi, 14; for something on the Synod of Elvira (c. 305) and Epiphanius, see Lowrie, *Art in the Early Church*, pp. 29, 34. The Catholics criticized Beza for employing Gregory the Great. What was at stake were several of Gregory's letters to Serenus, bishop of Marseilles, including his much-quoted "Pictures are used in the church, in order that those who are ignorant of letters may by merely looking at the walls read there what they are unable to read in books." Lowrie, *Art in the Early Church*, p. 36. See Calvin, *Institutes*, I, xi, 5, for more particulars. Beza's appeal to the fathers brought a reproach from Calvin. Beza, *Correspondance*, IV, 48, 68.

58. Este, *Négociations*, pp. 50-55; Valois, "conciliation," p. 268; *HE*, I, 787, 795. On the catacombs, see Joseph Wilpert, *Die Malereien der Katakomben Roms* (Freiburg, 1903). On Jean Pelletier, sometimes known as Pierre, see Beza, *Correspondance*, IV, 32, n. 11; Natalie Zemon Davis, "Peletier and Beza Part Company," *Studies in the Renaissance*, XI (1964), 192, n. 15.

59. Beza, *Correspondance*, IV, 30. Salignac had written Calvin an adulatory letter only the month before and became a Protestant within a few years. Calvin, *Opera*, XIX, 165-166; Haag, 1st ed., IX, 113-14.

60. Beza, *Correspondance*, IV, 30.

sidered inconsonant with the Huguenot's own recent appeals
for toleration.

The next day, February 1, they returned to the field.
Giustiniani, of Este's train, spoke, and "not without abil-
ity."[61] He argued that the prohibition of the Decalogue
applied only to the Old Testament, when it would have been
premature to represent the saints, as they had not yet tasted
the joys of paradise. Abuses in practice did not justify
prohibition in principle. Right preaching could dissipate any
errors. And he saw nothing scandalous in representing God
the Father, whom the prophet called "the Venerable One,"
under the aspect of an old man, the hair of whose head was
like "pure wool."[62]

But, as before, the divisions among the Catholic collocutors
served to undermine their own arguments. D'Espence spoke
next. Though he began by showing how the early Christians
rendered homage to the Cross, he gave considerable support
to Beza's interpretation of the Second Commandment. Like
Beza, he rejected the Second Council of Nicaea, the work of
Irene, "one of the most depraved women ever anointed." But
d'Espence concluded by accepting images provisionally. Beza
commented: "He copiously defended our cause, but he had
much less nerve than Salignac."[63] No doubt Beza enjoyed
hearing his cause defended by Catholics. Jean de Hans, a
popular Franciscan preacher, presented traditional arguments, announcing that he was "the least" of the company
assembled there.[64] That concluded the session.

The radical element received added support the following
day, February 2. Bouteiller, one of the Catholic five in the
petit colloque, adopted the strict interpretation of the Deca-

61. As Geisendorf, *Théodore de Bèze*, p. 188, put it.

62. Dan. 7: 9; B.N., MS. Moreau 740, fol. 52v°; Valois, "Conciliation," 269;
Beza, *Correspondance*, IV, 30.

63. Beza, *Correspondance*, IV, 31. For d'Espence, B.N., MSS. Moreau 740, fols.
54r°-55v°; *HE*, I, 710-711.

64. B.N., MS. Moreau 740, fol. 55r°.

logue. He indicated, like Beza, that he could not in good conscience tolerate images. Montluc spoke in the same way, though he would not oppose the submission of the matter to the general council.[65] A moment of relief was afforded when one of the doctors, Mouchy, tried to defend images by the curious argument that they had been honored in Paris at the time of Denis, the pseudo-Areopagite, as evidenced by the stained glass windows of St. Benedict. This anachronism provoked laughter, and Beza quipped that "his argument was of glass."[66] More sober was the argument of the liberal, Pierre Picherel. While he was repulsed by the abuses associated with images, he shrank from calling for their prohibition. If the clergy would properly instruct the faithful, images could be of positive service. Taking a page from Gregory the Great, he said that they could pass for "the books of the ignorant."[67]

By this time Catherine had witnessed enough of the *odium theologorum*. The conference seemed as far from agreement as ever, and only the first item of the agenda had been discussed. She again recommended conciliation, but ordered the various parties to submit their conclusions in writing.[68] The reports were offered at court on February 11.

The Catholics divided into two schools, following the lines drawn in the colloquy. The majority report upheld images in principle, but condemned certain practices, such as representing the saints in a way that could be considered immodest or the depicting of apocryphal miracles.[69] The minority report was drawn up by d'Espence, Salignac, Bouteiller, Montluc,

65. Santa Croce assigned this speech to February 4. *Archives curieuses*, ed. Cimber and Danjou, VI, 34.

66. *HE*, I, 693. But Beza's own historical knowledge could be no less faulty. Beza, *Correspondance*, IV, 67-68, and n. 3.

67. Petri Picherelli, *Opustula theologica* (Lyons, 1629), pp. 217 ff.; Valois, "Conciliation," p. 271.

68. Beza, *Correspondance,* IV, 52.

69. *Collection des procès-verbaux,* ed. Duranthon, I, 38-40.

and Picherel. This generally reproved the cult of images, recommending that the Cross alone should surmount the altars and that images be removed from the interior of churches, so that the people might neither "adore them, salute them, kiss them, adorn them with flowers, clothe them with finery, or burn candles before them." They also denounced the carrying of statues in processions and the depicting, among other things, of the Holy Trinity.[70] Este was obviously made uncomfortable by their report, but indicated he would make an effort to send a copy to Rome.[71] If Este was discomforted, d'Espence, who tendered the report, again suffered the martyrdom of the moderate: the next year he was "taken apart" by the Sorbonne for his role in the conferences. Lorraine mediated, and d'Espence made an indirect retraction.[72] Thereafter, d'Espence would be little more in the public eye. His kind of moderation was increasingly precarious—and outmoded.

The Calvinist report, given by Beza, was a long disquisition reviewing the various arguments on images. Simply put, it represented a request for the abolition of the cult of images, including the Cross. He dismissed the tradition that Helena, the mother of Constantine, had found "the true cross"; he expressed indignation over a certain hymn that salutes the Cross, "O crux, ave spes unica," as a detraction from the uniqueness of our only hope, Jesus Christ. As a token of goodwill, however, the Calvinists would accept the minority report of the liberals, qualified by the exclusion of the

70. *Ibid.*, 37-38; *HE*, I, 694-695; Picherelli, *Opustula theologica*, pp. 237-239. There are minor variations of detail. Feret, *La faculté*, I, 238, holds that only d'Espence and Bouteiller approved the minority report, and d'Espence himself says it was delivered on February 7 and indicates that it gained greater concurrence. See d'Espence's memorandum or *Discours* on this conference. A.N., G^8*589^a, fol. 83.

71. Este, *Négociations*, p. 60.

72. Feret, *La faculté* I, 239, II, 53. D'Espence died in 1571 and was buried in the Church of St. Cosmos, Paris. Jean Baptist Louis Crevier, *Histoire de l'Université de Paris* (7 vols., Paris, 1761), VI, 140-143.

Cross. Nothing came of this concession.[73] In general, the Huguenot would find God revealed only in the Bible, instead of in icons. Apart from the Bible, the sensible and the sacred were separate.

Even the Queen was now tiring of her well intentioned designs. She wrote Rennes, deploring "the hardness and obstinacy of both sides, who have combated lest they be conquered, rather than dispute and confer in order to submit to truth and reason."[74] On February 11 she ordered the collocutors to separate, asking them to submit their opinions on the other articles in writing, in order that the King might send them to Rome or to Trent.[75]

This was one consequence of the colloquy: Catherine's disenchantment with theological disputes induced her finally to fall in with Trent. A few days after the close of the colloquy, she issued the definitive order for the bishops to take the road to Trent.[76] A cycle was complete: the national council had failed; the general council was the only alternative. Trent was Catherine's last resort.

But Trent offered no resort to the Huguenots. There were last-minute efforts to persuade the Calvinists to bow to the council. Catherine hoped they would do so, and the now quixotic Lainez was hounding them all the way "to their beds," assuring them that the council would not be the tool of the Pope.[77] Though Beza had earlier indicated that he was prepared to brave a legitimate council, it was soon clear that this did not mean the Council of Trent. The Huguenots could

73. *HE*, I, 713-716; *Collection des procès-verbaux*, ed. Duranthon, I, 37.

74. *Lettres de Catherine de Médicis*, I, 276.

75. *Ibid.*, IV, 52; Valois, "Conciliation," p. 273.

76. Catherine to Rennes, Feb. 16, 1561, *Lettres de Catherine de Médicis*, I, 276. Only a month earlier Este had written with a pride tempered by ingenuousness: "All my rhetoric has not yet been able to make her change her will." Este, *Négociations*, p. 17.

77. *HE*, I, 716. At the same time Este inspired abortive hopes for English and German representation. Este, *Négociations*, p. 78.

not accept a council convoked by the Pope, presided over by the Pope or his party, and not governed by the principle of *sola scriptura.*[78] Recent experience had shown that these criteria were now impossible: reunion had become little more than a reverie. If the two sides could not agree in France, they could not, *a fortiori*, agree at Trent.

There was another consequence of the second colloquy, and one not dissimilar to that of Poissy. There was an immediate rash of iconoclasm throughout the realm. The emboldened Huguenots, emancipated by the Edict of January and reinforced by what they interpreted as a rejection of images by the Sorbonne and the bishops, pillaged churches and smashed images almost at will.[79] They presumed the permission of the King:

> Under you, sire, the Word of God has been publicly preached and heard, and the sacraments administered and received according to the true institution of Jesus Christ. Under you, the means to serve God in all purity and integrity has been once more deliberated, decreed and concluded, to chase out and extirpate the idolatry which, in the past, was too often commanded in this your kingdom. And nothing has been found more expedient than to remove the images and idols which are in the temples, indeed, a great abomination.[80]

This was, of course, to interpret the intent of the crown rather broadly.[81]

The Colloquy of Saint-Germain was not completely without consequence. We know that the majority report of the Catholics influenced the Tridentine formulation of the fol-

78. *HE*, I, pp. 716-720; Beza, *Correspondance*, IV, 52. It should be pointed out that it may well have been at this time that Calvin wrote the *Mémoire sur le concile*. See Beza, *Correspondance*, IV, 50, n. 5, and Chapter II, above. On these matters, see also Evennett, *Lorraine*, pp. 448-452, who is less than accurate in the one assertion that Rome accepted all the conditions of the Huguenots.

79. See Claude de Sainctes, *Les pillages et ruynes notables des églises de France, et en special du saccagement fait en ceste presente année 1562*, in *Archives curieuses*, ed. Cimber and Danjou, IV, 359-400.

80. From an unnamed remonstrance to the King, *ibid.*, IV, 379.

81. Jedin, *CC*, p. 151.

lowing year, which upheld images in principle, but sought to
eradicate the lascivious and the apocryphal. The Tridentine
spirit and its partisans, indeed, ushered in a new age in
religious art. Art became apologetics. It was enlisted in the
service of the polemics of the Reformation;[82] it was also put
on the defensive. Calvinists virtually denied the validity of
religious art; Catholics wanted it above reproach—faithful to
the letter of the sacred text. This made for self-consciousness
and constricted the imagination. Who today does not pity
Michelangelo when a connoisseur of orthodoxy like Gilio da
Fabriano could complain of *The Last Judgment*, probably
the most controversial painting of the period, that angels
should be represented with wings, that some of the figures
have windblown draperies though on Judgment Day wind
and storm shall cease, or that those trumpeting angels are
shown together though it is written that they are to be sent
to the four corners of the earth?[83] The spontaneity that is
indispensable for the purest expressions of the soul could not
survive such surveillance. As Émile Mâle put it so nostalgi-
cally, thus ended a "long tradition of legends, poetry and
dreams."[84] There would be few more such dreams until men
like Rouault and Shart.

The criticisms of the nudity in *The Last Judgment* are well
known. Vasari stated, and it has generally been thought, that
Paul IV, the putative personification of the Counter-Reformation, ordered the *imbraghettamento* (the covering of the
nudes), but this view has been definitely disproved. It is
curious that Paul actually extended more goodwill to
Michelangelo than his successor, Pius IV. And it was not
under the tyrannical Paul but under the prudent Pius that the

82. Émile Mâle, *L'art religieux après le Concile de Trente* (Paris, 1932), pp.
22-23.

83. For this and related matters, see Sir Anthony Blunt, *Artistic Theory in
Italy, 1450-1600* (Oxford, at the Clarendon Press, 1940), pp. 112-113. Federico
Zeri, *Pittura e Controriforma* (Turin, 1957), pp. 24 ff.

84. *L'art religieux de la fin du moyen âge en France* (4th ed., Paris: A. Colin,
1931), p. 483.

imbraghettamento was ordered,[85] symbolic proof of one of the incidental arguments of this book.

What is more fundamental, the Colloquy of Saint-Germain illustrates the larger failure to integrate Catholic substance and Protestant principle, iconophile and iconophobe, the tendency to objectification and its constructive and salutary criticism. No balance was found between the familiar and the alien, immanence and transcendence, and perhaps in some sense this exposed posterity to the twin perils of aestheticism and silence.

The silence in 1562 was of short duration: the quarrels of the theologians were about to be resolved by the arms of the princes. This was the final alternative.

It has been said that the Catholic party was prepared to go to war if Catherine put the Reformed faith on the same footing as Roman Catholicism.[86] This she had already done. Catherine offset the "feudal Triumvirate" of Guise, Montmorency, and St. André with a "Royal Triumvirate" of l'Hospital, Coligny, and Beza.[87] In October 1561 the Guises and their adherents had left the court, where Calvinism was the "reigning fashion."[88] Their retirement took place under threatening circumstances. Though the Duke of Guise, chief of the Triumvirate, would have it that he talked of nothing but "dogs and hawks,"[89] the very day he left court he sent a message to the Duke of Württemberg, militant Lutheran but old companion in arms from the Italian wars, with whom he had been in communication. He enclosed a copy of Lorraine's oration of September 16, so devoid of any mention of transubstantiation, and noted that there was considerable

85. Romeo de Maio, "Michelangelo e Paolo IV," in *Reformata Reformanda*, ed. Iserloh and Repgen, I, 640-641, 656; Pastor, *History of the Popes*, XII, 619.
86. Romier, *C&H* p. 281.
87. As put by Héritier, *Catherine de Medici*, p. 174.
88. Van Dyke, *Catherine de Médicis*, I, 222.
89. Guise to the Constable, quoted *ibid.*, I, 224. I cannot find this elsewhere. It should be noted that the Constable himself was one of the Triumvirate.

sentiment in France in favor of the Confession of Augsburg. He also mentioned that the prelates had been obliged to reject a eucharistic formula that came out of the final conferences at Saint-Germain, adding rather nonchalantly that this had been proposed by one of the Genevans.[90] Guise was obviously out to build up good relations with Lutheranism, perhaps to protect his flank.

This was the prelude to a remarkable and controversial interview between the Guises and the Duke of Württemberg at Saverne, in Alsace, in February 1562. The highlight of the meeting was a conference between Lorraine and Johann Brenz, a militant Lutheran theologian and a veteran of Marburg in 1529 and Trent in 1552. Therein Lorraine despaired of both the Calvinists and the Council of Trent and pledged instead a covert personal preference for the Confession of Augsburg.[91] No doubt Lorraine exaggerated and even dissimulated at Saverne in order to ingratiate himself with the Lutherans, but he apparently considered these base means justified by an irenical end. He contemplated some kind of ecumenical grand design for an international colloquy in Germany as a counterweight to Trent,[92] but this was a visionary scheme that bore no fruit.

Several weeks after Saverne, on March 1, the Duke of Guise

90. Duke of Guise to the Duke of Württemberg, Oct., 1561, *BSHPF*, XXIV, 78.

91. The only real record of the meeting is that published by A. Muntz, "Entrevue du duc Christophe de Wurtemberg avec les Guise, à Saverne, peu de jours avant la massacre de Vassy," *BSHPF*, IV (1855), esp. 191-193. This came at a time, of course, when the Huguenots as well as the Catholics were preparing for war. Beza, *Correspondance*, IV, 40, n. 22, 66, n. 15. Cf. views of Bernhard Kugler, *Christoph*, II, 339; Evennett, *Lorraine*, pp. 429-439. See also Beza, *Correspondance*, IV, 61, n. 2; De Thou, *Histoire universelle*, III, 128.

92. For some particulars, see *Die Römische Kurie*, ed. Šusta, II, 437-438; *BSHPF*, XXIV, 211; Evennett, *Lorraine*, pp. 455-458. It should be mentioned that as late as 1563 the Duke of Württemberg encouraged the Emperor to call an ecumenical general council the objective of which was reunion. Gustave Baguenault de Puchesse, "Le duc de Wurtemberg, les Guises et Catherine de Médicis (1561-63)," *Bulletin philologique et historique du Comité des Travaux Historiques et Scientifiques* (1915), p. 197.

was returning to Paris from his residence in Joinville. At Vassy, a small town on his lands, he came upon a congregation of Huguenots holding a service within the walls. In such a situation, the assembly was illegal. There was an altercation, and a terrible slaughter of Huguenots took place in which some sixty were killed. This is the famous, or infamous, Massacre of Vassy, "the Sarajevo of the Civil Wars."[93] The Reformed, rallied by Condé, took up arms, and Mars reigned in France for thirty years.

Catherine's tenuous and tortuous policy of peace was left in ruins—as would be much of France. Frenchmen generally were no more willing to tolerate than to conciliate. They had first to be schooled by war.

93. Evennett, *Lorraine*, p. 446.

VIII / The Case of the Cardinal of Lorraine

Charles Lorrain, le cardinal
Incestueux, abominable
S'est donné corps et âme au diable
Si, tant qu'il vivra, ne fait mal.
Anonymous Huguenot[1]

Combien que de toute virtu
Soit heuresement revistu
Ce prince tant doulx & amyable:
Si est il principalement
Orné d'un bon entendement
Et d'une prudence admirable.
Soeur Anne de Marguets[2]

In a whimsical scene of Christopher Marlowe's *Dr. Faustus,* the Pope and the cardinal of Lorraine enter the banquet hall only to have an invisible Faustus snatch away their dinners and, in a truly spectacular exit, scatter the hall with fireworks.[3] The cardinal of Lorraine has been surrounded by fireworks for 400 years. This is an effort to give him some peace at last.

Lorraine has borne a large share of the onus for the failure of the colloquy. This is because of the charge that he negotiated in bad faith, specifically in introducing the ostensibly alien subject of Lutheranism into a Calvinist-Catholic dialogue. The question is subject to two general lines of

1. *Recueil de poésies Calvinistes (1550-66)* ed. Prosper Tarbé (Reims, 1866), p. 30.
2. Sister Mary Hilarine Seiler, *Anne de Marquets, Poétesse religieuse du XVIe siècle* (Washington, D.C.: Catholic University of America, 1931), pp. 34-35.
3. *Marlowe's Doctor Faustus*, ed. W.W. Greg (Oxford: Clarendon Press, 1950), pp. 226-231.

thought: the one, that Lorraine introduced the matter of Lutheranism in good faith as a common ground for agreement, thereby obviating the need for the Huguenots to submit to completely Roman terms; the other, to the contrary, that Lorraine's injection of Lutheranism was a masterstroke of deceit, a ruse conspired to exacerbate the Evangelical-Reformed schism, a scheme to isolate the Huguenots and insulate the Gallican Church against friction with Lutheran Germany in the impending conflagration—in a few words, an effort to divide, and perhaps to conquer. It is both a critical and a complex matter for one can find evidence to support either interpretation.

The element of personality has doubtlessly played its role in particular interpretations. To the repressed Huguenot, Lorraine was Grand Inquisitor; to some of the older houses of France, an all too ambitious parvenu. Doubtless the Guises, as head of the party of the French Counter-Reformation, were fated to suffer some of their own slings and arrows at the hands of modern historiography. But more enlightened ages are not necessarily more discriminating, and perhaps there has been a tendency to read the Guises backward, roll them into one, and equate the generation of the "King of Paris" and that of the cardinal of Lorraine—for which there seems to be precedent in Marlowe himself in *The Massacre of Paris*.[4] The logic of the Huguenots' position prevented their attacking the crown, and so Lorraine served as their whipping boy. Moreover, the later question of Lorraine's exaggeration and even mendacity at the conference of Saverne must be understood against the background of his disillusionment with the failure of Poissy and the fact that all sides were then preparing for war. The maxim *Falsus in uno, falsus in*

4. *Dido Queen of Carthage and the Massacre at Paris*, ed. H.J. Oliver (London: Methuen and Co., 1968), p. 93.

omnibus has been applied too gratuitously. Lorraine was not at Vassy, and it is now held that the massacre there was not premeditated by the Guises.[5] In sum, Lorraine and Poissy are best understood by Lorraine at Poissy.

Lorraine has not generally had a good press. Pierre Bayle's judgment that Lorraine's conduct at Poissy was a case of "pure Machiavellianism"[6] was the usual one, with few exceptions, right up until the twentieth century. This found support in the published sources, generally written in a polemical spirit, the general reputation of the Guises for subterfuge and intolerance and, ironically, even by some Roman Catholics, in an age when extremism in defense of

5. Though some have held that Lorraine was at Vassy (e.g., Geisendorf, *Théodore de Bèze* p. 102, and even the editors of Beza, *Correspondance*, IV, 66, n. 10), a Protestant source clarifies that this was his brother, the cardinal of Guise. *BSHPF*, XXIV, 218. See also *BSHPF*, XXIV, 212 and Evennett, *Lorraine*, pp. 456-457. On the question of premeditation at Vassy, see Noël Valois, "Vassy," *Annuaire-bulletin de la Société de l'Histoire de France* (1913), 189 ff; Romier, *C&H*, 320-321. Geisendorf, *Théodore de Bèze*, p. 193, n. 1; Evennett, *Lorraine*, p. 439. The editors of Beza (*Correspondance*, IV, 61, n. 3, 72, n. 2, 257, n. 3) are ambiguous. It should be noted that well after Vassy Lorraine vigorously pursued various irenical projects. Later, at Trent in 1562-1563, he was the acknowledged leader of the rebellious ultramontane party, and he was also probably the foremost advocate of reunion with Protestants. He was so outspoken that at one point an exasperated papal legate said he sounded "like the Lutherans." Fra Paolo Sarpi, *The Historie of the Councel of Trent*, tr. Nathaniel Brent (London, 1676), p. 658; see also Jedin, *CC*, p. 105; *Instructions*, ed. Dupuy, pp. 335-340. With irenicism failing and circumstances adverse, he ultimately followed the lead of the Emperor and the directive of Catherine in making his peace with the Pope. For this very complicated and much misunderstood story, see Sarpi, *Historie*, p. 666; *Archives curieuses*, ed. Cimber and Danjou, VI, 146-147; Jedin, *CT*, II, 489; Jedin, *CC*, pp. 90-93; and Jedin, *Krisis und Wendepunkt des Trienter Konzils (1562-63). Die Neuendeckten Geheimberichte des Bischofs Gualterio von Viterbo an den heiligen Karl Borromaus* (Würtburg, 1941), pp. 81-93. The point to be stressed is that Lorraine was among the last to surrender the irenical ideal. One reason the French finally acceded to papal policy was to prevent the Pope from becoming completely dependent upon Spain. The imperial ambassador complained: "Almost all the theologians [at Trent] are from Spain, and they ignore completely the situation of the Church outside their country." Constant, *Concession*, I, 306. See Constancio Gutiérrez, *Españoles en Trento* (Valladolid, 1951), esp. pp. 1038-1042.

6. *Dictionaire historique et critique* (5th ed., 4 vols., Amsterdam, 1740), III, 161. Again, Jules Michelet, *Histoire de France* (19 vols., Paris, 1889-1891), XI, 214, 255, spoke of Lorraine as a "bad angel and demon."

the faith could be considered a matter for congratulations.[7] The twentieth century has seen the airing and publication of several sources[8] that have given new information on the old question, issuing in 1930 in the study of the late H. Outram Evennett of Trinity College, Cambridge, the first full-scale and systematic effort to rehabilitate the cardinal of Lorraine, but especially his role at Poissy.[9] Evennett's cardinal was mercurial and vain, but he was a genuine theological liberal and one who acted in good faith at Poissy. This view was opposed, however, rather than followed up, in a subsequent biography of Theodore Beza, chief spokesman for the Reformed at Poissy, by the late Paul F. Geisendorf[10] of Geneva who, despite a certain ambiguity, restated the old view. This was reinforced by an article in 1961 of the late Philippe de Félice, marking the fourth centenary of Poissy.[11] Thus, after 400 years of fireworks, the case of the cardinal of Lorraine still remains open: is Lorraine guilty or not guilty of perfidy at the colloquy?

The question must be broken into two parts: the one treats of Lutheran confessions; the other, Lutherans themselves. The first concerns Lorraine's demand of September 24, the third session of the colloquy, that the Huguenots subscribe to a Lutheran article or articles on the critical question of the Eucharist as a condition for the continuance of the colloquy; the second concerns an invitation to the German Lutherans

7. For example, the Spanish ambassador, Chantonnary. See his letter to Philip of Sept. 17, 1561, A.N., K 1494, No. 103; see also J.B. Bossuet, *Histoire des variations des églises protestantes* (2 vols., Paris, 1688), II, 74.

8. The *Diario* and d'Espence's *Discours*.

9. *Lorraine.* See also H. Outram Evennett, "The Cardinal of Lorraine and the Colloquy of Poissy," *Cambridge Historical Journal*, II (1927), 133-150. It would seem that Evennett's careful delineation of Lorraine's character reduces the necessity of reconsidering the element of personality and facilitates the concentration here upon the lingering textual problems. Let it simply be emphasized that Lorraine's reputation is largely a consequence of Reformation polemics.

10. Geisendorf, *Théodore de Bèze*, pp. 156-157.

11. "Le Colloque de Poissy," *BSHPF*, CVII (1961), 133-145; see also M. Mazauric, "À propos du Colloque de Poissy," *ibid.*, 222.

to send a delegation of their theologians to the colloquy. As regards the latter, there are recent indications of agreement that, though Lorraine may have favored the coming of the Germans, he did not himself invite them.[12] These are, of course, two different things. This facilitates concentration on the first point.

The matter of the Lutheran confession itself also resolves into two parts: first, did Lorraine use this perfidiously; second, what confession did he use? The points are related because there is a variety of *Augustanae*, and Calvin himself had subscribed to one version on several occasions.[13] At the same time, it seems apparent that Lorraine was basically a liberal in theology[14] and that he was possessed of a genuine taste for the Confession of Augsburg.[15]

The fact is that the prevailing mood of the court was one of theological experimentation and revisionism, and it was buzzing with talk of the Confession of Augsburg.[16] This

12. Beza, *Correspondance*, III, 198, n. 32, 150, n. 17, 131, n. 7; Kugler, *Christoph*, II, 304-306; Evennett, *Lorraine*, pp. 131-132.

13. The *Variata*. See Alain Dufour, "Deux lettres oubliées de Calvin à J. Andreae (1556-1558)," *BHR*, XXIV (1962), 378-379.

14. See Evennett, *Lorraine, passim*, and among some other particulars it is well to note that he had unorthodox views on such things as, for example, the question of icons. Jean Baptiste Louis Crevier, *Histoire de l'Université de Paris, depuis son origines jusqu'en l'année 1600* (7 vols., Paris, 1761), IV, 143. For more on Lorraine's theological liberalism, including strident conciliarism, see *Instructions*, ed. Dupuy, pp. 554-555; *Die Römische Kurie*, ed. Šusta, II, 437-438; *Suriano, Despatches,* p. 45; Throckmorton to Elizabeth, *CSP: Foreign*, June 23, 1561, No. 265(4); Francis Walsingham to Lord Burghley, *CSP: Foreign*, June 21, 1571, No. 1813; *Beiträge*, ed. Döllinger, I, 349, Jedin, *Krisis*, p. 42. Lorraine had long been in contact with Guillaume Postel and his *De orbis terrae concordiae.* Bouwsma, *Postel*, pp. 226, 239. Regarding the last, I have come upon a curious and apparently long-obscure tract of Postel written in 1561 expressly for Poissy: *Moyen proposé pour mettre en paix les Huguenots avec les Catholiques.* This is in the Bibliothèque Nationale, Moreau MS. 740, fols. 70-83, along with some other material pertinent to the colloquy. Perhaps this tract was in the hands of Lorraine at Poissy. We do know that Postel addressed Lorraine not long before the colloquy; see Bouwsma, *Postel*, p. 229, n. 53.

15. Beza, *Correspondance*, III, 169, n. 25.

16. For example, see *ibid.*, 144; De Thou, *Histoire universelle*, III, 177; and Romier, *C&H*, p. 205.

would not seem to make its employment at the colloquy—
which was the child of the court rather than the Church—
either extraordinary or pernicious, and even if the latter,
would make it difficult to situate the responsibility therefore
upon the shoulders of a single man. It is well to note,
furthermore, that Lorraine was among the earliest protagonists of the colloquy, that he was in the enterprise at his own
peril, running counter to the great majority of the prelates,
who were intransigently opposed to the very idea of a
colloquy, that in entering debate with the Protestants he had
exceeded his instructions and violated his own solemn
promise, and that he was in the colloquy in spite of the
bishops and presented the ultimatum because of them.[17] He
really had no alternative to the ultimatum, and to make him
assume sole responsibility skirts the entire setting of the
thing. These considerations put Lorraine in a somewhat
better light.

The requirements of the prelates vis-à-vis the Eucharist
cannot be exaggerated. They have been variously specified,
but they took their lead from Lorraine's initial address at the
colloquy and stipulated that the ministers must accept "the
existence of the flesh of the Lord in the Sacrament of the
Altar." That the requirements on the Eucharist sprang from
Lorraine's first oration[18] would seem to be significant, for
his approach here was not only un-Scholastic—lacking in
metaphysical subtleties—but was joined with a scarcely concealed appeal to Lutheranism as a kind of *via media*.[19] And
in eucharistic theology, Wittenberg *was* something of a
middle way between Geneva and Rome. Against this back-

17. Claude de Sainctes, *Responsio F. Claudii de Sainctes Parisien theologi ad
apologiam Theodori Bezae, editam contra examen doctrinae Calvinianae & Bezane
de coena Domini* (Paris, 1567), p. 63; *Diario*, p. 133. Bruslart even felt that
Lorraine was, in a general way, in danger of excommunication. *Condé*, I, 52.
There is no evidence for the opinion of Languet, *Arcana seculi*, III, 144, that
Lorraine was in secret accord with the bishops.
18. *Diario*, p. 124; François, *Tournon*, p. 413.
19. Beza, *Correspondance*, III, 156; *HE*, I, 550.

ground, then, Lorraine's utilization of a Lutheran text can be seen as only a logical extension of his first oration, a means of compliance with the requirements of the prelates, and a reflection and application of the atmosphere at court. No conspiracy thesis is necessary.

Lorraine has, moreover, a formidable battery of witnesses for the defense. Foremost among them is Claude d'Espence, who was first in Lorraine's counsels at Poissy and whose integrity is generally accepted by all. D'Espence disapproved of the "expedient" of introducing a Lutheran text into the colloquy, but maintained that it was done in good faith.[20] Claude de Sainctes, whose tactics annoyed Lorraine and who might have had grounds for resentment, also denied dissimulation.[21] Though the anonymous author of the *Diario* admits that Lorraine may have employed Lutheranism in order to intimidate the ministers, he twice contends that Lorraine's intent was to have the Huguenots accept the Real Presence in order to lead them more easily to transubstantiation.[22] The principal studies favorable to Lorraine are those by Romier and Evennett. The former argues with some force that if Lorraine's objective was to break up the colloquy, all he had to do was take the position of Tournon and oppose it.[23] To quote the pertinent passage from Lorraine's sympathetic biographer: "[The cardinal] had set his heart upon forcing the ministers' adhesion to a formula containing the essence of the Catholic doctrine, and if he chose a Lutheran formula it may have been partly to save them the shame of a complete submission to definitely Roman terms, partly also—no doubt—to emphasize their isolation and play upon their fears."[24] It should be observed

20. D'Espence, *Apologie*, pp. 597-600.
21. De Sainctes, *Responsio*, p. 68.
22. *Diario*, pp. 123, 133-135.
23. Romier, *C&H*, p. 230.
24. Evennett, *Lorraine*, p. 365.

that Evennett does not state his case monocausally, but concedes something to the consternation Lorraine's act was calculated to engender.

Yet the conspiracy thesis is a perennial and unavoidable fact of historiography. How, then, do we account for it? Apart from the nebulous element of personality, the principal remaining argument against Lorraine's sincerity is the charge—be it implicit or explicit—that his Lutheran text embodied the doctrine of Ubiquity. This is the vaulting doctrine, especially associated with the Württemberg theologian Johann Brenz that Christ's body is everywhere. As such, the doctrine was totally alien to the Calvinist spirit and was one that the ministers could *a fortiori* be calculated to reject. This would, then, underscore the case for Lorraine's duplicity. It is my understanding that Ubiquity was not introduced into the dialogue. The deductive argument for this is simply that, since Lorraine refrained from introducing transubstantiation into the colloquy, he would not have introduced Ubiquity. The more compelling inductive argument entails a long and technical analysis of the sources.

The *Histoire ecclésiastique*, of Genevan inspiration and one of the most influential of the sources, recounts that Lorraine presented the ministers with what is identified as Brenz's Confession of Württemberg of 1559. It should be noted, however, that the same source records that Lorraine required that the Huguenots subscribe to only "three or four lines" of the document's five pages—which are of unequal force—without revealing what the pertinent passage was.[25] Peter Martyr, the specialist on the Eucharist and counselor of the Reformed at Poissy, who could be expected to know, tells us that the passage read: "in sacramento adesse corpus Christi realiter vere ac substantialiter atque et exhiberi et sumi."[26]

25. *HE*, I, 587-588.
26. Calvin, *Opera*, XVIII, 767.

This formula would correspond well with the maximum requirement of the bishops, but there is one difficulty: the passage Martyr recites cannot be found in the Confession of Württemberg.[27] Yet it is clear that Lorraine did have a copy of that confession in his possession at the time of the colloquy.[28] There are several possible explanations: first, that Lorraine or Martyr modified the text of the confession; second, that the confession was not introduced into the colloquy; third, as would follow, that another, or perhaps several confessions, were introduced into the colloquy. A scrutiny of the sources shows that the last is the case, that is, there was more than one confession.

The work of Pierre de La Place, the *Commentaires de l'estat,* which is anterior to the *Histoire ecclésiastique* and from which the latter is partially derived, recounts the matter differently. In La Place, Lorraine presents Beza with the Confession of Augsburg and then, almost incidentally, with the confession of some ministers of "Wittenberg [*sic*]" of 1559.[29] It would seem safe to say that the second is the Confession of Württemberg. The editors of the splendid and recently published pertinent volume of the *Correspondance* of Beza are aware of the discrepancy between the two accounts, but prefer to follow that of the *Histoire ecclésiastique,* in saying, or at least implying, that there was only one confession and that this was the Confession of Württemberg. This conclusion is based on the ostensibly sound reason that Beza several times identified it as such.[30] Nevertheless, their argument in this case is weak. Taking their lead from the *Histoire ecclésiastique,*[31] they confuse a *third* confession,[32]

27. This confession was published by Christoph M. Pfaff, *Acta et scripta publica ecclesiae Wirtembergica* (Tübingen, 1720), pp. 340-344. I am grateful to the editors of Beza (III, 168 n. 18), for the reference. See Appendix B.
28. The Duke of Württemberg to the Duke of Guise, July 24, 1561, *BSHPF* XXIV, 76.
29. La Place, *Commentaires,* p. 192.
30. Beza, *Correspondance,* III, 168, n. 18.
31. *HE,* I, 588.
32. See Appendix C. That this was of Lorraine's composition, see also de

which is of Lorraine's own composition, with that of Würt-temberg. Needless to say, Lorraine's own text cannot be found in the Confession of Württemberg either.

There is other evidence that there was more than one confession. In the same letter in which Beza identifies the confession as that of Brenz, chief architect of the Confession of Württemberg, he himself speaks elsewhere of the Confession of Augsburg.[33] This could, of course, have been a mere conventional designation for any Lutheran confession. It is far more persuasive that, in a later speech at the colloquy, he makes reference to his having been asked by Lorraine to sign "the tenth part of an article."[34] But the tenth article of the Confession of Augsburg is just the one that treats of the Lord's Supper.[35] A cursory examination of the Confession of Württemberg will disclose that this could not have had reference to it.[36] Evennett also affirms that there were several confessions, including the Confession of Augsburg and the Confession of Württemberg.[37] In his appendix he publishes a passage, purportedly from the latter, which, he alleges, is the section that Lorraine used.[38] But, as was the

---

Sainctes, *Responsio*, p. 64; d'Espence, *Apologie*, p. 466; Jean Polanco in *MHSJ*, VIII, 756. This is materially different from the opening passage of the Confession of Württemberg that the editors of Beza cite (*Correspondance*, III, 168 n. 18), containing, as it does, the important verbs "esse et existere," from which the ministers shrank. De Sainctes, *Responsio*, pp. 64-65; *HE*, I, 604-605.

33. Beza, *Correspondance*, III, 162-163.

34. La Place, *Commentaires*, p. 195; *HE*, I, 594-595.

35. Appendix A.

36. Owing to its format, for unlike the Confession of Augsburg it is not itemized or otherwise enumerated. See Appendix B.

37. See the long footnote, p. 353, n. 5, in Evennett, *Lorraine*.

38. "De substantia Eucharistiae sentimus et docemus quod verum corpus Christi et verus sanguis ejus in Eucharistia distribuantur, et refutamus eos qui dicunt panem et vinum Eucharistiae esse tantum absentis corporis et sanguinis Christi signa. Credimus etiam omnipotentiam Dei tantam esse, ut possit in Eucharistia substantiam panis et vini vel annihilare vel in corpus et sanguinem Christi mutare." *Ibid.*, p. 499. This is actually from the *Confessio Wirtembergica* of 1552, as earlier set before the Council of Trent. Heinrich Heppe, *Die Bekenntnisschriften der altprotestantischen Kirche Deutschlands* (Cassel, 1855), pp. 514-515. It would be more likely that Lorraine would have used the more current confession of 1559.

case with Martyr and the *Histoire ecclésiastique*, a reading of the Confession of Württemberg again fails to reveal the passage cited. Like others, he apparently did not examine closely the confession itself. The fact is we do not know with certitude exactly what passage Lorraine used. It may be reasonably concluded that the confessions used in the course of the colloquy included those of both Augsburg and Württemberg.

Since Lorraine did somehow apparently introduce the Confession of Württemberg into the colloquy, does this not make a stronger case for his perfidy, that is to say, that he did not undertake this action in good faith? The argument does not follow. For while it is reasonably evident that Lorraine used, among other things, the Confession of Württemberg, it is likewise reasonably evident that he did not use a passage from it that dealt specifically with Ubiquity. This may be argued from the failure of any witness, including Beza, to charge that he did. And it is reasonable to expect that its introduction would have inspired proper comment.[39] Several days after he had examined the article, Beza wrote Calvin that Lorraine "Brentiana recitavit."[40] But he did not specify Ubiquity. The passages cited by Martyr, the *Histoire ecclésiastique*, and the *Correspondance* of Beza do not treat Ubiquity. It should be borne in mind that Lorraine was ostensibly trying to persuade the ministers to accept a real and substantial presence. The only two sources that describe the formula are Martyr and Jean Polanco, a Jesuit attending the colloquy. Though it is not absolutely certain that they

39. For they were well aware of the doctrine. That same year Martyr had written his *Dialogus de utraque in Christo natura*, against Ubiquity, which was actually a rejoinder to Brenz, the chief author of the Confession of Württemberg. And on August 23, weeks before the colloquy, he sent a copy of his tract against "that monstrous opinion" to the bishop of Norwich. Vermigli, *Common Places*, pp. 148-149. Beza would also write a tract against Brenz. The *HE*, I, 589, spoke of Brenz as "heretic, Eutychian, and Nestorian rolled into one!"

40. Beza, *Correspondance*, III, 162.

are speaking of the Württemberg Confession, both confirm that the key formula embodied a substantial presence.[41] It so happens that several passages in the Württemberg Confession satisfy this requirement, one of which could be described as "three or four lines," the length of the article Beza was asked to sign.[42] By the same token, the passages on Ubiquity do not teach a substantial presence; thus, there is no need to postulate that both subjects were introduced together. Given the absence of any positive evidence that Lorraine used Ubiquity, and at least indirect evidence that he did not, it would seem reasonable to conclude that Ubiquity was not introduced into the colloquy.

This analysis would seem to allow three principal objections. First, it could be argued that to Geneva, Brenz and Ubiquity were virtually interchangeable terms.[43] Hence, Beza need not *specify* Ubiquity. The reply is a simple return to the sources: none of the articles in any of the specified sources includes this doctrine. A second objection might be that the notion of Ubiquity is implicit in a real and substantial presence.[44] This would involve tortuous metaphysical subtleties, but it would seem quite safe to conclude that a consensus of theologians would not uphold such an equation. In fact, the reverse seems closer to the truth, insofar as one posits a change of substance as necessary for the presence of the body of Christ in the species. A conversion of substance

41. For Martyr, Calvin, *Opera*, XVIII, 767; for Polanco, see *MHSJ*, VI, 54. Polanco elsewhere notes a correspondence between the passage Lorraine used and one of Calvin himself that the liberal theologian, Claude d'Espence, had asked the ministers to approve: "donde pareze que confesa lo mesmo." *MHSJ*, VIII, 756. It goes without saying that this would make it incongruous for the passage to have included Ubiquity. For d'Espence and the pertinent passage, or, as it happens, passages of Calvin, see his *Apologie*, p. 498, and Beza, *Correspondance*, III, 168, n. 17.

42. For example: "Sed credimus & docemus, quemadmodum & substantia panis & vini in coena adiunt, ita & substantiam corporis & sanguinis Christi adesse, & cum Symbolis vere exhiberi & accipi." See Appendix B, second paragraph.

43. As seems to be the case in Beza, *Correspondance*, IV, 61, n. 5.

44. Alain Dufour to me, Dec. 3, 1965.

presumes precisely that Christ, in his human nature, is not everywhere, but, as some theologians put it, at the right hand of the Father.[45] Third, the argument that there was more than one confession involves, among other things, the assumption that the divines adhered closely to the original texts, without important terminological alteration.[46] Though this is not, for reasons indicated in the first objection, an indispensable part of the main thesis here, nevertheless it would seem that in a formal and critical exchange the theologians would have been scrupulous in any transcriptions of texts. If there were significant alterations in the texts, moreover, it would seem that the arguments on both sides— perfidy or mediation—would be undermined and neutralized. It would simply no longer be an authentic Lutheran text.

The question of Ubiquity involves a final and rather extraordinary revelation. My researches sent me to the long-overlooked manuscript of the first Huguenot account of the colloquy, the anonymous *Recueilli par les Calvinistes*. I examined numerous copies of this manuscript and was astonished to discover that, according to the original Calvinist account, it was the Huguenots themselves who presented the colloquy with what is apparently the Confession of Württemberg.[47] This is simply stated in the manuscript without elucidating comment. In view of the nature of the conclusion

45. See Hermann Sasse, *This Is My Body: Luther's Contention for the Real Presence in the Sacrament of the Altar* (Minneapolis, 1959), p. 150. Perhaps it should be pointed out that Ubiquity should not be understood in any crass or pantheistic sense. It would not seem germane to this paper, moreover, to consider whether or not Luther himself taught Ubiquity. *Ibid.*, pp. 155-160; and Edmund Schlink, *The Theology of the Lutheran Confessions*, tr. P.F. Keohneke and H.J.A. Bouman (Philadelphia, 1961), pp. 187-189. The articles in question here do not make general statements of a Christological nature. This excepts, of course, the Confession of Württemberg, already considered.

46. Dufour to me, Dec. 3, 1965.

47. The pertinent passage is set after Beza's reply to Lorraine of September 24 and reads: "Après cette harangue, les ministres presenterent leur confession de foy touchan le sacrament de l'Eucharistie: Et baillerent aussy avec ce quelques confessions de fit d'aucuns Ministres de Wittemberg, faites des l'année 1559 et fut ainsy mise fin au Colloque de ce jour." A.N., G8*589^a, fol. 176; see also A.N.,

about Lorraine that I feel the sources point to, it would be tempting to claim this as some kind of missing link providing final confirmation of the cardinal's innocence. But the statement in the *Recueilli* is so contrary to the other sources and to the whole sense of things at the colloquy that it would be extremely difficult to accept it as correct. It is more of a conundrum than a climax.

The question of which edition of the *Augustana* Lorraine used is not nearly so esoteric. We can presume that it was not the *Variata*—the softened edition of 1540—for Calvin himself several times explicitly approved this.[48] The ministers would likewise have accepted it. Moreover, the *Variata* does not disapprove other doctrines, as Beza maintained that the text presented to him on September 26 did.[49] This reduces the field to the original *Invariata* edition of 1530, which is expressly supported by an observer.[50] Finally, the *Invariata* conforms well with the requirement of the prelates that the ministers accept "the existence of the flesh of our Lord in the Sacrament of the Altar."

$G^{8*}589^b$, $G^8 589^d$; B.N. Fonds François 5812, fol. 34, 17813, fol. 130, Nîmes MS. 257, fol. 148; Lyon MS. 1044, fol. 95. There are no variations beyond spelling, for example, "Virtembert" in lieu of "Wittemberg." This would not seem significant for this is, in any event, a Lutheran document. The *Recueilli* was published in part as the mysterious propaganda piece, the *Ample discours des actes de Poissy*, without this section. La Place, *Commentaires*, p. 192, based his study partially on the *Recueilli* and used identical language in describing this phenomenon, except that he had Lorraine make this presentation. Present evidence indicates that this was a true emendation.

48. Calvin, *Opera*, XXXII, 148 ff; n. 13, above. See also W. Nijenhuis, "Calvin en de Augsburgse Confessie," *Nederlandsch Theologisch Tijdschrift*, XV (1960-1961), 416-433.

49. La Place, *Commentaires*, p. 195; *HE*, I, 594-595; Appendix A.

50. The *Journal*, p. 37, says that Lorraine used the Confession of Augsburg of the Naumburg convention of 1561, which is identical with the *Invariata*. Johann H. Gelbke, *Der Naumburger Fürstentag* (Leipzig, 1793), p. 191. The *Diario*, p. 133, has a somewhat obscure account in which the text is derived from Lüneburg, where some of the princes met in July to protest the Naumburg preface as too Calvinist. Robert Calinich, *Der Naumburger Fürstentag, 1561* (Gotha, 1870), pp. 259-262. It must be borne in mind that such diverse accounts as Jean Polanco, *MHSJ*, VIII, 756, and Martyr, in Calvin, *Opera*, XVIII, 767, did not view the text as embodying this kind of militancy.

Having said all this, I should point out that the explosive potential of the Lutheran texts could easily be exaggerated. Eucharistic controversy was raging in Germany at this time. As Calvin so familiarly put it, the Lutherans were "like cats and dogs." If the Lutherans could not agree among themselves, they could hardly take inordinate offense at Calvinist dissent from their confessions. Literate Germans were aware of Reformed difficulties with the *Augustana*. They had heard of Marburg. And so had Lorraine. But perhaps he did feel that the way to Rome was through Wittenberg. This is the construction that the textual evidence supports.

The conclusions should put Lorraine and Poissy into a broader context. This will make his conduct with reference to both Lutheran confessions and Lutherans all the more explicable. On the one hand, the German Lutherans themselves wanted to be included at Poissy just as ardently as the Calvinists wanted them excluded. The Duke of Württemberg, a zealous partisan of Lutheranism, himself took the initiative in the internationalization of Poissy; he has even been considered the one who inspired the colloquy.[51] The colloquy was an attempt at a national solution of what had become an international crisis. There were at least three interested parties, and it was unlikely that any third party would be indifferent to a settlement made independent of him. As such, dialogue seemed foredoomed to failure. Perhaps a trialogue *was* in order. On the other hand, Lorraine's conduct can be seen as an incident in what was becoming something of a tradition: alliance with German Lutheranism as a counterweight to Hapsburg power. The Duchy of Lorraine was on the periphery of France, and no doubt the Guises wanted the goodwill of Württemberg in the likely

51. Kugler, *Christoph*, pp. 291-293, 303-304. And Brenz, incidentally, had been mentioned as his collocutor there. S.A., Frankreich, A 115, Büschel 17, No. 79.

eventuality of war. They earlier gave their ardent support to Henry II's alliance with the Lutherans,[52] and Lorraine was scrupulous throughout in cultivating his relationship with the Germans. This does not necessarily mean that the cardinal's ecumenism was subordinate to his politics. It has been suggested that Lorraine "transformed Catherine's French irenicism into Imperial irenicism."[53] Perhaps it would be more appropriate to say that Lorraine's motives were probably mixed: a happy coincidence of political prudence and ecumenical virtue. In this view Lorraine, as it were, held forth an olive branch in one hand, while he held a sword in reserve in the other. Though this may not sound noble, it is not for that reason improbable.

While the sources would seem to argue for a better view of Lorraine and his conduct at Poissy, an element of ambiguity remains. He should be neither eulogized nor censured. The cardinal's is a gray innocence.

52. Romier, *Catherine de Médicis*, II, 262.
53. Héritier, *Catherine de Médicis*, p. 187. The author would not deny, however, that if Lorraine had any ecumenical preferences or priorities, they would probably be Lutheranism first, Calvinism second. But, then, was not Lutheranism closer to Catholicism?

IX / Conclusions

O Dieu, seul autheur de tous biens,
Regarde d'un oeil favorable
Ceste compaignie honorable
et qu'il te souvienne des tiens,
Leur faisant protester et croire
Ce qui est conforme à ta gloire.
                                    Anonymous[1]

In order to account for the failure of Poissy, insofar as any further accounting is necessary, one must go beyond the tactics of the cardinal of Lorraine and consider the entire situation. One cannot quantify the causes for the failure of the colloquy; indeed, one need not. First, like so many historic attempts of irenicism, the colloquy was inspired and managed by the secular arm, which, one might say, enlisted theology in its service. The princes could and did both foster and frustrate ecumenism, but even when good, their intentions were not pure. They did "the right thing for the wrong reason." This constricted enthusiasm for their cause. And if the princes preferred peace to truth, it is not sheer frivolity to assert that the theologians preferred orthodoxy to either. There was little of the spirit of *libre examen*. The sources do not permit a statistical study of the theologians, but both sides were generally intractable and triumphalist, viewing moderation as tantamount to treason. Both parties wanted unity, but on their own terms. And both were no doubt more interested in stealing sheep than in mending fences. The close union of church and state in the sixteenth century generally impeded and sometimes excluded organic reunion. These complications were made explicit at Poissy, where the one

1. *Pasquin pour le Concile national*, appended to the *Journal*, p. 50.

party had and the other party wanted—ultimately—an established church. Again, one must consider the character of so many of the irenicists of Poissy: the pragmatic Catherine, the *politique* l'Hospital, the irresolute Navarre, the mercurial Lorraine, and the almost chameleon-like Baudouin. Baudouin himself seems to foreshadow a future where irenicism would become increasingly eccentric and utopian.

Innumerable other factors were involved in the failure of the colloquy. There was, for example, the competition between a dubiously legal national council and a technically ecumenical general council. Again, Poissy marks the high tide of French Protestantism, and though Beza's opening oration was prefaced by a beautiful paean to ecumenism, it seems patent that he was content to vindicate his cause and publicize his faith[2] before court and commoners. In other words, it was perhaps vain to expect the vibrant and expansive Huguenots to compromise the purity of a newly discovered Gospel. Moreover, Beza himself has been considered "one of the founders of Protestant Scholasticism."[3] This means, among other things, that Protestantism was becoming relatively less an inspiration and relatively more an organization. The organization of thought inevitably reduces plasticity. Perhaps most of all, one must consider the passions engendered by Catholic persecution and the consequent Calvinist outrages. The theologians called each other "serpents" and "wolves" behind the mask of Scripture—not to mentioned under a flag of truce. Catherine not only failed to understand dogma; she also underestimated the profound and mutual hatred which demarcated the two parties. Poissy really lacked any consensus; failure seemed to lie in its very nature. There was no psychological readiness. There was no *kairos*.

2. Beza, *Correspondance*, III, 165.
3. See, e.g., the comments of the editors in Beza, *Correspondance*, IV, 9.

This assessment seems confirmed by a metahistorical consideration. If there had been accord at Poissy, would this have meant Christian reunion in France? There is good reason to reply in the negative. The conciliatory Cardinal Contarini's concessions at the abortive meeting at Ratisbon in 1541 were later repudiated by Pope Paul III. Geisendorf illuminates the subject from the Reformed point of view. He says that, had the ministers accepted Lorraine's formula on September 26, the Protestant churches would have repudiated their representatives, and disorder would have resulted.[4] And for the Catholics, reunion with the Calvinists would probably only have been won at the price of schism with Rome.

Poissy really provides an object lesson in how not to conduct a colloquy. And if, at this point, we were to deduce a few laws from its experience, they might be as follows: one, expanding forces are disinclined to compromise; two, religious establishments are disinclined to accept challengers as equals. Perhaps we should add a rider: studies in irenicism are apt to rehabilitate the irenical party. But this invites some commentary.

It is axiomatic that history is written by its winners. Hence, the properly deserved praise for a Luther or a Loyola. They were heroic men of profound spiritual insight. But in the perspective adopted by such studies as the present one, a d'Espence can seem much more attractive than a Tournon or a Martyr. This should not be surprising; it only suggests how far we have forgotten the unitive ideal of the early Reformation. Luther and others shared this ideal, to which historiography has preferred accomplished fact. The failure of Poissy can be seen in terms of the supersession of the ideal by hard facts. It came at a time when the memories of a common past were receding; the schism between Protestantism and Rome could be seen as a part of the natural order. To be sure, there

4. Geisendorf, *Théodore de Bèze*, p. 158.

were chains rattling in some cellars, which would be echoed in the ubiquitous theological overreaction. But a new generation was maturing in which the all too human nostalgia for continuity need no longer mean organic continuity within Christendom, but continuity with one's given confessional loyalties. The faith of our fathers can exclude that of our grandfathers. And lost causes have a way of getting lost.

Poissy inevitably leads to Trent. There was, of course, a considerable interaction between the two. Poissy did not "cause" Trent. Pius' initial plans for a council were anterior to the particular plans of the French court. But Poissy influenced the form that the council took. Poissy forced the hand of the Pope and prompted his decision to hold it in the unfortunate location of Trent. It is even possible that the council would have lost its raison d'être without the threat of the colloquy. And the obstructionist policy of the French was a major factor in driving the Pope into the arms of Philip. Whereupon Philip's posture ensured that the council would be largely a convention of the Latin world.

It hardly needs saying that Trent influenced Poissy—the relationship was reciprocal. Trent inhibited and haunted the colloquy; the prelates felt guilty to be there and anxious to leave. Trent provided the rationale for Lainez' case against the colloquy. Finally, the failure of Trent as a medium of reconciliation enhanced the potentiality of Poissy. The colloquy was the last resort of European ecumenism.

The previous chapter suggested that, inasmuch as the Reformation had become international and multiconfessional, perhaps a trialogue was in order. And perhaps a general council would have been the ideal place for such a convention. Protestants were invited to all three phases of the council, but relations had deteriorated so much that there was only a rather nominal Protestant representation during the second period. The general prospects of the time were summed up by Francisco Vargas, Spanish jurist and imperial envoy. Anxiously and ardently awaiting the Protestants, he wrote in a rather pathetic letter of 1551 about the need of "a miracle" or "some extraordinary stroke of Providence."[5] It was not forthcoming, Providence having apparently delegated the worst part of these affairs to men.

There might have been another opportunity early in the reign of Pius IV. He initially possessed the necessary liberality and goodwill, but only the most naïve could expect that the cup or comparable concessions would be a panacea for religious divisions. What was needed was a whole new spirit jealous to assimilate the Protestant genius and a thoroughgoing reform of the Church in head and in members. But the Pope reportedly said that he would go "so far and no farther."[6] This was obviously not far enough.

It would seem, nevertheless, that there was reciprocal responsibility. If Pius can be accused of a failure to exercise heroic, imaginative, and generous leadership, Protestants can be accused of not being responsive. It would be interesting to speculate on the consequences of a massive Protestant presence at Trent. By sheer force of numbers they might have intimidated the fathers there into taking them into counsel. Throckmorton wrote one of the last appeals to Elizabeth, and, in turn, to the Protestant princes, to send representatives to the council. As he put it, "Protestants are so strong in all states that they shall either cause some good to be done, or impeach any harm."[7] Given the relatively modest attendance at the council, there might have been more danger to the Catholics than to the Protestants. But neither side was sufficiently responsive. They made great refusals. Trent, then, could not excise members who had already withdrawn. It simply made the severance official and complete.

5. *CT*, XI, 691.
6. Jedin, *CC*, p. 79. The positive accomplishments of this last assembly at Trent would, nevertheless, be considerable. See, e.g., *ibid.*, pp. 115, 137.
7. *CSP: Foreign*, Feb. 16, 1562, No. 892.

Some might see a sort of poetic restitution in that a Pope who bore the name of Medici should resuscitate and ratify the Council of Trent, for in the popular mind the name summons an image of the Renaissance Papacy at its most permissive and pleasure loving. Certainly Pius IV is among the most critical personages in this study and was, perhaps, the most important Pope of the century. At his inception in 1559 the future seemed to belong to Protestantism. England's definitive defection dates from the Act of Supremacy of that year, the Huguenots were emboldened to hold their First National Synod all but under the nose of the King, John Knox returned to Scotland that year and Protestantism was established the next, Germany was predominantly Protestant, Lutheranism was established in Scandinavia, and Protestantism was making powerful inroads in Eastern Europe.

Under Pius the tide would turn. Catholicism would finally awaken from its long slumber and take the initiative. This involved far more than the Council of Trent. There were many other factors, including the negative consideration of the inability of Protestants to unite. Positively, and perhaps fundamentally, Pius normalized relations with the great Catholic powers. Hitherto it had generally been either Hapsburg or Valois in the forefront. His patient and astute diplomacy managed to obtain the patronage of Spain without alienating France and the Emperor. The champion of Catholicism in the previous generation, Charles V, generally had poor relations with Rome. Pius effected a convergence of papal leadership with the champion of Catholicism of the next generation, Philip II, appreciating that there was a fundamental parallelism of interests that transcended particular differences. His deference to Philip was such that, taking it together with political and religious influences, we might almost speak of the Hispanicization of Roman Catholicism. Pius helped resolve the paralyzing ambivalence of so many Catholics toward Protestantism—conciliation or conquest?—

in favor of the latter. He deferred to Philip on the quality of the council and the question of concessions. The later grant of the cup to Ferdinand was no more than gesture. And the council would be instrumental in the rehabilitation of papal leadership. It effectively acknowledged the primacy of Rome, and Rome reserved the right to interpret its decrees. The Pope lent new prestige to the Jesuits, who would provide so much of the manpower for the reform movement, and appropriated the critical services of people like Lainez. Finally, Pius promoted his young nephew, Charles Borromeo. As Secretary of State, Borromeo played an intimate role in the diplomatic negotiations before Trent and later, as archbishop of Milan, realized the Tridentine ideal and became the acknowledged model bishop of the Catholic Church.[8] Borromeo symbolizes an age when the problem was no longer dialogue but the cure of souls. The new pastoral ideal was hierarchic, systematic, sacramental, kerygmatic—and late.

Men were entering a new age. The attitude at Rome and at Trent on the question of concessions was one of reluctance to yield an iota, lest the entirety be lost—a petrification into theological positivism. This movement, which had earlier antecedents, superseded the, at least theoretically upheld, philosophical or speculative theology of the Middle Ages. It found a foremost exponent in Melchior Cano, theological adviser to Philip, who has been called "the beginning of modern theology."[9] It can be seen in the decisive stress upon

8. Giuseppe Alberigo, "Carlo Borromeo come Modello di vescovo nella Chiesa post-Tridentina," *Rivista storica italiana* LXXIX (1967), p. 1031, stresses the importance of Borromeo as a fountainhead. The historian Angelo Giuseppe Roncalli, later known as Pope John XXIII, wrote that San Carlo was "il maestro" of the bishops. *Gli atti della visita apostolica di S. Carlo Borromeo a Bergamo (1575)* Florence, 1936), p. xxxiv, quoted in Alberigo, "Carlo Borromeo," p. 1035. See also André Deroo, *Saint Charles Borromée, Cardinal réformateur, docteur de la pastorale (1538-1584)* (Paris, 1963).

9. Albert Lang, *Die Loci Theologici des Melchior Cano und die Methode des dogmatischen Beweises*, in *Münchener Studien zur historischen Theologie*, VI, 6,

the magisterium best illustrated by Loyola and the Jesuits. And it can be seen in the promulgation of the decrees of Trent, the long-gestated reply to Protestantism, and a reply that obviated any need for future dialogue.

Whether it was intrinsic, extrinsic, or both, there seems to have been a distinct development in the orientation of Pius in the years that separated the conclave and the council. In the conclave he could be "reputed a Lutheran"; at the council he might be characterized as a Spanish Pope. There was no longer any question whether he would be a Pope of the Renaissance or a Pope of reconciliation. He was a Pope of the Counter-Reformation. This means that the Counter-Reformation was born not in the deafening and divisive thunderbolts of the titanic Paul IV, but in the muted, measured, and consensus-minded polity of his prudent and politic successor.[10] To be sure, this was due partly to the man, partly to the imponderables of the time. But unlike his predecessor, Pius was sensitive and receptive enough to register and perhaps ratify the shifting dynamics of his age. Pius may not have had the spiritual qualities and force of character of his great successors like Pius V, Gregory XIII, and Sixtus V, but he was a decisive figure at the moment when the Church was charting a new course.

Let us return to Poissy and underscore its broader relevance, bringing these reflections together. We have seen a study in sixteenth-century ecumenism become a study in the Counter-Reformation. Poissy represents the point where

cited in Julian H. Franklin, *Jean Bodin and the Sixteenth-Century Revolution in the Methodology of Law and History* (New York: Columbia University Press, 1963), p. 104, n. 2, which is also good for bibliography, p. 103, n. 1.

10. Pastor, *History of the Pope*, XVI, 402, sees Paul IV "as the incarnation of Catholic reform in its highest and most ideal form" and Pius IV as "little imbued with the new ecclesiastical spirit." Idealism apart, these views might almost be reversed. Jedin, *CC*, p. 1, wrote that the pontificate of Pius IV was "epoch-making in the history of the church."

Catholicism cut its losses and consolidated its ecclesiastical assets. And united against Poissy was a coalition of Pope, Trent, Spain, and Jesuit. This might well be considered a characteristic formula of the Counter-Reformation: spiritual leadership of the Papacy, Spanish might, Jesuit élan, and Tridentine doctrine. This is not to postulate a static concept for a dynamic and variegated movement. The Counter-Reformation was probably more a *modus operandi* than a holy alliance. But the Counter-Reformation emerged—for better or for worse.

Poissy marks a kind of watershed in the history of religious reform in the sixteenth century, which was the result of a conjunction of circumstances: the Catholic standard passed from Charles V, who ruled and responded to an empire of mixed religious loyalties, to Philip II and Spain, monolithically and uncompromisingly Catholic; there was, of course, the rise of the Jesuits, who were characteristic of a certain new tough-mindedness. Both Spain and Jesuits espoused Trent and its anathemas, and the council became a barrier rather than a bridge. Reform popes replaced Renaissance popes. On the other side, Calvinism replaced Lutheranism as the ascendant Protestant movement, and it was expansive, uncompromising, and truly international. The two forces— revived Catholicism and emergent international Protestantism—met at Poissy in the last great religious colloquy of the sixteenth century. Poissy and its failure mark the waning of moderation and irenicism, the breakdown of communication, the loss of contact, the hardening of religious frontiers, estrangement.

Epilogue: A Concluding Unscientific Postscript

May [this book] lead not to theological disputation but to a theological life.
Erasmus, Preface to the *Enchiridion*

No book on peacemaking should end on a bittersweet note: today we are moving from estrangement to reconciliation. At this point, moreover, the author, like so many before him, has experienced the wisdom of Eccles. 12:12: "One last thing, my son, be warned that writing books involves endless hard work, and that much study wearies the body." And, after seven years of hard labor on the strictly academic problem of sixteenth-century ecumenism, he may be entitled to a few highly condensed comments and questions of an existential nature on the contemporary ecumenical opportunity or predicament.

Contemporary ecumenism is only a renaissance of a Reformation ideal. And inasmuch as the objective of history is to enlarge our memory and extend our experience, it may be hoped that, having appropriated the experience of our ancestors, we might avoid their failures and find their prize. This study involves no effort to transpose heroes and villains. It seeks only to redress a historiographical imbalance, as, on a much larger scale, it may be for the twentieth century to redress the imbalance of the sixteenth. As I have put it elsewhere, we should advance, Holy Writ in one hand and Herodotus in the other.

There are numerous auguries that we shall advance farther. First, it is hatred that is blind and love that illuminates and unites, and the rediscovery of love in our time is a reformation almost as impressive as that of the sixteenth century. Second, the great theme now is neither faith nor works (which would be a caricature of the issues even for the sixteenth century), but hope (Rom. 8:24). The dynamism implicit in eschatology favors ecumenism, for it can move mountains, even the mountain of Trent. It raises our eyes to the mountains, where everything that rises converges.

Finally, much has been written in these pages on the subtleties of the Eucharist, and it is perhaps unfortunate that so much theological focus traditionally has been upon what Christ said, not upon what Christ did. Was not the original Eucharist, perhaps most fundamentally, a model of sacrifice? And does not the ecumenical ideal solicit a similar sacrifice, a similar consummation? Is not its consummation in consummation? While we know today that unity is not the same as uniformity, we also know that the great but separate Christian traditions are interdependent and require reintegration. And if compatibility is enough for others, can a Christian be satisfied with anything less than communion? The task is formidable, but, after all, Christianity is a religion of miracles.

Appendixes, Bibliography, Index

Appendix A

I. THE CONFESSION OF AUGSBURG OF 1530 (*INVARIATA*)

De Coena Domini docent, quod corpus et sanguis Christi vere adsint, et distribuantur vescentibus in Coena Domini; et improbant secus docentes.

Concerning the Lord's Supper, they teach that the body and blood of Christ are truly present, and are distributed [communicated] to those that eat in the Lord's Supper. And they disapprove of those that teach otherwise.[1]

II. THE CONFESSION OF AUGSBURG OF 1540 (*VARIATA*)

De Coena Domini docent, quod cum pane et vino vere exhibeantur corpus et sanguis Christi vescentibus in Coena Domini.

Concerning the Lord's Supper, they teach that with bread and wine are truly exhibited the body and blood of Christ to those that eat in the Lord's Supper.[2]

1. Philip Schaff, *The Creeds of Christendom* (3 vols., 6th rev. ed., New York and London, 1919), I, 241, III, 13.
2. *Ibid.*

Appendix B

CONFESSIO ET DOCTRINA THEOLOGORUM ET MINISTRORUM
VERBI DEI, IN DUCATU WIRTEMBERGENSI,
DE VERA PRAESENTIA CORPORIS ET
SANGVINIS JESU CHRISTI IN
COENA DOMINICA.

Tubingae, Anno 1561.

CONFESSIO FIDEI
DE
COENA DOMINICA.

Firmiter credimus & docemus in coena Domini, cum pane & vino, virtute verbi, seu institutione Christi, verum corpus & verum sanguinem Domini nostri Jesu Christi vere ac substantialiter exhiberi omnibus coena Domini utentibus: ut quemadmodum ministri manu exhibentur, ita ore manducantis & bibentis accipiantur.[1] Nam quod ad substantiam Sacramenti attinet, verbis Christi instituentis perspicue docetur Ecclesia, panis & vini substantiam non mutari,[2] sed in hunc usum verbo Domini consecrari, ut dispensationi corporis & sanguinis Christi in coena serviant.

Corpus vero Christi & sanguinis in coena, non solum Symbolis adumbrantur, ita ut in verbis coenae per corpus & sanguinem Christi figura aut signum corporis & sanguinis intelligatur: Sed credimus & docemus, quemadmodum & substantia panis & vini in coena adiunt, ita & substantiam corporis & sanguinis Christi adesse, & cum Symbolis vere exhiberi & accipi.[3]

Dum vero hanc veri corporis & sanguinis Christi veram praesentiam statuimus, nullam corporis & sanguinis ejus cum pane & vino commixtionem, nullam in pane localem inclusionem assetimus, sed sacramentali unione talem praesentiam docemus, quae verbo Christi desinita

---

1. Passage perhaps used by the Cardinal of Lorraine.
2. Denial of Transubstantiation.
3. Passage perhaps used by the Cardinal of Lorraine.

est. Accipiens enim panem, dixit. Hoc est corpus meum: Accipiens calicem dixit. Hic est sanguis meus.

Et quoniam Christus, priusquam panem & vinum ad hunc usum consecraret, mandatum dedit, manducate, inquit, & bibite ex hoc omnes: docemus extra usum non esse Sacramentum. Sic in substantia coenae docemus, haec tria concurrere, panem & vinum, corpus & sanguinem Domini, & externum Socramenti (sic) usum, qui in manducando consistit & bibendo. Ideoque, si panis & vinum in sua substantia non permaneant, aut corpus & sanguis Christi non adsint, aut usus externus non accedat, sacramentum esse negamus, cujus substantia in his tribus consistit, quae non sunt ab hominibus consista, sed verbo Instituentis expressa.

Quia vero ab his, qui veram in coena Domini Corporis & sanguinis Christi praesentiam negant, Articulus fidei de ascensu Christi in coelum, & sessione ejus ad dexteram Dei Patris opponitur, quoniam in coelo est, in coena praesens esse negetur:[4]

Nos hunc fidei Articulum non nostris, sed Apostoli verbis, quam simplicissime explicamus, ubi scribit: Qui descendit, idem ille est, qui etiam ascendit supra omens coelos ut impleret omnia. Non enim sic in editiorem aliquem locum aeris vel firmamenti ascendit, ut ibi haeteret, sed etiam in eam Majestatem & gloriam ingressus est, quae teste Apostolo, est super omnem Principatum, & Potestatem, & virtutem, & Dominationem, & omne nomen, quod nominatur, non solum in hoc seculo, sed etiam in futuro. Itaque nullam humanae naturae dissusionem, aut membrorum Christi distraetionem imaginamur, sed hominis Christi Majestatem imaginamur, sed hominis Christi Majestatem explicamus, qua ad dexteram Dei collocatus, non solum Divinitate sua, sed homo Christus quoque implet omnia, modo coelesti, & humanae rationi imperscrutabili, qua Majestate, praesentia ejus in coena non tollitur, sed confirmatur. Atque hoc modo per verba Christi in coena docemur, ubi corpus Christi quaerendum, & ad salutem nostram sumendum sit.[5]

Quemadmodum igitur in coena, veritate verbi Dei, corporis & sanguinis ejus praesentiam asserimus, quod ratio humana assequi nequit: Ita & ascensum Christi in coelum, & sessionem ejus ad dexteram Dei, Apostoli verbis explicamus, qui eo in loco, ubi dicit: Christum ascendisse supra omnes coelos, ut omnis impleret, non loquitur de vaticiniorum impletione, sed de Majestate Christi, qua nunc in gloria patris

4. Denial of *sursum corda*.
5. Paragraph treating doctrine of Ubiquity.

omnibus rebus praesens est, & res omnes illi praesentes. Quod Mysterium, ut reliquos fidei Articulos, non ratione sed sola fide compraehendimus.

Quia vero necesse est, de judicio quoque recte doceri Ecclesiam, quod juxta Apostolum sibi manducant impii, indigni, & hypocritae quos tanquam indignos ab usu coenae arcere oportebat, (nisi Hypocrisi aut vanis persuasionibus suam impietatem tegerent) credimus & confitemur, corpus & sanguinem Christi in coena, non solum a piis & dignis, sed etiam ab impiis & infidelibus Hypocritis sumi. Supra enim ex verbis Christi demonstratum est, substantiam sacramenti coenae, extra usum (qui in edendo & bibendo consistit) non definiri.

Cum ergo, quod ad substantiam coenae attinet, non solum panis & vinum, sed una cum his, juxta veritatem verbi Christi, verum corpus, & verus sanguis ejus, omnibus coena utentibus offerantur, nec extra usum (qui non solum in exhibitione, sed etiam in sumptione consistit, quemadmodum verba Christi clare sonant) sacramentum dici queat, (qua significatione vocabuli nunc utimur) docemus, Christum in coena tam adesse impiis & infidelibus Hypocritis, quam fidelibus & electis Christi membris.

Nullo modo autem sequitur, propterea impios quoque vivificari, quod Christum, qui vita est, praesentem habent. Vivicatio enim non una solum, sed duabus causis definitur, efficiente scilicet, quae est Christus, & instrumentali, quae est Fides. Christus enim sine fide nos non vivificat, sicut scriptum est: Justus ex fide vivet. Et iterum: Fide purificans corda eorum. Nec fide sine Christo vivificamur, quemadmodum scriptum est: Inhabitans Christus per fidem in cordibus nostris.

Similiter & judicium non una causa definiendum est, sed duabus: causa, propter quam indigne manducantes judicantur, non est in Christo, qui in se vita est & salus, sed in homine, impietas scilicet & incredulitas eorum. Causa vero efficiens est ipse Christus praesens impietatem hominis puniens, qui jam judicii & justitiae Dei executor est.

Cum ergo impii fide careant, Sacramento tamen utuntur, cujus substantia in usu consistit, hoc est, manducando & bibendo, praesente Christo non vivificantur, sed juxta Apostolum judicantur, propter suam impietatem & incredulitatem, cujus impietatis ultor est praesens Christus, verus Deus & homo, cui omne judicium traditum est a Patre, ut quemadmodum sua gratia per fidem electos vivificat & salvat, ita sua justitia propter impietatem & incredulitatem impios Hypocritas judicat & damnat.

Et hoc modo rei fiunt praesentis corporis & sanguinis Christi, qui Sacramento utentes promissioni fidem non habent; qua promissione offeruntur remissio peccatorum & vita aeterna. Et quoniam in Christo non minor laus est justitiae quam bonitatis, gloriae ac Majestati ejus nihil detrahitur, quod patitur sese sumi ab impiis & indignis. Nec lethalis est caro Christi, quae aeternae morti impios tradit, sed hac coenae prophanatione impii Hypocritae, sua impietate polluti, & propter suam incredulitatem jam judicari, judicium sibi manducant, hoc est, iram Dei cumulant & augent.

Haec simplex, perspicua, vera & orthodoxa est de substantia coenae Domini confessio, non rationibus humanis, sed Scripturae sacrae verbis & testimoniis, non coactis aut depravatis, confirmata. Quemadmodum & haec nostra declaratio de hoc articulo in sensu atque effectu consentanea est & conformis Augustanae, & Illustrissimi Principis nostri Confessioni, Synodo Tridentinae oblatae, quam sicut per gratiam Dei semel defendendam amplexi sumus, ita, eodem adjuvante, in ejus pio consensu nos perseveraturos profitemur.

Quod vero ad rationem dispensationis attinet hujus Sacramenti, & quod non solum una ejus parte, sed integro Sacramento omnibus utendum sit, & quae sint utilitates & fructus ejus, si vera fide accipiatur: quia non controvertitur, non judicamus opus esse aliquid dicere. Nunc enim de substantia solum coenae, & quae ad ejus explicationem necessaria sunt, nostram sententiam recitare voluimus, quam speramus omnibus piis, pacis & veritatis studiosis, probatum iri.

1. Rector Academicae Tubingensis.
2. Abbates & Praepositi.
3. Decanus & Facultas Theologica Scholae Tubingensis.
Generales & Speciales Superattendentes Ecclesiarum in Ducatu Wurtembergensi.

Actum Stutgardiae 19. die Mensis Decembris,
Anno Domini 1559.[6]

6. Christoph M. Pfaff, *Acta et scripta publica ecclesiae Wirtembergica* (Tübingen, 1720), pp. 340-344.

Appendix C

Firma fide confitemur in augustissimo eucharistiae sacramento verum Christi corpus et sanguinem realiter et substantialiter esse et existere, exhiberi, et sumi a communicantibus.[1]

1. *Discours*, p. 62.

Appendix D

Credimus in usu Coenae Dominicae vere, re ipsa, & substantialiter, id est in ipsa substantia, verum corpus & sanguinem Christi spirituali & ineffabili modo esse, exhiberi, sumi a fidelibus communicantibus.[1]

1. *HE*, I, 604-605.

Appendix E

Nous disons que nostre seigneur Jésus Christ est en l'usage de la saincte Cène, en laquelle il nous présente, donne & exhibite veritablement sons corps & son sang par l'opération du S. Esprit, & que nous recevons, mangeons, & beuvons spirituellement & par foy, ce propre corps qui a esté livré à la mort pour nous, & ce propre sang qui a esté respondu pour nous, pour estre os de ses os & chair de sa chair, afin d'en estre vivifiés & percevoir tout ce qui est requis pour nostre salut.[1]

1. *HE*, I, 595-596; *Diario*, p. 134.

Bibliography

MANUSCRIPTS

Paris

A.N. Correspondence of Thomas de Chantonnay with Philip II. K 1492-1495 (the originals were recently returned to Spain and Simancas.) The other major sources have been published. The *Procès-verbaux des assemblées générales du clergé* provide plentiful copies of the *Journal*, the *Discours*, the *Recueilly par les Calvinistes*, and a memorandum or *Discours* of d'Espence on the conference on icons. See G^8*588, G^8*589a, G^8*589b, G^8*589c (containing a beautiful copy of the *Journal* and the letter of Armagnac to d'Espence of 1570, supporting that d'Espence was the author), G^8*590, G^8*591, and G^8*596b.

B.N. Mss. Moreau 740 contains a relation of the conference on icons and a little-known irenical tract of Guillaume Postel of 1561: *Moyen proposé pour mettre en paix les Huguenots avec les Catholiques*. Fonds Français 15494 contains Jacques de Montagne's *Histoire de l'Europe*, useful for occasional detail. Pertinent in the same collection would be: 3955, 5812, 17813 (fine copies of *Discours* and *Journal*), 6618, 8685 (for *Actes du synode de Poissy*), and 3870 and 8927 for the cahiers of Pontoise. See also Fonds Dupuy 309, 641, and 10331 and Française nouvelles acquisitions 7117 on the subvention and 20597 for some correspondence between the court and Rome and Trent.

Stuttgart

S.A. Frankreich. For a listing of the relevant documents, see *BSHPF*, XXII, 312-331. See also the important correspondence between the Duke of Guise and Württemberg: "Correspondance de François de Lorraine, Duc de Guise, avec Christoph, Duc de Württemberg (1561-1562)," *BSHPF*, XXIV (1875), 71-83, 113-122, 209-221, and 499-511.

Modena, Rome, and Naples

A discussion of the relevant sources will be found in Roserot de Melin's preface to the *Diario*, pp. 57-90. I found nothing of singular importance in these archives that cannot otherwise be found in the printed sources.

PRINTED SOURCES

Ample discours des actes de Poissy. n.p., 1561.

Annales ecclesiastici ab anno MCXCVIII.; ubi desinit cardinalis Baronius, auctore Odorico Raynaldo . . . accedunt in hac editione notae chronologicae, criticae, historicae . . . auctore Joanne Dominico Mansi. 15 vols. Luca, 1747-1756.

Aymon, Jean. *Tous les synodes nationaux des églises Réformées de France, auxquels on a joint des mandemans roiaux et plusieurs lettres politiques (du cardinal de Sainte-Croix au cardinal Borromée.* 2 vols. The Hague, 1710.

Beza, Theodore. *Correspondance de Théodore de Bèze.* Collected Hippolyte Aubert. Eds. Henri Meylan and Alain Dufour *et al.* 6 vols. to date. Geneva: Droz, 1960-1970. Vols. III-IV.

————*Tractationum theologicarum, in quibus pleraque Christianae religionis dogmata adversus haereses nostris temporibus renovat ac solide ex verbo Dei defenduntur.* 3 vols. in 1, 2nd ed. Geneva, 1582.

Brantôme, Pierre de Bourdeilles de. *Oeuvres complètes.* 13 vols. Paris, 1858-1895.

Bruslart, Pierre. *Des choses plus remarquables arrivées en France depuis la mort d'Henry second, arrivée le dernier de Juin MDLIX jusques à la bateille de Montcontour, laquelle eust donnée le 3 Octobre MDLXIX.* (See *Condé*, Louis I of Bourbon, I, 1-211.)

Calendar of Letters and State Papers relating to English Affairs, Preserved Principally in the Archives of Simancas. 4 vols. London: Public Record Office, 1892-1899.

Calendar of State Papers and Manuscripts, relating to English Affairs, Existing in the Archives and Collections of Venice, and in Other Libraries of Northern Italy. 38 vols. London: Public Record Office, 1864-1940.

Calendar of State Papers, Foreign Series, of the Reign of Elizabeth. 23 vols. London: Public Record Office, 1863-1950.

Calendar of State Papers, relating to English Affairs, Preserved Principally at Rome, in the Vatican Archives and Library. 2 vols. London: Public Record Office, 1916-1926. 15 vols.; 2nd Ser., 8 vols. Paris, 1834-1839. Vols. IV and VI of 1st Ser.

Concilium Tridentinum: Diariorum, actorum, epistularum, tractatuum, nova collectio. Ed. Stephanus Ehses and Sebastianus Merkle. 10 vols. Freiburg-im-Breisgau: Görres-Gesellschaft, 1901-1919.

Condé, Louis I of Bourbon. *Mémoires de Condé, Ou Recueil pour servir à l'histoire de France, contenant ce que s'est passé de plus mémorables dans le royaume, sous le regne de François II, & sous une partie de celui de Charles IX où trouvera des preuves de l' histoire de M. de Thou.* 6 vols. London, 1743-1745.

Dareste, R. (ed.). "François Hotman, sa vie et correspondance," *Revue historique*, II (1876), 1-59.

Desjardins, Abel (ed.). *Négociations diplomatiques de la France avec la Toscane*. 6 vols. Paris, 1859-1886.

Diario dell' Assemblea de' Vescovi à Poissy. Ed. and preface Joseph Roserot de Melin. *Mélanges d'archéologie et d'histoire*, XXXIX (1921-1922), 47-151.

Döllinger, J.J. (ed.). *Beiträge zur politischen, kirchlichen und Kulturgeschichte dem sechs letzen jahrhunderten*. 3 vols. Ratisbon and Vienna, 1863-1882.

Dupuy, Pierre. (ed.). *Instructions et lettres des rois très-Chrestien, et de leurs ambassadeurs, et autres actes concernant le concile de Trente*. 4th ed. rev. Paris, 1654.

Duranthon, Antoine (ed.). *Collection des procès-verbaux des assemblées générales du clergé de France*. 8 vols. Paris, 1767-1768.

Ehses, Stefan. "Die letzte Berufung des Trienter Konzils durch Pius IV," *Festschrift G. von Hertling* (Kempten, 1913), pp. 139-162.

Espence, Claude d'. *Apologie contenant ample discours, exposition, response, & deffense de deux conférences avec les ministres extraordinaires de la religion prétendue réformée en ce royaume*. Paris, 1569.

_____*Continuation de la tierce conférence avec les ministres extraordinaires de la religion prétendue réformée en ce royaume, touchant l'efficace & vertu de la parole de Dieu ès saincts sacremens de l'église*. Paris, 1570.

_____*Traicté de l'efficace et vertu de la parole de Dieu au ministère des saincts sacremens de l'église*. Paris, 1563.

_____*Traicté en forme de conférence avec les ministres de la religion prétendue réformée, touchant l'efficace & vertu de la parole de Dieu aux ministère & usage des saincts sacrements de l'église*. Paris, 1566.

_____*Discours*. (See Evennett, H.O.)

_____*Journal*. (See Ruble, Baron Alphonse de.)

Este, Hyppolite d'. *Négociations, ou lettres d'affaires ecclésiastiques, et politiques. Excrittes au pape Pie IV, et au cardinal depuis saint Borromée, par Hyppolite d'Est, cardinal de Ferrare, légat en France au commencement des guerres civiles*. Tr. J. Baudoin. Paris, 1650.

Evennett, H.O. "Claude d'Espence et son 'Discours' au Colloque de Poissy," *Revue historique*, CLXIV (1930), 40-78.

François, Michel (ed.). *Correspondance du cardinal François de Tournon*. Paris: Honoré Champion, 1946.

Gachard, Louis. (ed.). *Correspondance de Marguerite d'Austriche duchesse de Parme avec Philippe II*. 3 vols. Brussels, 1867-1881.

García Cuéllar, Fidel. "Política de Felipe II en torno a la convocación de la tercera etapa del Concilio de Trento," *Miscelánea conmemorativa del Concilio de Trento (1563-1963)*. Madrid and Barcelona, 1965, pp. 25-60.

Grisar, Hartman (ed.). *Jacobi Lainez disputationes Tridentinae*. 2 vols. Innsbruck, 1884.

Guise, François de Lorraine, duc d'Aumale et de Guise. "Correspondance de François de Lorraine, duc de Guise, avec Christophe, duc de Würtemburg: Conférence de Saverne; Massacre de Vassy," *BSHPF*. XXIV (1875), 71-83, 113-122, 209-221, 499-511.

_____ *Mémories*. Ed. J.F. Michaud and J.J.F. Poujoulet. *Mémoires pour servir à l'histoire de France*, VI (1839).

Haton, Claude. *Mémoires, Contenant le récit des événements accomplie de 1553 à 1582* 2 vols. Ed. Félix Bourquelot. Paris, 1857.

Histoire ecclésiastique des églises réformées au royaume de France. Ed. G. Baum and Ed. Cunitz, 3 vols, Paris, 1883–1889.

Jedin, Hubert. *Krisis und Wendepunkt des Trienter Konzils (1562-63). Die neuendeckten Geheimberichte des Bischofs Gualterio von Viterbo an den heiligen Karl Borromaus*. Würtzburg: Rita-Verlag, 1941.

Journal (See Ruble, Baron Alphonse de.)

Kausler, Eduard von E., and Theodor Schott. *Briefwechsel zwischen Christoph Herzog zur Württemberg and P.P. Vergerio*. Stuttgart, 1895.

Kluckholn, August. *Briefe Friedrich des Frommen Kürfursten von der Pfalz, 1559-1566*. 2 vols. Braunschweig, 1868-1870.

La Bourdaisière, Philibert Babou de. *Correspondance*. Ed. E. Henry and Loriquet. *Travaux de l'Académie Impériale de Reims*, XXVII (1859).

Languet, Hubert. *Arcana seculi decimi sexti. Epistolae secretae ad principem suum Sax. ducem & S.R.I. septemvirum*. 3 vols. in 1. Halle, 1699.

La Place, Pierre de. *Commentaires de l'estat de la religion et république sous roys Henry et François seconds et Charles neufviesme*. Ed. J.A.C. Buchon. *Choix de chroniques et mémoires sur l'histoire de France*. Paris, 1836.

La Planche, Louis Regnier, Sieur de. *A Legendarie, Containing an Ample Discourse of the Life and Behavior of Charles Cardinal of Lorraine, and of his Brethren, of the House of Guise*. Under pseud. Francis de Lisle. Geneva, 1577.

_____ *Histoire de l'estat de France, tant de la république que de la religion: Sous le règne de François II*. Ed. J.A.C. Buchon. *Choix de Chroniques et Mémoires sur l'histoire de France*. Paris, 1836.

L'Aubespine, Sébastien de. "Dépêches de Sébastien de l'Aubespine, ambassadeur de France en Espagne sous Philippe II," *Revue d'histoire diplomatique*, XIII (1899), 583-607, XIV (1900), 289-302.

L'Hospital, Michel de. *Oeuvres Complètes*. Ed. P.J.S. Dufey. 3 vols. Paris, 1824.

Le Plat, Jodoci. *Monumentorum ad Historiam concilii Tridentini*. 7 vols. Louvain, 1781-1787.

Médicis, Catherine de.*Lettres*. Ed. Hector de la Ferrière. 10 vols. Paris: Imprimerie Nationale, 1880-1909.

Melanchthon, Philip. *Opera quae supersunt omnia*. Ed. Carolus Gottlieb Bretschneider. In *Corpus Reformatorum*. 21 vols. Halle, 1834-1854.

Montluc, Jean de. *Apologie contre certaines calomnies mises sus à la desfaveur & desavantage de l'estat des affaires de ce roiaume*. N.p., 1562.

Monumenta historica societatis Jesu. Especially Vol. VII, *Lanii monumenta epistolae et acta patris Jacobi Lanii secundi praeposita generalis societatis Jesu*. 93 vols.to date. Madrid: G. López del Horno, 1894-1965.

Muntz, A. (ed.). "Entrevue du duc Christophe de Wurtemberg avec les Guise, à Saverne, peu de jours avant le massacre de Vassy," *BSHPF*, IV (1855), 184-196.

Paris, Louis (ed.). *Négociations lettres et pièces diverses relatives au règne de François II*. Paris, 1841.

Paschal, Pierre de. *Journal de ce qui s'est passé en France durant l'année 1562*. Ed. Michel François. Paris: *Société de l'Histoire de France*, 1950.

Pasquier, Estienne. *Oeuvres.* 2 vols. Amsterdam, 1723.

Picherelli, Petri. *Opuscula theologica*. Lyons, 1629.

Quick, John (ed.). *Synodicon in Gallia reformata: or, The Acts, Decisions, Decrees and Canons of the Seven Last National Councils of the Reformed Churches in France: A Work never before Extant in any Language. Collected and Composed out of the Original Manuscript Acts of those Councils*. 2 vols. London, 1682.

Registres de la Compagnie des Pasteurs de Genève au temps de Calvin. Ed. Robert M. Kingdon, with the collab. of Jean François Bergier and Alain Dufour. 2 vols. Geneva: Droz, 1962.

Ribier, Guillaume. *Lettres et mémoires d'estat, des roys, princes, ambassadeurs, et autres ministres, sous les règnes de François premier, Henry II, and François II*. 2 vols. Paris, 1666.

Ruble, Baron Alphonse de. *Le Colloque de Poissy* (the *Journal*) in *Mémoires de la Société de l'histoire de Paris et de l'Isle de France*, XVI (1889), 1-56.

Sainctes, Claude de. *Confession de la foy Catholique contenant en brief la réformation de celle que les ministres présentèrent au roy, en*

l'assemblée de Poissy, addressée au peuple de France. Paris, 1561.
———*Responsio F. Claudii de Sainctes Parisien theologi ad apologiam Theodori Bezae, editam contra examen doctrinae Calvinianae & Bezane de coena Domini.* Paris, 1567.
Schaff, Philip. *The Creeds of Christendom, with a History and Critical Notes.* 3 vols. 6th ed. rev. New York: Harper and Brothers, 1919.
Serres, Jean de. *Histoire des choses mémorables avenues en France, depuis l'an 1547 jusques au commencement de l'an 1598, sous le règne de Henry II, François II, Charles IX, Henry III, & Henry IV, contenant infinies merveilles de notre siècle.* Paris, 1599.
Steinherz, Stefan (ed.). *Nuntiaturberichte aus Deutschland 1560-1572 nebst ergänzenden Actenstücken.* 2 vols. Vienna: Kaiserlichen Akademie der Wissenschaften, 1897-1903.
Suriano, Michele. *Despatches of Michele Suriano and Marc' Antonio Barbaro: Venetian Ambassadors at the Court of France, 1560-63.* Ed. Sir Henry Layard. Lymington: Printed for the Huguenot Society of London, 1891.
Šusta, Josef (ed.). *Die Römische Kurie und das Konzil von Trient unter Pius IV. Actenstücke zur Geschichte des Konzils von Trient.* 4 vols. Vienna: A. Hölder, 1904-1914.
Tarbé, Prosper. *Recueil de poésies Calvinistes 1550-66.* Reims, 1866.
Vermigli, Peter Martyr. *The Common Places of the most Famous and Renowned Divine Doctor Peter Martyr, Divided into Foure Principall Parts: With a large edition of manie Theologicall and Necessarie Discourses, Some never Extant before.* Tr. Anthonie Marten. London, 1583.
Weiss, Charles (ed.). *Papiers d'estat du Cardinal de Granvelle.* 9 vols. Paris, 1841-1852.

SECONDARY WORKS:

Books

Amphoux, Henri. *Michel de l'Hospital et la liberté de conscience au XVIe siècle.* Paris: Fischbacher, 1900.
Aumale, M. le duc d'. *History of the Princes of Condé in the XVIth and XVIIth Centuries.* Tr. Robert B. Borthwick. 2 vols. London, 1872.
Bataillon, Marcel. *Érasme et l'Espagne.* Paris: Droz, 1937.
Baum, Johann. *Theodor Beza nach handschriftlichen Quellen dargestellt.* 2 vols. Leipzig, 1843-1851.
Bayne, C.G. *Anglo-Roman Relations 1558-1565.* Oxford: Clarendon Press, 1913.
Beame, Edmond M. "The Development of Politique Thought during the French Religious Wars (1560-1595)," unpub. diss., University of Illinois, 1959.

Berthoud, Gabrielle (ed.). *Aspects de la propagande religieuse.* Geneva: Droz, 1957.

Bizer, Ernst. *Confessio Virtembergica: Das Württembergische Bekenntnis von 1551.* Stuttgart: Quell-Verlag, 1952.

Bories, Edmond. *Histoire de la ville de Poissy.* Paris: H. Champion, 1901.

Bouwsma, William J. *Concordia Mundi: The Career and Thought of Guillaume Postel (1510-1581).* Cambridge, Mass.: Harvard University Press, 1957.

————— *Venice and the Defense of Republican Liberty: Renaissance Values in the Age of the Counter Reformation.* Berkeley: University of California Press, 1968.

Braudel, Fernand. *La Méditerranée et la monde Méditerranéen à l'époque de Philippe II.* 2 vols. 2nd ed. Paris: A. Colin, 1966.

Buisson, Albert. *Michel de l'Hospital.* Paris: Hachette, 1950.

Calinich, Robert. *Der Naumburger Fürstentag, 1561.* Gotha, 1870.

Capraiis, Vittorio de. *Propaganda e pensiero politico in Francia durante le guerre di religione.* Naples: Edizioni scientifiche italiane, 1959.

Cardauns, Ludwig. *Zur Geschichte der kirchlichen Unions und Reformbestrebungen von 1538-1542.* Rome: W. Regenberg, 1910.

Cereceda, Feliciano. *Diego Lainez en la Europa religiosa de su tiempo 1512-1565.* 2 vols. Madrid: Ediciones Cultura Hispánica, 1945-1946.

Champion, Pierre. *Charles IX, la France et le Contrôle de l'Espagne.* 2 vols. Paris: B. Grasset, 1939.

Chevreul, Henri. *Hubert Languet.* Paris, 1856.

Constant, Gustave. *Concession à l'Allemagne de la communion sous les deux espèces: Études sur les débuts de la réforme Catholique en Allemagne (1548-1621).* 2 vols. Paris: E. de Boccard, 1923.

Crevier, Jean Baptiste Louis. *Histoire de l'Université de Paris, depuis son origines jusqu'en l'année 1600.* 7 vols. Paris, 1761.

Decrue, Francis. *Anne Duc de Montmorency, connétable et pair de France sous Henri II, François II et Charles IX.* Paris, 1889.

Delaborde, Jules. *Gaspard de Coligny, amiral de France.* 3 vols. Paris, 1879-1882.

Denzler, Georg. *Kardinal Guglielmo Sirleto (1514-1585): Leben und Werk. Ein Beitrag zur nachtridentinischen Reform.* Munich: Hueber, 1964.

Deroo, André. *Saint Charles Borromée, Cardinal réformateur, docteur de la pastorale, 1538-1584.* Paris: Édition Saint-Paul, 1963.

Dolan, John P. *The Influence of Erasmus, Witzel and Cassander in the Church Ordinances and Reform Proposals of the United Duchess of Cleve during the Middle Decades of the 16th Century.* Münster: Aschendorff, 1957.

Duffield, G.E. (ed.). *John Calvin.* Grand Rapids, Mich.: William B. Eerdmans Publishing Co., 1966.

Dupront, Alphonse. *Les conciles de l'Église modernes et contemporaine.* Paris: Centre de Documentation Universitaire, 1963.

Elliott, J.H. *Imperial Spain 1469-1716.* New York: New American Library, 1966.

Evennett, H. Outram. *The Cardinal of Lorraine and the Council of Trent.* Cambridge, Eng.: Cambridge University Press, 1930.

————— *The Spirit of the Counter-Reformation.* Ed. with a postscript by John Bossy. Cambridge, Eng.: Cambridge University Press, 1968.

Feret, Pierre. *La faculté de théologie de Paris: Époque moderne.* 4 vols. Paris: Picard, 1900-1907.

Fernández Álvarez, Manuel. *Político mundial de Carlos V y Felipe II.* Madrid: C.S.I.C., Escuela de Historia Moderna, 1966.

Forneron, Henri. *Les ducs de Guise et leur époque: Étude historique sur le seizième siècle.* 2 vols. Paris, 1877.

Fouqueray, Henri. *Histoire de la Compagnie de Jésus en France des origines à la suppression, 1528-1762.* 5 vols. Paris: Picard, 1910-1925.

François, Michel. *Le Cardinal François de Tournon: Homme d'état, diplomate, mécène et humaniste 1489-1562.* Paris: Bibliothèque des Écoles Françaises d'Athènes et de Rome, 1951.

Gardy, Frédéric. *Bibliographie des oeuvres théologiques, littéraires, historiques et juridiques de Théodore de Bèze.* Geneva: Droz, 1960.

Geisendorf, Paul F. *Théodore de Bèze.* Geneva: Labor & Fides, 1949.

Gelbke, Johann Heinrich. *Der Naumburgische Fürstentag.* Leipzig, 1793.

Guillemin, J.J. *Le Cardinal de Lorraine, son influence politique et religieuse au XVIe siècle.* Paris, 1847.

Gutiérrez, Constancio. *Españoles en Trento.* Valladolid: Consejo Superior de Investigaciones Científicas, 1951.

Haag, Eugène and Émile. *La France Protestante.* 9 vols. Paris, 1846-1859. 2nd ed. 6 vols. Paris, 1877-1888.

Hauser, Henri. *Les sources de l'histoire de France. XVIe siècle.* 4 vols. Paris: Picard, 1906-1915.

Hefele, Karl Joseph von. *Histoire des conciles d'après les documents originaux.* Tr. H. Leclercq. 9 vols. Paris: Letouzey et Ané, 1907-1931.

Heidenhain, Arthur. *Die Unionspolitik Landgraf Philipps von Hessen.* Halle, 1890.

Heppe, Heinrich. *Die Bekenntnisschriften der Altprotestantischen Kirche Deutschlands.* Cassel, 1855.

————— *Geschichte des Deutschen Protestantismus in dem Jahren 1555-1581.* 4 vols. Marburg, 1852-1859.

Héritier, Jean. *Catherine de Medici.* Tr. Charlotte Haldane. New York: St. Martin's Press, 1963.

Hogu, Louis. *Jean de l'Espine.* Paris: E. Champion, 1913.

Hoogstra, Jacob T. (ed.). *John Calvin, Contemporary Prophet: A Symposium.* Grand Rapids, Mich.: Baker Book House, 1959.

Hopfen, O.H. *Kaiser Maximilian II. und der Kompromisskatholizismus.* Munich, 1895.

Imbart de la Tour, Pierre. *Les origines de la Réforme.* 4 vols. Paris: Hachette, 1905-1935.

Iserloh, Erwin, and Konrad Repken (eds.). *Reformata Reformanda: Festgabe für Hubert Jedin.* 2 vols. Münster: Aschendorff, 1965.

Jedin, Hubert. *A History of the Council of Trent.* Tr. Dom Ernest Graf. 2 vols. to date. St. Louis, Mo.: Herder, 1957-1961.

_____ *Crisis and Closure of the Council of Trent.* (Tr. N. D. Smith.) London and Melbourne: Sheed and Ward, 1967.

_____ *Ecumenical Councils of the Catholic Church.* Tr. Dom Ernest Graf. New York: Herder and Herder, [1960].

Jensen, De Lamar. *Diplomacy and Dogmatism: Bernardino de Mendoza and the French Catholic League.* Cambridge, Mass.: Harvard University Press, 1964.

Kingdon, Robert M. *Geneva and the Coming of the Wars of Religion in France, 1555-1563.* Geneva: Droz, 1956.

Klipffel, Henri. *Le Colloque de Poissy.* Paris, 1867.

Kluckholn, August. *Friedrich der Fromme, Kurfürst von der Pfalz, der Schutzer der Reformirten Kirche, 1559-1579.* Nördingen, 1879.

Köhler, Walther. *Das Marburger Religionsgespräch 1529.* Leipzig: M. Heinsius, 1929.

Kugler, Bernhard. *Christoph, Herzog zu Wirtemberg.* 2 vols. Stuttgart, 1872.

Laferrière, Julien. *Le contrat de Poissy.* Paris: L. Larose et L. Tenin, 1905.

Lavin, Michael O.H. "Franco-Spanish Rivalry from the Treaty of Cateau-Cambrésis to the Death of Charles IX," unpub. diss., Stanford University, 1956.

Lecler, Joseph. *Histoire de la tolérance au siècle de la Réforme.* 2 vols. Paris: Aubier, 1954.

Lefevre, Louis-Raymond. *Les Français pendant les guerres de religion: Le tumulte d'Amboise.* Paris: Gallimond, 1949.

Lutz, Heinrich. *Christianitas Afflicta. Europa, das Reich und die päpstliche Politik im Niedergang der Hegemonie Kaiser Karls V., 1552-1556.* Göttingen: Vandenhoeck & Ruprecht, 1964.

MacCaffrey, Wallace. *The Shaping of the Elizabethan Regime.* Princeton, N.J.: Princeton University Press, 1968.

McDonnell, Kilian, O.S.B. *John Calvin, the Church, and the Eucharist.* Princeton, N.J.: Princeton University Press, 1967.

McLelland, Joseph. *The Visible Words of God: An Exposition of the Sacramental Theology of Peter Martyr Vermigli A.D., 1500-1562.* Grand Rapids, Mich.: William B. Eerdmans Publishing Co., 1957.

McNair, Philip. *Peter Martyr in Italy*. Oxford: Clarendon Press, 1967.
McNeill, John T. *Unitive Protestantism: The Ecumenical Spirit and Its Persistent Expression*. Rev. ed. Richmond, Va.: John Knox Press, 1964.
Major, J. Russell. *Representative Institutions in Renaissance France, 1421-1559*. Madison: University of Wisconsin Press, 1960.
_____ *The Estates General of 1560*. Princeton, N.J.: Princeton University Press, 1951.
Mâle, Émile. *L'art religieux après le Concile de Trente*. Paris: A. Colin, 1932.
Marchand, Abbé Charles. *Le maréchal François de Spéceaux de Viellement et ses mémoires*. Paris, 1893.
Matheson, Peter. *Cardinal Contarini at Regensburg*. Oxford: Clarendon Press, 1972.
Matthisius, Ioannes. *Quaestiones eucharisticae . . . colloquio inter Cardinalem Lotharingum et Theodorum Bezum, 1561*. Basel, 1589.
Méaly, Paul F.M. *Origines des idées politiques libérales en France: Les publicistes de la Réforme sous François II et Charles IX*. Paris: Fischbacher, 1903.
Merriman, R.B. *The Rise of the Spanish Empire in the Old World and the New*. 4 vols. New York: Macmillan, 1918-1934.
Müller, Theodor. *Das Konklave Pius' IV*. Gotha, 1888.
Nieto, Jose C. *Juan de Valdes and the Origins of the Spanish and Italian Reformation*. Geneva: Droz, 1970.
Nijenhuis, W. *Calvinus Oecumenicus*. The Hague: M. Nijhoff, 1959.
Pacifici, Vincenzo. *Ippolito II d'Este, Cardinale di Ferrara*. Tivoli: Società di storia e d'arte in Villa d'Este, 1920.
Pastor, Ludwig von. *The History of the Popes, from the Close of the Middle Ages*. 34 vols. 5th ed. St. Louis, Mo.: Herder, 1923-1941.
Pelikan, Jaroslav. *Obedient Rebels: Catholic Substance and Protestant Principle in Luther's Reformation*. New York: Harper and Row, 1964.
Peyrat, Napoléon. *Le Colloque de Poissy et les conférences de Saint-Germain en 1561*. Paris, 1868.
Polman, Pontien. *L'élément historique dans la controverse religieuse du XVIᵉ siècle*. Gembloux: J. Duculot, 1932.
Rocquain, Félix. *La France et Rome pendant des guerres de religion*. Paris: Édouard Champion, 1924.
Roelker, Nancy Lyman. *Queen of Navarre, Jeanne d'Albret, 1528-1572*. Cambridge, Mass.: Harvard University Press, 1968.
Rogger, Igino. *Le nazioni al Concilio di Trento durante la sua epoca imperiale, 1545-1552*. Rome: Orbis Catholicus, 1952.
Romier, Lucien. *Catholiques et Huguenots à la cour de Charles IX*. Paris: Perrin, 1924.

_____ *La carrière d'un favori: Jacques d'Albon de Sainte-André, maréchal de France (1512-1562)*. Paris: Perrin, 1909.
_____ *La conjuration d'Amboise. L'aurore sanglante de la liberté de conscience. Le règne et la mort de François II*. Paris: Perrin, 1923.
_____ *Le royaume de Catherine de Médicis: La France à la veille des guerres de religion*. 2 vols. Paris: Perrin, 1922.
_____ *Les origines politiques des guerres de religion*. 2 vols. Paris: Perrin, 1913-1914.
Roserot de Melin, Joseph. *Antonio Caracciolo, évêque de Troyes, 1515?-1570*. Paris: Letouzey et Ané, 1923.
Rouse, Ruth, and Stephen Charles Neill (eds.). *A History of the Ecumenical Movement, 1517-1948*. 2nd ed. London: S.P.C.K., 1967.
Ruble, Baron Alphonse de. *Antoine de Bourbon et Jeanne d'Albret*. 4 vols. Paris, 1881-1886.
_____ *Jeanne d'Albret et la guerre civile*. Paris, 1897.
_____ *Le Traité de Cateau-Cambrésis*. Paris, 1889.
Salig, Christian August. *Vollständige Historie der Augspurgischen Confession und derselben Apologie*. Halle, 1730.
Sarpi, Fra Paolo. *The Historie of the Councel of Trent*. Tr. Nathaniel Brent. 1st ed., 1619. London, 1676.
Sasse, Hermann. *This Is My Body: Luther's Contention for the Real Presence in the Sacrament of the Altar*. Minneapolis, Minn.: Augsburg Publishing House, 1959.
Sattler, Christian Friedrich. *Geschichte des Herzogthums Würtemberg unter der Regierung der Graven*. 4 vols. Tübingen, 1767-1768.
Schickler, Fernand de. *Les églises du refuge en Angleterre*. 3 vols. Paris, 1892.
Schlink, Edmund. *The Theology of the Lutheran Confessions*. Tr. P.F. Keohneke and H.J.A. Bouman. Philadelphia: Muhlenberg Press, 1961.
Schreiber, Georg. *Das Weltkonzil von Trient, sein Werden und Wirken*. 2 vols. Freiburg: Herder, 1951.
Serbat, Louis. *Les assemblées du clergé de France: Origines, organisation, développement, 1561-1615*. Paris: Honoré Champion, 1906.
Shimizu, J. *Conflict of Loyalties: Politics and Religion in the Career of Gaspard de Coligny, Admiral of France, 1519-72*. Geneva: Droz, 1970.
Soldan, Wilhelm. *Geschichte der Protestantismus in Frankreich bis zum Tode Karl IX*. 2 vols. Leipzig, 1855.
Stupperich, Robert. *Der Humanismus und die Wiedervereinigung der Konfessionen*. Leipzig: Schriften der Vereins für Reformationsgeschichte, 1936.
Tarander (pseud.). *Les actes de Poissy mys en ryme Françoyse par*

Tarander, plus trois cantiques dont le premier est au nom des fideles de France, les deux derniers sont faits au nom d'un prince Chrestien estant en affliction. N.p., n.d.
Thou, Jacques-August de. *Histoire universelle.* 11 vols. The Hague, 1740.
Van Dyke, Paul. *Catherine de Médicis.* 2 vols. New York: Charles Scribner's Sons, 1928.
Vivanti, Corrado. *Lotta politica e pace religiosa in Francia fra cinque e seicento.* Turin: Biblioteca di cultura storica, 1963.
Voss, Wilhelm. *Die Verhandlungen Pius IV. mit den katholischen Mächten über die Neuberufung des Tridentiner Concils im Jahre 1560.* Leipzig, 1887.
Wendel, François. *Calvin: The Origins and Development of His Religious Thought.* Tr. Philip Mairet. New York: Harper and Row, 1963.
Whitehead, A.W. *Gaspard de Coligny, Admiral of France.* London: Methuen, 1904.
Zeri, Federico. *Pittura e Controriforma.* Turin: G. Einaudi, 1957.

Articles

Alberigo, Giuseppe. "Carlo Borromeo come Modella di vescovo nella Chiesa post-Tridentina," *Rivista storica italiana,* LXXIX (1967), 1031-1052.
Baguenault de Puchesse, Gustave. "La politique de Philippe II dans les affaires de France, 1559-1598," *Revue des questions historiques* XXV (1878), 1-66.
_____ "Le duc de Württemberg, les Guises et Catherine de Médicis (1561-63)," *Bulletin philologique et historique du Comité des Travaux Historiques et Scientifiques,* 1915, 173-197.
Bonnet, Jules. "Le massacre fait à Vassy le premier jour de Mars 1562," *BSHPF,* XXXI (1882), 49-60.
Bossert, Gustav. "Die Reise der württembergischen theologen nach Frankreich im Herbst 1561," *Württembergische Vierteljahrhefte für Landesgeschichte,* VIII (1898-1899), 351-442.
Dannreuther, H. "Le martyr Augustine Marlorat et son frère Martin," *BSHPF,* XL (1891), 2-22.
Dareste, R. "Charte relative à François Baudouin 1563," *BSHPF,* I (1853), 147-50.
Davis, Natalie Zemon. "Peletier and Beza Part Company," *Studies in the Renaissance.* XI (1964), 188-222.
Delaborde, Jules. "Les Protestants à la cour de Saint-Germain lors du Colloque de Poissy," *BSHPF,* XXII (1873), 385-400, 481-505, 529-45, XXIII (1874), 49-63.
Droz, E. "L'Imprimeur de l'histoire ecclésiastique (1580)," *BHR,* XXII (1960), 371-376.
_____ "Notes sur Théodore de Bèze," *BHR,* XXIV (1962), 392-412.

Dufour, Alain. "Deux lettres oubliées de Calvin à J. Andreae (1556-1558)," *BHR*, XXIV (1962), 375-384.

Dupront, Alphonse. "Du Concile de Trente: Réflections autour d'un IVe Centenaire," *Revue historique*, CCVI (1951), 262-280.

Duquesne, J. "François Baudouin et la Réforme," *Bulletin de l'Académie Delphinale* (1917), 55-108.

Evennett, H.O. "The Cardinal of Lorraine and the Colloquy of Poissy," *Cambridge Historical Journal*, II (1927), 133-150.

Félice, Philippe de. "Le Colloque de Poissy," *BSHPF*, CVII (1961), 133-145.

_____ "Odet de Coligny: Cardinal de Châtillon, *BSHPF*, CVII (1961), 1-12.

Hauser, Henri. "Antoine de Bourbon et l'Allemagne," *Revue historique*, XLV (1891), 54-61.

Jedin, Hubert. "Die Deutschen am Trienter Konzil, 1551-52," *Historische Zeitschrift*, 188 (1959), 1-16.

_____ "Ist das Konzil von Trient ein Hindernis der Wiedervereinigung?" *Ephemerides theologicae Lovaniensis*, 38 (1962), 841-855.

Keller, Abraham-Charles. "Michel de l'Hospital and the Edict of Toleration of 1562," *BHR*, XIV (1952), 301-10.

Kingdon, Robert M. "Some French Reactions to the Council of Trent," *Church History*, XXXIII (June 1964), 149-156.

_____ "The Political Resistance of the Calvinists in France and the Low Countries," *Church History*, XXVII (Sept. 1958), 220-233.

"Le protestantisme en Champagne au XVIe siècle: Documents inédits et originaux," *BSHPF*, XII (1863), 349-366.

Lulvès, Jean. "Päpstliche Wahlkapitulationen. Ein Beitrag zur Entwickelungsgeschichte des Kardinalats," *Quellen und Forschungen aus Italienischen Archiven und Bibliotheken herausgegeben vom Koenigl. Preussischen Historischen Institut in Rom*, XII (1909), 212-235.

MacCaffrey, W.T. "Elizabethan Politics: The First Decade, 1558-68," *Past & Present*, XXIV (Apr., 1963), 25-42.

Mackensen, Heinz. "Contarini's Theological Role at Ratisbon in 1541," *ARG*, LI (1960), 36-57.

McNeill, John T. "Calvin as an Ecumenical Churchman," *Church History*, XXXII (Dec. 1963), 379-391.

Maurer, Wilhelm. "Confessio Augustana Variata," *ARG*, LIII (1962), 97-151.

Mazauric, M. "À Propos du Colloque de Poissy," *BSHPF*, CVII (1961), 222.

Meyer, Helmut. "Die deutschen Protestanten an der Zweiten Tagungsperiode des Konzils von Trient 1551-52," *ARG*, LVI (1965), 166-209.

Nugent, Donald. "A Parisian Colloquy of 1566: Holy Spirit or Holy

Church," *Renaissance Quarterly*, XXIII (Spring 1970), 25-36.
────── "The Cardinal of Lorraine and the Colloquy of Poissy," *Historical Journal*, XII (No. 4, 1969), 596-605.
────── "The Erasmus Renaissance," *Month*, CCXXIX (Jan. 1970), 36-45.
────── "The Historical Dimension in Reformation Theology," *Journal of Ecumenical Studies*, V (Summer 1968), 555-571.
Paist, Benjamin F. "Peter Martyr and the Colloquy of Poissy," *Princeton Theological Review*, XX (1922), 212-231, 418-447, 616-646.
Philippson, Martin. "Philipp II von Spanien und das Päpstthum," *Historisches Zeitschrift*, XXXIX (1878), 269-315, 419-457.
Plèche, J. "L'évêque Jean de Montluc et la Réforme à Valence (1560)," *BSHPF*, LXXVII (1928), 31-35.
"Questions et réponses—correspondance," *BSHPF*, XIII (1864), 284.
Roehrich, L. "Les Protestants à Poissy," *BSHPF*, XXVII (1878), 141-144.
Saulnier, V.L. "Autour du Colloque de Poissy: Les avatars d'une chanson de Saint-Gelais à Ronsard et Théophile," *BHR*, XX (1958), 44-76.
Stupperich, Robert. "Die Reformation und das Tridentium," *ARG*, XLVII (1956), 20-63.
Sutherland, N.M. "Calvinism and the Conspiracy of Amboise," *History*, XLVII (1962), 111-138.
────── "The Origins of Queen Elizabeth's Relations with the Huguenots," *Proceedings of the Huguenot Society of London* XX (1966), 626-648.
Swierenga, Robert P. "Calvin and the Council of Trent: A Reappraisal (III)," *Reformed Journal*, XVI (May-June 1966), 20-23.
Valois, Noël. "Les essais de conciliation religieuse au début du règne de Charles IX," *Revue d'histoire de l'église de France*, XXXI (1945), 236-276.
────── "Les états de Pontoise," *Revue d'histoire de l'église de France*, XXIX (1943), 237-256.
────── "Vassy," *Annuaire-bulletin de la Société de l'histoire de France* (1913), 189-236.
Van Dyke, Paul. "The Estates of Pontoise," *English Historical Review*, XXVII (1913), 472-495.
Waddington, A. "La France et les Protestants Allemands sous Charles IX et Henri III: Hubert Languet et Gaspard de Schomberg," *Revue historique*, XLII (1890), 241-277.
Weber, Bernard C. "The Council of Fontainebleau (1560)," *ARG*, XLV (1954), 43-62.

Index

Adrian VI, 2, 29
Albret, Jeanne d', 16, 73
Anthony, king of Navarre: opposition to Guise, 14, 16, 21; appointed lieutenant general, 21; religion of, 23, 71n, 186; and Europeanization of colloquy, 24, 25, 58–59, 117
Armagnac, Cardinal, 74n, 81
Augustine, St., and Eucharist, 98n, 99n, 111–112, 132n, 133

Barbaste, Arnaud-Guillaume, 191
Baudouin, Francis, 24–25, 117, 177; and utopianism, 221
Beza, Theodore, 15n, 22–23; arrival and introduction, 68–71; preliminary encounter with Lorraine, 85–89; hopes, 93; exchange with Tournon, 93; opening oration, 96–103, and Confession of Augsburg, 127; second oration, 129–134; debates, 138–139, 140, 141, 157–159; and Lorraine's ultimatum, 143–152 *passim;* and *petit colloque,* 165, 166, 168; and Colloquy of Saint-Germain, 193–198 *passim;* rejection of Trent, 198–199; and text used in Lorraine's ultimatum, 212–217 *passim;* and Protestant Scholasticism, 221
Borromeo, Charles, 28, 43, 226
Bourbon, cardinal of, 71, 105
Bourbon, *see* Anthony, king of Navarre; Bourbon, cardinal of; Louis, prince of Condé
Bouteiller, Jean, 78; radical views of, 80, 127, 163; and icons, 195–196
Brenz, Johann, 200, 211, 214, 215
Bretagne, Jacques, 84
Bucer, Martin, 8, 135

Calvin, John: as ecumenical figure, 1–2, 6, 9, 54–55, 208, 217; Beza

preferable for colloquy, 70; on prospects, 89; on Eucharist, 99n, 104n, 137, 152n, 153n, 165, 208; warns of Confession of Augsburg, 116–117, 127, 143
Cano, Melchior, 40, 226
Caraccioli, Antonio, 79, 80, 180
Carranza, Bartolomé, 38, 40–41
Cassander, George, 23, 24–25, 177
Catherine de' Medici: rise to regency, 17, 18, 20; favors Protestants, 17, 20–22, 82, 85, 182, 201; expedient ecumenist, 23–24, 127, 161, 221; convokes national council, 26, 61; opposes Pope, 36, 52, 61–62, 64–66; and spoliation of church property, 78, 83, 179; on Beza's first oration, 103–104; and Martyr, 107–108, 121–122; subvention and reform canons of national council, 178–179; favors concessions, 183–184; and toleration, 189–190; accepts Trent, 198
Catholics, representatives of at conferences, 75, 94, 128, 162, 191
Cecil, William, 57
Chantonnay, Thomas de: complaints of, 22, 64, 82, 91; and *Diario,* 76n
Charles V, 7, 8, 9, 61; and Paul IV, 28; and Philip II, 38–41
Charles IX, 20, 23, 95
Charles, cardinal of Lorraine: opposite Bourbons, 14; criticized by Catholics, 22, 50, 60, 115, 146–147, 170, 209n; on his ecumenicity, 23, 79, 82, 114, 117, 126–127, 206n, 208n; convokes national council, 42–43, 52n; inquisitor-general, 44; speaker, 79; support of colloquy, 81–82, 91, 104–105, 122, 123, 126, 209; preliminary encounter with Beza, 85–89; opening oration, 108–116; ultimatum of, 142–144, 146–147, 209; and Sav-

Harvard Historical Studies

OUT OF PRINT TITLES ARE OMITTED

33. *Lewis George Vander Velde.* The Presbyterian Churches and the Federal Union, 1861-1869. 1932.

35. *Donald C. McKay.* The National Workshops: A Study in the French Revolution of 1848. 1933.

38. *Dwight Erwin Lee.* Great Britain and the Cyprus Convention Policy of 1878. 1934.

48. *Jack H. Hexter.* The Reign of King Pym. 1941.

58. *Charles C. Gillispie.* Genesis and Geology: A Study in the Relations of Scientific Thought, Natural Theology, and Social Opinion in Great Britain, 1790-1850. 1951.

60. *Robert G.L. Waite.* Vanguard of Nazism: The Free Corps Movement in Postwar Germany, 1918-1923. 1952.

62, 63. *John King Fairbank.* Trade and Diplomacy on the China Coast: The Opening of the Treaty Ports, 1842-1854. One-volume edition. 1953.

64. *Franklin L. Ford.* Robe and Sword: The Regrouping of the French Aristocracy after Louis XIV. 1953.

66. *Wallace Evan Davies.* Patriotism on Parade: The Story of Veterans' and Hereditary Organizations in America, 1783-1900. 1955.

67. *Harold Schwartz.* Samuel Gridley Howe: Social Reformer, 1801-1876. 1956.

69. *Stanley J. Stein.* Vassouras: A Brazilian Coffee Country, 1850-1900. 1957.

71. *Ernest R. May.* The World War and American Isolation, 1914-1917. 1959.

72. *John B. Blake.* Public Health in the Town of Boston, 1630-1822. 1959.

73. *Benjamin W. Labaree.* Patriots and Partisans: The Merchants of Newburyport, 1764-1815. 1962.

74. *Alexander Sedgwick.* The Ralliement in French Politics, 1890-1898. 1965.

75. *E. Ann Pottinger.* Napoleon III and the German Crisis, 1865-1866. 1966.

76. *Walter Goffart.* The Le Mans Forgeries: A Chapter from the History of Church Property in the Ninth Century. 1966.

77. *Daniel P. Resnick.* The White Terror and the Political Reaction after Waterloo. 1966.

78. *Giles Constable.* The Letters of Peter the Venerable. 1967.
79. *Lloyd E. Eastman.* Throne and Mandarins: China's Search for a Policy during the Sino-French Controversy, 1880-1885. 1967.
80. *Allen J. Matusow.* Farm Policies and Politics in the Truman Years. 1967.
81. *Philip Charles Farwell Bankwitz.* Maxime Weygand and Civil-Military Relations in Modern France. 1967.
82. *Donald J. Wilcox.* The Development of Florentine Humanist Historiography in the Fifteenth Century. 1969.
83. *John W. Padberg, S.J.* Colleges in Controversy: The Jesuit Schools in France from Revival to Suppression, 1813-1880. 1969.
84. *Marvin Arthur Breslow.* A Mirror of England: English Puritan Views of Foreign Nations, 1618-1640. 1970.
85. *Patrice L.R. Higonnet.* Pont-de-Montvert: Social Structure and Politics in a French Village, 1700-1914. 1971.
86. *Paul G. Halpern.* The Mediterranean Naval Situation, 1908-1914. 1971.
87. *Robert E. Ruigh.* The Parliament of 1624: Politics and Foreign Policy. 1971.
88. *Angeliki E. Laiou.* Constantinople and the Latins: The Foreign Policy of Andronicus, 1282-1328. 1972.
89. *Donald Nugent.* Ecumenism in the Age of the Reformation: The Colloquy of Poissy. 1974.